PREFACE TO PLATO

PREFACE TO PLATO

ERIC A. HAVELOCK

THE BELKNAP PRESS OF
HARVARD UNIVERSITY PRESS
CAMBRIDGE, MASSACHUSETTS
AND LONDON, ENGLAND

Printed in the United States of America
10   9   8   7   6

Leisure for the completion of this work was indirectly afforded the author during the course of an appointment as visiting fellow in the Ford Humanities Project administered by the Council of the Humanities of Princeton University. His debt to the Council and its officers, to Princeton University, and also to the Ford Foundation is gratefully acknowledged.

Library of Congress Catalog Card Number 62—13859
ISBN 0-674-69906-8

TO MY FATHER

FOREWORD

THE present volume is offered as the first of what it is hoped will be a series of studies designed to demonstrate what may be called the growth of the early Greek mind. By this I do not mean another history of Greek philosophy in the accepted sense of that term. All human civilisations rely on a sort of cultural 'book', that is, on the capacity to put information in storage in order to reuse it. Before Homer's day, the Greek cultural 'book' had been stored in the oral memory. Discoveries and conclusions associated with the recent decipherment of 'Linear B', fascinating and fashionable though they are, must not be allowed to obscure this essential fact. Between Homer and Plato, the method of storage began to alter, as the information became alphabetised, and correspondingly the eye supplanted the ear as the chief organ employed for this purpose. The complete results of literacy did not supervene in Greece until the ushering in of the Hellenistic age, when conceptual thought achieved as it were fluency and its vocabulary became more or less standardised. Plato, living in the midst of this revolution, announced it and became its prophet.

Direct evidence for mental phenomena can lie only in linguistic usage. If such a revolution as outlined did take place in Greece, it should be attested by changes in the vocabulary and syntax of written Greek. The semantic information hitherto compiled in Greek lexicons will not help us much, in so far as the various significations of words are arranged for the most part analytically rather than historically, as atoms of finite meaning suspended in a void, rather than as areas of meaning which are contained and defined by a context. The effect is to foster the unconscious assumption that the Greek experience from Homer to Aristotle forms a cultural constant capable of being represented in a sign system of great variety, to be sure, but consisting merely of sets of interchangeable parts.

The enterprise which lies ahead would therefore be to seek to document the growth of an abstract vocabulary in pre-Platonic Greek, considered not as an addition to the tongue (though this also must be taken into account) but as a remodelling of existing resources.

Such an enterprise to be worth anything must be built on foundations laid by others, and indeed my debts are diverse, for the synthesis here offered has relied on many separate findings of classical scholarship in fields at first sight unrelated. Any attempt to reinterpret the history of the Greek mind as a search for concepts not yet realised and for a terminology not yet invented confronts a formidable obstacle in the traditional reports preserved in Hellenistic and Roman antiquity. These assume that the earliest philosophers of Greece were engaged from the first with metaphysical problems, and formulated solutions which presuppose a mastery of the abstract: that in fact they were philosophers in the modern sense of that word. The publication of Diels' *Doxographi Graeci* in 1879, while it demonstrated the dependence of these reports upon the metaphysical portions of the lost history of the physical philosophers by Theophrastus, did nothing to impair their ultimate authority, as can easily be seen from an inspection of the pages of such a work as Burnet's *Early Greek Philosophy*. After all, what could be a sounder authority than this work of Theophrastus, Aristotle's pupil and successor, and a pioneer historian of thought? The findings of Cherniss (1935) established the conclusion that the metaphysical interpretations of pre-Platonic thinkers which are found in Aristotle's own works are in large measure accommodated to the problems and indeed the terminology of his own system. It remained for McDiarmid in 1953 to point out that the Theophrastean account of the First Causes which formed the underpinning of the whole later tradition appears itself to have been based on a collation of Aristotle's own notices, and could therefore claim an authority no greater than do they. At a stroke, one may say, an elaborate structure, which has enjoyed prestige in modern scholarship at least since the first appearance of Zeller's magisterial history of ancient philosophy, fell to the ground in pieces. If the doxography depends on Theophrastus, if Theophrastus in turn is a mirror of Aristotle's historical opinions, and if these place early Greek thought in a context of problems which are Aristotelian but not Presocratic, then the tradition cannot be historical. This conclusion is still unpalatable to many scholars, but it is difficult to see how it can be evaded. Familiarity is no guarantee of fidelity.

The next task might seem to be to construct a corrected account of the metaphysical positions of early Greek thinkers. My reader will realise that in the light of these findings I have felt it possible to take a more radical step, and to call in question the whole assumption that early Greek thought was occupied with metaphysics at all, or was capable of using a vocabulary suitable for such a purpose. It becomes possible to remove a screen of sophistication which has hitherto intervened between the modern historian and the early Greek mentality, and to view the latter afresh as a phenomenon of essential naïveté, the nature of which began to be partly visible to the modern eye as soon as Diels published in 1903 the first edition of the *Fragmente der Vorsokratiker*, for in that work, by organising the *ipsissima verba* on the one hand and the tradition on the other in mutually exclusive sections, he revealed a linguistic conflict between the two which might be judged irreconcilable.

But if the early Greek mentality was neither metaphysical nor abstract, what then was it, and what was it trying to say? The resources of epigraphy, marshalled in the first instance by Carpenter, supplied the next clue. For epigraphy pointed to the conclusion that the Greek culture was maintained on a wholly oral basis until about 700 B.C. and if this were true, then the first so-called philosophers were living and speaking in a period which was still adjusting to the conditions of a possible future literacy, conditions which I concluded would be slow of realisation, for they depended on the mastery not of the art of writing by a few, but of fluent reading by the many.

Those few who had elected themselves to be the prototypes of future philosophers did so by virtue of their attempt to rationalise the sources of knowledge. What then had been the shape of knowledge when preserved in the oral memory and stored there for re-use? At this point, I turned to the work of Milman Parry, and thought I saw the outline of the answer, and an answer also to the problem of why Xenophanes, Heraclitus and Parmenides, to take the first three thinkers who survive, spoke in the curious ways they did. The formulaic style characteristic of oral composition represented not merely certain verbal and metrical habits but also a cast of thought, or a mental condition. The Presocratics themselves were essentially oral thinkers, prophets of the concrete linked by long habit to the past, and to forms of expression which were also forms of experience, but they were trying to devise a vocabulary and syntax for a new future, when thought should be expressed in categories organized in a syntax suitable to abstract statement. This was their fundamental task, and it absorbed most of their energies. So far from inventing systems in the later philosophical manner, they were devoted to the primary task of inventing a language which would make future systems possible. Such, in simplified outline, was the new picture which began to emerge. I think that even so I would not have been so ready to undertake the responsibility of drawing these implications from Parry's work had it not been for a prophetic article by Nilsson, published in 1905, which speculatively set forth the probably oral character of early Milesian publication.

These were the original guide posts which pointed along the path of this investigation. That which in my book will appear first in exposition, namely the Platonic attack on the Greek poetic tradition, came last in realisation. Meanwhile, fresh support for a re-examination of the history of what is called early 'philosophy' has begun to appear in a new quarter, with the appearance of several studies of early vocabulary usage. It was Burnet's article 'The Socratic Doctrine of the Soul' which here broke new ground, when it demonstrated that a notion normally taken as fundamental to any kind of speculative activity was in fact probably invented in the last half of the fifth century. Stenzel's monograph on Socrates which appeared in Pauly-Wissowa in 1927 supplemented this insight by proposing the general thesis that Socraticism was essentially an experiment in the reinforcement of language and a realisation that language had a power when effectively used both to define and to control action. Studies by Snell and von Fritz have drawn attention to the fact that the terminology which in Plato and Aristotle seeks to define with precision the various operations of the consciousness, in categories which we usually take for granted, had in fact to pass through a considerable period of development before reaching such precision. It is a fair presumption that until the fit word is present, you do not have the idea, and the word to become fit requires a suitable contextual usage. Signs are not wanting that scholarship is now preparing itself for the same genetic-historical approach in other areas of terminology and of thought, as for instance in seeking to understand original Greek conceptions of time.

One should of course here acknowledge the general stimulation given to this type of study in the classical field which has been imparted from other disciplines, particularly those of comparative anthropology and analytic psychology. Historians of early Greek thought do not have to accept all the theories of Lèvy-Bruhl in order to prove their debt to him. If in early Greek rationalism there can still be seen the persistence of religious symbolism and ritual tabu, if the worlds of Homer and Plato can be viewed in terms of a contrast between shame culture and guilt culture, such general theses do nothing to impair the purport of the present work, but rather give it a certain support. Nevertheless, it remains true that the crux of the matter lies in the transition from the oral to the written and from the concrete to the abstract, and here the phenomena to be studied are precise, and are generated by changes in the technology of preserved communication which are also precise.

My manuscript was read in draft by Professors Christine Mitchell, Adam Parry and A. T. Cole, and their numerous corrections and improvements, here gratefully acknowledged, are incorporated in the text. It is impossible that in an enterprise which cuts so wide a swathe error should be lacking, but I may hope that its correction by others will lead to further investigation of problems here partially exposed and no doubt imperfectly solved.

E. A. H.

Cambridge, Mass.
April 1962.

CONTENTS

Part One

THE IMAGE-THINKERS

Part Two

THE NECESSITY OF PLATONISM

NOTES

Modern authorities have for brevity's sake been identified for the most part only by surname and pagination. To complete the identification, the reader is referred to the bibliography. Where distinction is needed between two or more works by the same author, his surname identifies the work listed first under his name and for the others abbreviated titles or dates have been added.

I

THE IMAGE-THINKERS

CHAPTER ONE

Plato on Poetry

IT sometimes happens in the history of the written word that
an important work of literature carries a title which does not
accurately reflect the contents. A part of the work has become
identified with the whole, or the meaning of a label has shifted
in translation. But if the label has a popular and recognisable ring,
it can come to exercise a kind of thought control over those who
take the book in their hands. They form an expectation which
accords with the title but is belied by much of the substance of
what the author has to say. They cling to a preconception of his
intentions, insensibly allowing their minds to mould the content
of what they read into the required shape.

These remarks apply with full force to that treatise of Plato's
styled the *Republic*. Were it not for the title, it might be read for
what it is, rather than as an essay in utopian political theory. It is
a fact that only about a third[1] of the work concerns itself with
statecraft as such. The text deals at length and often with a great
variety of matters which bear on the human condition, but these
are matters which would certainly have no place in a modern
treatise on politics.

Nowhere does this become more evident to the reader than
when he takes up the tenth and last book. An author possessing
Plato's skill in composition is not likely to blunt the edge of what
he is saying by allowing his thoughts to stray away from it at
the end. Yet this terminal portion of the *Republic* opens with an
examination of the nature not of politics but of poetry. Placing
the poet in the same company with the painter, it argues that the
artist produces a version of experience which is twice removed
from reality; his work is at best frivolous and at worst dangerous

both to science and to morality; the major Greek poets from Homer to Euripides must be excluded from the educational system of Greece. And this extraordinary thesis is pursued with passion. The whole assault occupies the first half of the book. It is clear at once that a title like the *Republic* cannot prepare us for the appearance in this place of such a frontal attack upon the core of Greek literature. If the argument conforms to a plan, and if the assault, coming where it does, constitutes an essential part of that plan, then the purpose of the whole treatise cannot be understood within the limits of what we call political theory.

To the overall structure of the work we shall return a little later. Let us for a moment consider further the tone and temper of Plato's attack. He opens by characterising the effect of poetry as 'a crippling of the mind'.[2] It is a kind of disease, for which one has to acquire an antidote. The antidote must consist of a knowledge 'of what things really are'. In short, poetry is a species of mental poison, and is the enemy of truth. This is surely a shocker to the sensibilities of any modern reader and his incredulity is not lessened by the peroration with which, a good many pages later, Plato winds up his argument: 'Crucial indeed is the struggle, more crucial than we think—the choice that makes us good or bad—to keep faithful to righteousness and virtue in the face of temptation, be it of fame or money or power, or of poetry—yes, even of poetry.'[3] If he thus exhorts us to fight the good fight against poetry, like a Greek Saint Paul warring against the powers of darkness, we can conclude either that he has lost all sense of proportion, or that his target cannot be poetry in our sense, but something more fundamental in the Greek experience, and more powerful.

There has been natural reluctance to take what he says at face value. Plato's admirers, normally devoted to his lightest word, when they reach a context like the present start looking around for an escape hatch, and they find one which they think he has provided for them. Just before this peroration, has he not said that poetry may offer a defence of herself if she can? Has he not

confessed to her overpowering charms? Does he not admit
reluctance to expel her, and does this not mean that in effect he
recants? He does indeed so confess, but to think that his confes-
sion amounts to a recantation profoundly mistakes his intention.
Indeed, the terms in which he makes the concession to poetry, to
plead her case if she chooses, are themselves damning. For he
treats her in effect as a kind of prostitute, or as a Delilah who may
seduce Plato's Samson if he lets her, and so rob him of his
strength. She can charm and coax and wheedle and enthral, but
these are precisely the powers that are so fatal. If we listen, we
dare to do so only as we counter her spell with one of our own.
We must repeat over and over to ourselves the line of reasoning
we have previously followed. We must keep on our guard:
'We have our city of the soul to protect against her.'[4]

The mood of this passage uncovers the heart of the difficulty.
Plato's target seems to be precisely the poetic experience as such.
It is an experience we would characterise as aesthetic. To him it is
a kind of psychic poison. You must always have your antidote
ready. He seems to want to destroy poetry as poetry, to exclude
her as a vehicle of communication. He is not just attacking bad
poetry or extravagant poetry. This is made even clearer during
the course of the argument he builds against her. Thus the poet,
he says, contrives to colour his statement by the use of words and
phrases[5] and to embellish it by exploiting the resources of meter,
rhythm and harmony.[6] These are like cosmetics applied as an
outward appearance which conceal the poverty of statement
behind them.[7] Just as the graphic artist employs illusionism to
deceive us,[8] so the acoustic effects employed by the poet confuse
our intelligence.[9] That is, Plato attacks the very form and substance of the poetised statement, its images, its rhythm, its choice
of poetic language. Nor is he any less hostile to the range of
experience which the poet thus makes available to us. He can
admittedly represent a thousand situations and portray a thousand
emotions.[10] This variety is just the trouble. By his portrayal he
can unlock a corresponding fund of sympathetic response in us

and evoke a wide range of our emotions.[11] All of which is dangerous, none of it acceptable. In short, Plato's target in the poet is precisely those qualities we applaud in him; his range, his catholicity, his command of the human emotional register, his intensity and sincerity, and his power to say things that only he can say and reveal things in ourselves that only he can reveal. Yet to Plato all this is a kind of disease, and we have to ask why.

His objections are taken in the context of the standards he is setting for education. But this does not help us one bit to solve what seems at least a paradox in his thought, and perhaps, if judged by our values, an absurdity. For him, poetry as an educational discipline poses a moral danger, and also an intellectual one. It confuses a man's values and renders him characterless and it robs him of any insight into the truth. Its aesthetic qualities are mere frivolities and provide unworthy examples for our imitation. Thus argues the philosopher. But we surely, in estimating the possible role of poetry in education, would turn these judgments upside down. Poetry can be morally uplifting and inspire us to the ideal; it can enlarge our moral sympathies; and it is aesthetically truthful in the sense that it often penetrates to a reality as to a mystery which is denied to prosaic intellects. It could do none of these things in our eyes without the language and the images and the rhythm which are its peculiar possession, and the more of this kind of language you can put into a humane educational system the better.

Small wonder, as we have said, that Plato's interpreters have been reluctant to take him at face value. The temptation in fact to do otherwise is overwhelming. Was not the master a great poet himself, commanding a style which if it chose could abandon abstract argument in order to appeal to all the resources of the imagination either by vivid portraiture or by symbolic myth? Could a writer of such sensitive prose have really been indifferent, nay hostile, to the rhythmic arrangement and the verbal imagery which are the secrets of the poetic style? No, he must have been ironic or temporarily petulant. He cannot, surely, have meant

what he said. The attack on poetry can and must be explained
away, cut down to size, rendered innocuous enough to fit our
conception of what Platonism stands for.[12]

So runs subconsciously the argument, and like all such it
reflects the modern prejudice which finds it necessary from time
to time to save Plato from the consequences of what he may be
saying in order to fit his philosophy into a world agreeable to
modern taste. This may be called the method of reduction—a
type of interpretation that can be applied also to certain facets of
his politics, psychology and ethics—and it consists in pruning his
tall trees till they are fit to be transplanted into a trim garden of
our own making.

The pruning process has been applied quite liberally to that
section of the *Republic* which we are looking at now. Several
types of instrument have been used for the purpose, and applied
to different parts of the argument. On the overall issue, Plato
is accommodated to modern taste by arguing that the programme
of the *Republic* is utopian and that the exclusion of poetry applies
only to an ideal condition not realisable in the recognisable future
or in earthly societies.[13] One might reply that even in that case
why should the Muse of all people be selected for exclusion from
Utopia? But in fact this kind of evasion of Plato's argument
depends as we have said upon the assumption that the *Republic*
(so-called) is all about politics. Is that not the label on the bottle?
Yes, it is, but we must recognise that the contents of the bottle
when tasted in this instance report a strong flavour of educational
but not of political theory. The reforms which are proposed are
considered to be urgent in the present and are not utopian.
Poetry is not charged with a political offence but an intellectual
one, and accordingly the constitution which has to be protected
against her influence is twice defined as 'the polity within the
soul'.[14]

The critics have sought another instrument of evasion by supposing that the more extreme parts of Plato's polemic are directed
against a passing fashion in literary criticism which had been

fostered by the Sophists. They, it is argued, had sought to use the poets artificially as a source of instruction in all useful subjects, and had pushed these claims to absurdity.[15] This explanation will not work. Plato to be sure speaks of the 'champions' of poetry[16] but without identifying them as professionals. They seem rather to be the more vocal representatives of common opinion. He also speaks of these claims as though Homer himself were pushing them; that is, as though public opinion shared this exaggerated opinion of Homer.[17] As for the Sophists, it is not usually remarked, as it ought to be, that Plato's argument here counts them not as his enemies but as his allies in the educational battle he is waging against the poets.[18] This may not conform to the critics' usual preconception of where to place the Sophists in relation to Plato, but for the moment at least Plato has placed them in a context which prohibits the belief that in attacking poetry he is attacking their view of poetry.

Defensive criticism has yet another weapon in its armoury: this is to argue that Plato's target, at least in part of what he says, is not to be identified with poetry as such but is to be confined to drama and even to certain forms of the drama which followed a current fashion of extreme realism.[19] The text however simply cannot stand dismemberment in this fashion, as though Plato at one point focused on Homer, Hesiod and drama, and at another point on drama alone. It is true that tragedy is in the forefront of his mind, simply because, we suggest, it is contemporary. But the striking thing is his constant refusal to draw a formal distinction between epic and tragedy as different genres, or between Homer and Hesiod on the one hand (for Hesiod is also mentioned)[20] and the tragic poets on the other. At one point he even uses language which suggests that 'tragedy', that is drama, is a term by which to define all poetry, applying equally to 'epic and iambic'.[21] It makes no difference, he seems to imply, whether we mean Homer or Aeschylus. He defines the subject matter of the target he is attacking as: 'Human action, whether this action be autonomous, or the result of external compulsion, and also including what men think or feel about their actions; that is, how they interpret their effect in terms of weal or woe to themselves, and their corresponding joys and sorrows.' This definition applies as vividly to the *Iliad* as to any stage play.[22] Indeed, Plato goes on to illustrate what he means by citing the poet's description of a father's grief at the loss of his son. This plainly is a reminiscence of an instance cited earlier in the *Republic*, where Plato is thinking of Priam's collapse at the loss of Hector.[23]

Scholars would not have been tempted to confine Plato's target in these contexts to the drama were it not for the fact that the philosopher does seem to be occupied to a rather extraordinary extent with the emotional reaction of an audience to a public performance. The reason for this preoccupation will be unfolded in a later chapter. It does indeed supply one of the clues to the whole puzzle of what Plato is talking about. In our modern experience the only artistic situation which can provoke such public response as he describes would be the performance of a stage play. So we are tempted to conclude that Plato has his eye exclusively on the stage, forgetting that in Greek practice epic recital equally constituted a performance, and that the rhapsodist[24] apparently exploited a relationship to his audience analogous to that of an actor.

These attempts to lessen the impact of Plato's assault do so by trying to disperse it over a variety of targets. They are well-meaning, but they misconceive the whole spirit and tenor of the argument. It forms a unity; it is launched, as we shall notice in a later analysis, first against the poetised statement as such and second against the poetic experience as such, and it is conducted with intense earnestness. Plato speaks passionately in the tones of a man who feels he is taking on a most formidable opponent who can muster the total forces of tradition and contemporary opinion against him. He pleads, he argues, he denounces, he cajoles. He is a David confronting some Goliath. And he speaks as though he had no choice but to fight the battle to a finish.

There is some mystery here, some historical puzzle. It cannot

be solved by pretending it does not exist, that is, by pretending
that Plato cannot mean what he says. It is obvious that the poetry
he is talking about is not the kind of thing we identify today as
poetry. Or more properly that his poetry and our poetry may
have a great deal in common, but that what must have changed
is the environment in which poetry is practised. Somehow,
Plato is talking about an over-all cultural condition which no
longer exists. What are the clues to this mystery which has so
altered our common values that poetry is now esteemed as one
of the most inspiring and profitable sources for the cultivation of
mind and heart?

Before seeking an answer to this problem it will be necessary
to enlarge it. Plato's polemics against poetry are not confined to
the first half of the last book. Indeed he reminds us as much in
his preface to the book which recalls that poetry 'so far as
mimetic'[25] had already been refused acceptance. The reference is
to an analysis of the *lexis* or verbal mechanisms of poetry which
had been offered in the third book of the *Republic* and which
itself followed a previous attack upon poetry's content (*logoi*).[26]
This attack had begun before the end of Book Two,[27] when Plato
proposed a policy of stern and sweeping censorship of the Greek
poets, both past and present. What guidance, he asks himself and
his readers, can traditional poetry give us in morality? His
answer is: very little; that is, if we take the stories told of the
gods, heroes and ordinary men at all seriously. They are full of
murder and incest, cruelty and treachery; of passions uncon-
trolled; of weakness, cowardice and malice. Repetition of such
material can only lead to imitation by unformed and tender minds.
Censorship is the sole resort. Plato's position is not very different, in short, from those who have advocated a similar editing of
the Old Testament for younger readers, except that, the condition
of Greek mythology being what it was, his proposals had to be
more drastic.

So far, the philosopher's objectives are understandable, whether
or not we think they are mistaken. But he then turns from the

content of the stories told by the poets to consider the way that
they are told. The problem of substance is succeeded by the
problem of style, and it is at this point that the sympathetic
reader begins to feel mystified. Plato proposes a useful if rather
simple classification of poetry under three heads:[28] either it reports
what is happening through the mouth of the poet, or it dramatises what is happening by letting the characters speak in their
own person, or it does both. Homer is here again in the forefront
of the philosopher's mind; he is an exponent of the mixed style,
whereas tragedy is wholly devoted to the dramatic. We shall have
to notice this analysis more closely in the next chapter. For the
present it suffices to observe that Plato obviously is hostile to the
dramatic style as such. To be sure, as it turns out, he will tolerate it;
that is, he will tolerate the poetry of dramatised situation and
speech provided the characters thus presented are ethically
superior. But by the time he recalls this context at the beginning
of the tenth book he has forgotten[29] he was even as tolerant as that.
Through most of what he says in Book Three there persists a
strong undercurrent of suspicion and dislike for the dramatic
empathy as such. A purely descriptive style he seems to think is
always preferable, and he suggests that if Homer were paraphrased to produce a purely descriptive effect, what he is saying
would reduce itself to insignificance.[30] We cannot, that is, evade
the feeling that even in this discussion, so much less drastic in its
proposals than that of Book Ten, Plato is revealing a fundamental
hostility to the poetic experience *per se* and to the imaginative
act which constitutes such a large part of that experience. And
this should be puzzling.

An approach to a solution of the puzzle must begin by first
taking the *Republic* as a whole and getting it into perspective, in
order to ask: What is the overall role which poetry plays in this
treatise? Is it confined to the passages so far reviewed, which
give analytic attention to what the poet says? No, it is not. The
formal thesis which is to be demonstrated and defended in the
body of the *Republic* is proposed for discussion at the opening of

Book Two.[31] 'Socrates' is challenged to isolate the principle of morality in the abstract, and as it may exist as a moral imperative in the soul of man. It is to be defined and defended for its own sake; its rewards or penalties are to be treated as incidental, and it is to be demonstrated that this pure type of morality is the happiest human condition.[32] This challenge dominates the plan of the entire work,[33] and while it is formally answered by the end of Book Nine it continues as the moving cause of the argument of Book Ten.[34]

Why is the challenge so crucial? Surely because it marks an innovation. Such a pure morality has never before been envisaged. What Greece has hitherto enjoyed (says Adeimantus in a passage of great force and sincerity)[35] is a tradition of a half-morality, a sort of twilight zone, at best a compromise, at worst a cynical conspiracy, according to which the younger generation is continually indoctrinated in the view that what is vital is not so much morality as social prestige and material reward which may flow from a moral reputation whether or not this is deserved. Or else (and this is not inconsistent) the young are insensibly warned that virtue is the ideal, of course, but it is difficult and often unrewarding. For the most part a lack of principle proves more profitable. Do not the gods so often reward the unrighteous? And immoral conduct in any case can be expiated quite easily by religious rites. The over-all result is that the Greek adolescent is continually conditioned to an attitude which at bottom is cynical. It is more important to keep up appearances than to practise the reality. Decorum and decent behaviour are not obviously violated, but the inner principle of morality is.

This is an indictment of the Greek tradition and the Greek educational system. The chief authorities cited in support of this type of twilight morality are the poets. Homer and Hesiod are named and quoted, as well as others. It would thus appear that the *Republic* sets itself a problem which is not philosophical in the specialised sense of that term, but rather social and cultural. It questions the Greek tradition as such and the foundations on

which it has been built. Crucial to this tradition is the condition
and quality of Greek education. That process, whatever it is, by
which the mind and attitude of the young are formed lies at the
heart of Plato's problem. And at the heart of this process in turn
somehow lies the presence of the poets. They are central to the
problem. They emerge even here at the beginning of the treatise
as 'the enemy', and that is how they are made to play out their
role in Book Ten.

Once the *Republic* is viewed as an attack on the existing educational apparatus of Greece, the logic of its total organisation becomes clear. And once it is appreciated that the poets are central to
the educational apparatus,[36] the successive critiques of poetry fall
into place. That part of the argument which deals directly with
political theory occupies only about a third of the nine books,[37] and
when it interposes itself, it is to provide successive excuses for progressive discussions of educational theory.[38] The political framework may be utopian; the educational proposals certainly are not.
Thus in Book Two, the problem having been proposed, a problem which concerns the construction of justice in the soul of the
individual, the device is used of describing first a political society
in the large, which shall then correspond to the individual in the
small. The evolution of this society is pursued to the point where
a 'guardian class' emerges as the key class in the state. Whereupon
the argument promptly turns to consider their education, and we
get in effect a programme of revised elementary and secondary
education for existing Greek practice. This concluded, the argument reverts briefly to politics, in order to describe the three-class
state and its virtues in precise detail. Then comes the psychology
of the individual soul, a theory obviously devised to conform to
Plato's educational objectives. Some more political, social and
economic theory then follows—the equality of the sexes, the
communisation of the family, and the role of limited war—until
the paradox is proposed that the only safe and suitable recipient
of political power is the philosopher. This is a novelty. Native
philosophers are to say the least a minority group, and their

character is defined in explicit contrast to that of the theatregoer, the audience at dramatic performances and the like. Once more, by implication, the poets emerge as the enemy.[39] Then, after a picture of the present ambiguous status of the philosopher in existing societies, according to which he is now a fool and now a criminal, we are confronted with the problem of his proper education, and are introduced to the secret of the fount of true knowledge upon which his intellectual integrity is built. And then in the seventh book, the most important book in the *Republic*, there follows the elaborate curriculum which is to train him for his task. It ascends through mathematics to dialectic, and it is to be made available[40] to the age-group between twenty and thirty-five, and it is to be obtained only on a competitive basis, which at successive stages weeds out the lesser abilities.[41] This concluded, the argument through Book Eight reverts to political theory. The degeneration of societies and of individuals from the ideal is presented in four successive stages before, in Book Nine, Plato returns to his original question.[42] Absolute morality as opposed to current morality has now been defined; it is the condition of the true philosopher. Is it also the happiest condition for men? And after answering yes, Plato in the tenth book turns back to a piece of unfinished business. He had defined the new curriculum of the Academy,[43] but he had not explained the total absence therein of poetry.[44] Its exclusion has now become logical and inevitable for its genius is wholly incompatible with the epistemology which lies behind the new programme. So the poets, revealed briefly in Book Five as the enemies of the philosophers, are now in Book Ten fully exposed and expelled from the discipline that must reign over the philosophic stage of instruction.

From this perspective, the educational argument of the *Republic* moves through two main stages: the primary and secondary curriculum, called *mousike*, and the university[45] curriculum of Book Seven. For each of these, a political excuse is furnished, by the introduction of the guardians in Book Two, and of the philosopher-kings in Book Five. At the first level, the traditional poetic curriculum is to be retained but purged, and purged according to principles which seem to us a little curious; at the second level it is to be unceremoniously thrown out.[46]

This is a great and a splendid argument, a major document in the history of European culture. It marks the introduction of the university system into the west. But it proposes for the modern mind several problems which are historical. Why in the first place, in the existing educational system of Greece, is poetry treated as so absolutely central? It appears, if we are to follow Plato, to enjoy a total monopoly. Why in the second place does Plato propose such curious reforms in the field of poetic style? Why is dramatisation so significant, and why does he think it is so dangerous? And thirdly why does he feel it is essential to throw poetry out of the university curriculum altogether? Which is exactly the place where modern taste and practice find it possible in humane studies to exploit the full possibilities of the poetic experience. Why does Plato feel so committed to a passionate warfare upon the poetic experience as such? The answers to these questions may not be irrelevant to a history of the Greek mind.

NOTES

[1] Cf. note 37 below.

[2] 595b5 λώβη . . . τῆς τῶν ἀκουόντων διανοίας.

[3] 608b4 μέγας γάρ, ἔφην, ὁ ἀγὼν κτλ.

[4] 608b1 περὶ τῆς ἐν αὑτῷ πολιτείας δεδιότι cf. 605b7 κακὴν πολιτείαν ἰδίᾳ ἑκάστου τῇ ψυχῇ ἐμποιεῖν.

[5] 601a4-5.

[6] 601a8.

[7] 601b2 ἐπεί γυμνωθέντα γε τῶν τῆς μουσικῆς χρωμάτων τὰ τῶν ποιητῶν, αὐτὰ ἐφ'αὑτῶν λεγόμενα, οἶμαι σε εἰδέναι οἷα φαίνεται.

[8] 602d1-4.

[9] 603b6-d3.

[10] 604e1-2 οὐκοῦν τὸ μὲν πολλὴν μίμησιν καὶ ποικίλην ἔχει, τὸ ἀγανακτητικόν.

[11] 605d3-4.

[12] What might be called the magisterial scholarship on Plato (Zeller, Nettleship,

Wilamowitz, Shorey, among others), confronting what seems surprising or unpalatable in the first half of Book Ten, has continued to insist that a spade should be called a spade. Nettleship, for example, avoiding the temptation to reduce Plato's target, identifies it as 'imaginative literature' (pp. 349, 351) citing the contemporary (Victorian) novel as a parallel. Others who take the target equally seriously have nevertheless resorted to ingenuities. Thus Ferguson (*Introd.*, p. 21) proposes that 'the aesthetic criticism of the *Republic* is almost certainly inherited by Plato from Socrates', and supports the suggestion by an implausible description of a Socrates who could be drawn to a book 'as a carrot draws a donkey'. According to Friedlaender, on the other hand, the mimetic poet of Book Ten is to be equated with the author of Plato's own dialogues; cf. also Lodge, pp. 173-4, who however tries to elevate the dialogues in the metaphysical scale, whereas Friedlaender (if I follow him correctly) depresses them. (At *Laws* 811c, however, the dialogues are recommended as a type of composition which should *replace* poetry.) Such explanations at least have the merit of realising Plato is in earnest. The alternative course, and the scholarship which has pursued it, is reviewed below cap. 2, n. 37. Small wonder that the temptation to judge the matter ambiguously becomes great (cf. Atkins, pp. 47-50, who expresses both willingness and unwillingness to take what Plato says 'at its face value').

[13] Greene, pp. 55-6 (who however refuses to tamper with the plain sense of Book Ten, taken by itself: 'It is clearly his purpose in this place to damage the cause of poetry as much as he can') and Grube, p. 203: 'They are all banished from the ideal state. But this is, I repeat, the ideal state.'

[14] Above, n. 4.

[15] Cornford, p. 322: 'The main object of the attack . . . is the claim currently made by sophists . . . that Homer in particular and in a less degree the tragedians were masters of all technical knowledge.' Cf. ibid., p. 333, n. 2. Ferguson (notes on 598d4 and 606e1) nominates Antisthenes for the role of ἐπαινέτης Ὁμήρου.

[16] 598c7 and d8, 606e1, 607d6 τοῖς προστάταις αὐτῆς.

[17] 599c6 ff.

[18] 600c6 ff.

[19] Webster, 'Gk. Theories', pp. 166-7, who is followed by Cornford, pp. 324 and 335, n. 1.

[20] 600d6.

[21] 602b8-10.

[22] With 603c4 πράττοντας, φαμέν, ἀνθρώπους μιμεῖται ἡ μιμητικὴ βιαίους ἢ ἑκουσίας πράξεις . . . cf. 606e2 πεπαίδευκεν οὗτος ὁ ποιητὴς καὶ πρὸς διοίκησίν τε καὶ παιδείαν τῶν ἀνθρωπίνων πραγμάτων. . . .

[23] 603e3 ff. refers back (ἐλέγομεν) to Book 2, 387d ff., and particularly to 388b4 ff.

[24] At 600d6 Plato uses ῥαψῳδεῖν to describe the activity of both Homer and Hesiod.

[25] 595a5; cf. below, n. 29.

²⁶ 392c6 *Τὰ μὲν δὴ λόγων πέρι ἐχέτω τέλος· τὸ δὲ λέξεως . . . μετὰ τοῦτο σκεπτέον.*

²⁷ 377b5 ff.

²⁸ 392d2 ff.

²⁹ 595a1-5, where *τὸ μηδαμῇ παραδέχεσθαι αὐτῆς* (sc. *τῆς ποιήσεως*) *ὅση μιμητική* seems to be stated as though it were the principle already advocated in Book 3. This phraseology of Plato's has provoked two distinct problems of interpretation: (i) Not all mimetic poetry was banned in Book 3. How explain the apparent contradiction between 3 and 10? (This has encouraged the deduction that Book 10 is an afterthought, and that the connection is careless; cf. below, n. 46.) (ii) As the argument of Book 10 develops, it becomes clear that *mimesis* is to be treated as equivalent to all poetry and not just to part (denied by Collingwood, but at cost of maltreating Plato's text, as pointed out by Rosen, pp. 139-40). How then explain this second apparent contradiction within Book 10 itself? The common solution to both questions lies in the fact that Plato's perspective on poetry is controlled by his educational programme (below, n. 36). At the élite level, there is no room for poetry, as there had been at the school level. Hence the phrase here used at 595a2 *παντὸς ἄρα μᾶλλον ὀρθῶς ᾠκίζομεν τὴν πόλιν* refers to the programme of Book 7, and particularly to 7. 521b13 ff., where gymnastics and music are both dismissed as inadequate for this programme, music failing to provide *ἐπιστήμη* (522a5), and then Plato adds: *μάθημα δὲ πρὸς τοιοῦτον τι ἄγον, οἷον σὺ νῦν ζητεῖς, οὐδὲν ἦν ἐν αὐτῇ.* It is precisely the fundamental lack of this *mathema* within 'music' which is exposed completely in Book 10. But at the university level, Plato does have to consider the role of his own dialogues, especially the *Republic*. They remain a valid educational alternative to 'music'; are they or are they not a form of *poiesis*? They indeed are (on *poiesis*, cap. 2, n. 37; Friedlaender seems to have appreciated this fact, but not the implicit distinction between the prose dialogue and poetry; cf. above, n. 12). Plato with characteristic looseness of terminology is here thinking of *poiesis* generically, and now is prepared to demonstrate that one of its species—namely the traditional poetic curriculum—must be expelled from higher education.

³⁰ 601b2 ff.; cf. 393d8 ff.

³¹ Cornford, p. 41: 'The case which Socrates has to meet is reopened by Glaucon and Adeimantus.'

³² Cf. below, cap. 12, pp. 220 ff..

³³ Below, cap. 12, notes 13, 20.

³⁴ But explicitly recalled only in connection with the second half of Book 10, at 612b2 ff.

³⁵ 362e1-367a4.

³⁶ Anxiety to accommodate the doctrine of Book 10 to a theory of art (below, cap. 2, n. 37) promotes a reluctance to accept priority in Plato's mind of educational over aesthetic purposes; cf. Verdenius, p. 9: 'Plato likes to disguise his theoretical views by his pedagogical zeal'; p. 19: 'the deficiencies of poetry . . . are exaggerated by Plato for his pedagogical purpose'; and p. 24 ' . . . a fatal return to the educationalist position'.

18   PREFACE TO PLATO

³⁷ Book I is certainly 'political', in the sense that the challenge of Thrasymachus depends essentially on his view of how governments are formed and how states are actually governed, and it seems to ignore the educational problem (though in fact it poses almost *ab initio*, 331e ff. the problem of the authority of the poets; cf. Atkins, p. 39). Its character has helped to condition readers to accept the *Republic* as an essay in political theory. But originally the book may have been composed as a separate 'aporetic' dialogue (cf. Cornford, *C.Q.* 1912, p. 254, n. 3), and I have statistically excluded it, to expose the homogeneity of plan in the next nine. In them, political theory is presented in Book 2 368e-374e, Book 3 412b to Book 4 434a, Book 5 449a-473b, Book 8 543a to Book 9 576b. This amounts to roughly 81 Stephanus pages out of 239.

³⁸ At 374d8 (in a political context) the *phylakes* are introduced; at 374e4-376d their human 'type' (*physis*) corresponding to their function is defined, until at 376e2 the question is asked τίς οὖν ἡ παιδεία; How is this type to be trained? The answer terminates at 412b2 οἱ μὲν δὴ τύποι τῆς παιδείας τε καὶ τροφῆς οὗτοι ἂν εἶεν. This concludes the revision of the existing school curriculum. At 473c11 (in a political context) the *philosophos* is introduced; at 474b4 the problem of his human type is first raised, and though the answer becomes involved in the Theory of Forms, it is resumed at Book 6 485a4 ὃ τοίνυν ἀρχόμενοι τούτου τοῦ λόγου (viz. at 474b4) ἐλέγομεν, τὴν φύσιν αὐτῶν πρῶτον δεῖ καταμαθεῖν. The answer to this problem, including the definition of the *physis* and the qualifications required by the definition (Is the philosopher as a type useless or dangerous?), and the possibilities of ever finding such a type, are then pursued through Book 6 to 502c; whereupon at 502c10 three questions are asked: τίνα τρόπον ἡμῖν καὶ ἐκ τίνων μαθημάτων τε καὶ ἐπιτηδευμάτων οἱ σωτῆρες ἐνέσονται τῆς πολιτείας, καὶ κατὰ ποίας ἡλικίας ἕκαστοι ἑκάστων ἁπτόμενοι. These questions presume the answers supplied by the three parables, by the curriculum, and by the age requirements which occupy the rest of Book 6 and all of Book 7. Thus the two educational programmes are in argument organised symmetrically. In each case, a political excuse is furnished for providing a given type of human being suitable for a given political function. That type is then given psychological definition (which in the case of the philosopher has to be elaborated) and the definition is followed by a programme of training.

³⁹ Cf. below, cap. 13, notes 26-31.

⁴⁰ 537b8-539 e2.

⁴¹ The process of selection continues even after the descent into *empeiria* (539e5-540a5).

⁴² 588b 1-4.

⁴³ Friedlaender, p. 92: 'The education of the guardians (sc. in Book 7) cannot differ very significantly from that of the students at the Academy'; cf. also Grube, p. 240.

⁴⁴ The *Protagoras* (347c-348a) anticipates the *Republic* by demonstrating that the attempt by adults to deal seriously with the poets is mistaken; their mental needs require a dialectical discipline. The *Laws* retains this premiss, but focuses main attention on the school curriculum ('Art as a whole is relegated to the

education of the young and the relaxation of adults'—Grube, p. 207, where for 'art' read 'poetry'; cf. also Gould, p. 118, who suggests that as Plato finished the *Laws*, he 'thought of the Nocturnal Council as pursuing a course of study almost identical with that of the Guardians in the *Republic*'). This marks no change: poetry is to be tolerated and indeed used by the legislator at the primary and secondary level of education, even when expelled from the university; Marrou p. 488.

⁴⁵ For the qualifications which necessarily limit the use of this word as applied to the Academy see Cherniss, pp. 61-70.

⁴⁶ The cumulative logic of this arrangement disposes of the argument that 'the attack on poetry in this part has the air of an appendix, only superficially linked with the preceding . . .', and renders unnecessary the speculation that 'the strictures on dramatic poetry . . . had become known and provoked criticism to which Plato rushed to reply' (Cornford, p. 321, and cf. Nettleship, pp. 340-1). Even if either half of the tenth book lacks some internal revision (so Nettleship, pp. 341, 355) this would not affect the overall structure of the treatise. The expulsion of poetry from higher education cannot be defended until that education has been defined, and any actual rewards that may accrue to justice cannot be suggested until after justice has first been established as autonomous. As early as 1913, Hackforth, replying to Cornford, had argued (a) that there were 'no important points in which the educational scheme of 6-7 is incompatible with that of 2-4', but (b) that the two parts nevertheless represented 'two radically different lines of thought'. He however identified the difference as originating in metaphysics rather than in the wish to add to the existing Greek apparatus of education; but cf. Havelock, 'Why was Socrates Tried', p. 104.

CHAPTER TWO

Mimesis

WE have spoken of the undercurrent of Plato's hostility to the poetic experience as such—a phenomenon so disconcerting to the Platonist, who may feel that at this point in his thinking the master has let him down. Plato's critique of poetry and the poetic situation is in fact complicated, and it is impossible to understand it unless we are prepared to come to terms with that most baffling of all words in his philosophic vocabulary, the Greek word *mimesis*.[1] In the *Republic* Plato applies it in the first instance as a stylistic classification defining the dramatic as opposed to descriptive composition. But as he goes on he seems to enlarge it to cover several other phenomena. As these are comprehended, some of the clues to the character of the Greek cultural situation begin to emerge.

The word is introduced[2] as he turns in Book Three from the kind of tale narrated by the poet to the problem of the poet's 'technique of verbal communication'. This cumbrous phrase may be adequate to translate the overtones of the Greek word *lexis*, which, as is made clear when Plato proceeds, covers the entire verbal apparatus, rhythmic and imagistic, at the poet's disposal. The critique which now follows, on careful inspection, divides into three parts. Plato begins by examining the case of the poet *per se*,[3] his style of composition and the effects he may achieve. In the middle of his argument he switches to consider problems connected with the psychology of the 'guardians',[4] that is, of his citizen soldiers, problems which he regards as related, but which certainly pertain to a different class in the community, for citizen soldiers cannot be said by any stretch of the imagination to be poets. Later still,[5] he turns back again to the problem of poetic composition and style, and the poet rather than the guardian once more occupies the field of vision. Let us survey first what is said in the two passages on the poets and their poetry.

Plato begins by arguing in effect that in all verbal communication there is a fundamental distinction between the descriptive method and that of dramatisation. Homer is still the prototype of both. His poems divide into the speeches which are exchanged, as between actors, and the statements which intervene, spoken by the poet in person. The former are examples of *mimesis*, of dramatic 'imitation' or 'impersonation', the latter are examples of 'simple rehearsal'[6] or as we might say, straight narrative in the third person. Epic is thus *in toto* an example of the mixed mode of composition, whereas drama exemplifies only mimetic composition. Plato's words make it clear that he is not interested in the distinction between epic and tragedy as genres, which we find familiar, but in basic types of verbal communication. Drama according to his classification is comprehended under epic, as is narrative. He hints as much when, in answer to the suggestion of Adeimantus that he is preparing to exclude drama from his ideal state, he replies: 'Perhaps; but perhaps also my target is bigger. I don't yet know. We have to proceed whither the logic of our argument carries us':[7] a hint which looks forward to the more fundamental critique of Book Ten, and warns us that the formal distinction between epic and drama is not in itself relevant to his philosophic purpose.

So far, we conclude, the term *mimesis* has been usefully and rather precisely applied to define a method of composition. But there is slipped in, during the course of this part of the argument, a very curious statement: 'When the poet speaks a speech in the person of another, he makes his verbal medium (*lexis*) resemble the speaker'—and then Plato continues: 'Any poet who makes himself resemble another in voice or gesture is imitating him' (and hence practising *mimesis*).[8] Now, this on the face of it is a *non-sequitur*. The missing link which has slipped out between these two statements would run as follows: 'Any poet who makes his verbal medium resemble the speaker is making himself resemble the speaker.'[9] Now this, if applied to the creative act of composition on the part of the poet, is patently untrue. The poet applies his conscious skill to choosing words temporarily appropriate to Agamemnon. So far from 'imitating' Agamemnon in his own character, he must keep his own artistic integrity detached, for in a moment the same skill is to be employed to put appropriate words in the mouth of Achilles. But Plato's supposition would be approximately true if it were applied not to the creation of a poem but to an actor or reciter who recites it. He in a measure does have to 'identify' with the original supplied to him by the creative artist. He has to throw himself into the part precisely because he is not creating it but reproducing it, and this reproduction is for the benefit of an audience whose interest and attention he must engage. He can refuse to 'imitate', and get only a lukewarm response.

The first puzzle concerning *mimesis* as the word is used by Plato has now already appeared. Why use it to describe both an act of composition which constitutes an act of creation, and a performance by an actor who is a mouthpiece or a reciter? Is this a loose and confusing use of the word, or is Plato expressing faithfulness to a cultural situation which is alien to our own?

When in the last third[10] of his argument Plato returns to the poet's case, the ambiguity between the situation of the creative artist and that of the actor or performer is maintained. It is impossible to be sure which of them in any given sentence is more prominently before the philosopher's eye. Considered as an 'orator', our Platonic poet will prefer a style with a minimum of *mimesis* and a maximum of description. His indulgence in extreme forms of *mimesis*, extending even to the growls and squeals of animals, will be in direct proportion to his inferiority as a poet. And then Plato adds a comment which is in part a stylistic analysis and in part a philosophic judgment: 'The dramatic-mimetic mode involves all-various shapes of changes.'[11] It is polymorphous and, we might say, exhibits the characteristics of a rich and unpredictable flux of experience. The descriptive mode cuts this tendency down to a minimum. Are we then to admit the performance of that kind of versatile poet whose skill can enable him to be any kind of person and to represent any and everything?[12] Emphatically no. Clearly, then, the situation of the creative artist and of the performer of a work of art still overlap each other in Plato's mind.

But this peroration raises still another problem which we have touched on in the previous chapter. Why is the philosopher so profoundly hostile to the range and versatility which dramatisation makes possible? It has been argued that his target is merely the extreme and uncouth realism of some contemporaries.[13] But philosophic objection is taken to variety and range in principle, and will apply to good drama as well as bad. How comes it that a poetic virtue (in our eyes) which enlarges both range of meaning in the product and emotional sympathy in the audience is converted by Plato precisely into a vice?

In the intervening section of his argument Plato suddenly turns from the poets and performers to consider the young guardians of his state, and applies the mimetic situation to their case. Are they to be mimetic? he asks.[14] Now they presumably are not going to be either poets or actors, but citizen soldiers, and in that case, how can the problem of *mimesis*, if it be a matter of artistic style and method, affect them at all? The clue lies in the 'occupations', 'pursuits', 'procedures', or 'practices' (all of these are possible translations of the single Greek word *epitedeumata*) which are admittedly central to the life of these young men.[15] They have as adults to become 'craftsmen of freedom'[16] for the state. But they also have to learn this trade, and they learn by practice and by performance, in fact by an education in which they are trained to 'imitate' previous models of behaviour.[17] Hence *mimesis* now becomes a term applied to the situation of a student apprentice, who absorbs lessons, and repeats and hence 'imitates' what he is told to master. The point is made all the clearer when Plato recalls that earlier social and educational principle which required

division of labour and specialisation.[18] The young guardians pose
a problem of training. Their assigned task will not be narrowly
technical but one which requires character and ethical judgment.
These he says are precisely the result of a training which employs
constant 'imitation' carried out 'from boyhood'.[19] Clearly therefore the context of the argument has shifted from the artistic
situation to the educational one. But this only complicates still
further the mystery of the ambivalence of *mimesis*. Why should
Plato, not content with applying the same word both to the
creation and to the performance of the poem, also apply it to the
learning act achieved by a pupil? Why in fact are the situations
of artist, of actor and of pupil confused? Nor does this exhaust
the ambiguities of the word. For as he warms to his theme of the
pupil-guardian and how his moral condition depends on the
correct kind of 'imitations', the pupil seems to turn into a grown
man[20] who for some reason is continually engaged in reciting or
performing poetry himself which may involve him in unfortunate types of imitation. He had better, says Plato, be on his
guard to censor his own performance. In short, not only is the
poetic situation confused with the educational, but the educational
is then confused with the recreational, if that is the correct word
by which to describe the mood of adult recitation.

It is therefore not much wonder if scholars and critics have had
difficulty in deciding precisely what Plato does mean by *mimesis*.[21]
And before we leave Book Three, there is still one more complication we have to notice. The word as introduced was used to
define only one *eidos*[22] or species of composition, namely the
dramatic, to which was opposed both the 'simple' style of direct
narration and the 'mixed' style which employs the two together.
To this meaning it adheres through most of the argument on
style. But before the end is reached, Adeimantus without objection from Socrates can speak of that 'imitation of a virtuous
model which is simple'.[23] Is this a slip, or are we to infer that
imitation is a term which is also applicable to non-dramatic types
of poetry? And so to all poetry *qua* poetry?

This is precisely the turn given to the word as the argument of Book Ten unfolds itself. True, the poetry to be banned is at first qualified as 'poetry in so far as it is mimetic,' but this qualification then appears to be dropped.[24] Plato as he says himself has now sharpened his vision of what poetry really is.[25] He has transcended the critique of Book Three, which confined itself to drama as its target. Now, not only the dramatist, but Homer and Hesiod come into question. Nor is the issue any longer confined to protecting the moral character. The danger is one of crippling the intellect. And why this? The answer, he replies, will require a complete and exhaustive definition of what *mimesis* really amounts to.[26] This answer depends on whether we accept[27] the Platonic doctrine, established in the intervening books, that absolute knowledge, or true science if we so choose to call it, is of the Forms and of the Forms alone, and that applied science or skilled technique depends on copying the Forms in artifacts. The painter[28] and the poet achieve neither. Poetry is not so much non-functional as anti-functional. It totally lacks the precise knowledge that a craftsman for example can apply to his trade,[29] still less can it employ the precise aims and goals which guide the skilled educator in his training of the intellect. For this training depends on the skill of calculation and measurement; the illusions of sensible experience are critically corrected by the controlling reason. Poetry *per contra* indulges in constant illusionism, confusion and irrationality.[30] This is what *mimesis* ultimately is, a shadow-show of phantoms, like those images seen in the darkness on the wall of the cave.[31]

We have summarised the decisive part of this argument. In a later chapter we shall return to it in more detail. But it is now obvious that *mimesis* has become the word *par excellence* for the over-all linguistic medium of the poet and his peculiar power through the use of this medium (meter and imagery are included in the attack) to render an account of reality. For Plato, reality is rational, scientific and logical, or it is nothing. The poetic medium, so far from disclosing the true relations of things or the true definitions of the moral virtues, forms a kind of refracting screen which disguises and distorts reality and at the same time distracts us and plays tricks with us by appealing to the shallowest of our sensibilities.

So *mimesis* is now the total act of poetic representation, and no longer simply the dramatic style. On what grounds could Plato apply the same word first in the narrower sense and then in the broader? And how, we repeat, can we explain in this broader sense the fundamental philosophic hostility to the poetic experience as such?

As he dissects the poetic account, so he also seeks to define that part of our consciousness to which it is designed to appeal,[32] and to which the poetic language and rhythm are addressed. This is the area of the non-rational, of the pathological emotions, the unbridled and fluctuating sentiments with which we feel but never think. When indulged in this way they can weaken and destroy that rational faculty in which alone lies hope of personal salvation and also scientific assurance.[33] *Mimesis* has just been applied to the content of the poetised statement. But as he considers the appeal of this kind of statement to our consciousness, he is drawn back into portraying the pathology of the audience at a performance of poetry, and *mimesis* resumes one of those meanings it had assumed in Book Three. It now is the name of the active personal identification by which the audience sympathises with the performance.[34] It is the name of our submission to the spell. It describes no longer the artist's imperfect vision, whatever that may be, but the identification of the audience with that vision.

For this meaning of *mimesis*, Book Three, we repeat, had prepared us, and if Plato had used the word only or mainly in this sense we would have less difficulty in understanding the usage. 'Imitation', regarded as a form of impersonation, is an understandable conception. Though we might argue that the good actor may recreate his part anew, in general his performance is readily viewed as an act of imitation. We raise our eyebrows, or should, at the further application of the word to the involvement of the audience in a performance. Plato's descriptions in this context have a ring of mob psychology about them. They do not sound too much like the mood and attitude in which modern theatre-goers attend a play, still less like the kind of attention a pupil gives to his lesson. We in fact have to notice here a hint of a curious emotionalism on the part of the Greeks which is alien to our experience. It is all part of the larger puzzle still unresolved.

But nothing is quite so hard to digest, if modern values and sensibilities are taken into account, as that picture of *mimesis* which Plato gives when he applies the word to the very content of the poetic communication, the genius of the poetised experience. Why on earth, we wish to ask, should he attempt to judge poetry as though it were science or philosophy or mathematics or technology? Why demand that the poet 'know', in the sense that the carpenter knows about a bed? Surely this is to degrade the standards of poetic creation by submitting them to criteria which are unworthy or at least improper and irrelevant. Need the poet be an expert in the matter that he sings of? Such a presupposition does not make sense.

This however is precisely the supposition that Plato in Book Ten adopts without question and it brings us to confront our last and most crucial problem in the search for clues as to what all this means. We saw in our review of the treatise as a whole that, as educational theory is central to the plan of the *Republic*, so also poetry is central in the educational theory. It occupied this position so it seems in contemporary society, and it was a position held apparently not on the grounds that we would offer, namely poetry's inspirational and imaginative effects, but on the ground that it provided a massive repository of useful knowledge, a sort of encyclopedia of ethics, politics, history and technology which the effective citizen was required to learn as the core of his educational equipment. Poetry represented not something we call by that name, but an indoctrination which today would be comprised in a shelf of text books and works of reference.

Plato in the tenth book is quite explicit: 'Our next task is a critical examination of tragedy and Homer the prototype thereof. We are told in certain quarters that these poets possess the know-how of all techniques and all human affairs pertaining to vice and virtue, not to mention divine matters.' These claims in Plato's eyes are impossible to maintain. Let us however, he says, ignore for the moment the claim to technical competence and come instead 'to those major matters of supreme value on which Homer undertakes to speak, warfare, military leadership, politics and administration, and the education of men'. Thus phrased, the claim becomes Homer's own. That is, Plato is reporting the traditional estimate placed upon his poetry, and that estimate crystallised itself in the conception of Homer as the Hellenic educational manual *par excellence*. He proceeds to expose it as false and asks rhetorically 'if he had really been able to educate men and make them better, . . . then who have been his pupils and his protégés?' The Sophists have their following, which at least proves their educational effectiveness. But where are Homer's followers, or Hesiod's?[35]

The question sounds too much like an *argumentum ad hominem*. Plato at any rate turns from rhetoric back to dialectic, and proceeds to demonstrate at length the complete gulf between the truth, as understood by reason, and the illusions effected by poetry. And then, as he begins to approach the terminus of his polemic, he cites once more that conception of Homer which he finds so impossible: 'When you encounter encomiasts of Homer who say that this poet has educated Hellas for the purpose of administration of human affairs and of education therein; that he is the correct authority to be taken up and learnt, since this poet can guide the conduct of man's entire life . . . '—in the face of this claim one can only reply gently—'You may be as good a man as is possible under the circumstances . . .' (that is, as a product of Homeric education); but nevertheless, Homer as we have him is not admissible. Yet how hard it is to do this, exclaims Plato. Don't we all feel Homer's spell? But still our feeling for him, though traditional and deep, is a love that we have to renounce, so dangerous it is:

'Our *eros* for this kind of poetry is bred in us by the educational nurture characteristic of the better polities.' But it is perilous, and we shall say over to ourselves our rational antidote to it, 'taking great care less we fall back again into this immature passion which the many still feel'.[36]

It is clear from these statements that the poets in general and Homer in particular were not only considered as the source of instruction in ethics and administrative skills but also enjoyed a sort of institutional status in Greek society. This status received, as it were, state support, because they supplied a training which the social and political mechanism relied on for its efficient working.

All this forces us to realise that Plato assumes among his contemporaries a view of the poet and his poetry which is wholly unfamiliar to our way of thinking. We assume that the poet is an artist and his products are works of art. Plato seems at one point to think so too, when he compares the poet to the visual artist, the painter. But he does not make this comparison on aesthetic grounds. In fact, it is not too much to say that the notion of the aesthetic as a system of values which might apply to literature and to artistic composition never once enters the argument. Plato writes as though he had never heard of aesthetics, or even of art.[37] Instead he insists on discussing the poets as though their job was to supply metrical encyclopedias. The poet is a source on the one hand of essential information and on the other of essential moral training. Historically speaking, his claims even extend to giving technical instruction. It is as though Plato expected poetry to perform all those functions which we relegate on the one hand to religious instruction or moral training and on the other to classroom texts, to histories and handbooks, to encyclopedias and reference manuals. This is a way of looking at poetry which in effect refuses to discuss it as poetry in our sense at all. It refuses to allow that it may be an art with its own rules rather than a source of information and a system of indoctrination.

This is to us an astonishing assumption, but once accepted, it provides the logical excuse for Plato to apply to poetry that philosophic critique which he does by placing poetry in relation to the Theory of Forms. The Theory is epistemological; it seeks to define the character of that knowledge which we would call universal, exact and final. Mathematical science will in this instance suffice as an example. Applied science is not alien to this theoretic kind of knowledge. On the contrary it applies it by using the unique and exact Forms as models which are copied in existing material products. Beds in the plural are the carpenter's copies of the unique Form of bed. But the poet simply talks about a bed in his poetry without knowing anything about it or attempting to make it. This kind of argument is perhaps fair to Homer if Homer is really pretending to be a manual on the manufacture of beds and the like. For if so it is a bad manual, says Plato. It is not composed by that kind of man who technically understands beds or ships or horses or anything else. On the contrary what he is doing is simply painting word-portraits of what beds look like in a thousand different confusing situations and he is effective only in the illusions he is able to create by verbal and rhythmic images, not in exact procedures for manufacture.

This is the 'mimesis at second remove'[38] to which Plato consigns the poet in the more fundamental part of his critique in Book Ten. This use of mimesis essentially indicates that the poetic statement is mummery; it is illusionism, as opposed to the carpenter's mechanical exactitude and faithfulness,[39] and the term is applied to the entire basic content of the poetised statement as such and not just to drama.

Such is the last and final metamorphosis of mimesis at Plato's hands. It is truly a protean word. But behind the puzzle of its application in the sense of total poetic illusionism is that second puzzle which gives rise to the first. This is, we repeat, to us the

astonishing presumption that poetry was conceived and intended
to be a kind of social encyclopedia. If it was so designed, it was
obviously by Plato's day doing a very poor job. It could not
carry out this task according to the standards which Plato required in the Academy. The hallmark of his own curriculum is
conveyed in the Greek term *episteme* for which our word science
is one possible equivalent. The graduate of the Platonic academy
has passed through a rigorous training in mathematics and logic
which has equipped him to define the aims of human life in
scientific terms and to carry them out in a society which has been
reorganised upon scientific lines. The poet as a possible claimant
to fulfil this role thus becomes an easy target; we feel too easy.
He should never have been placed in such an inappropriate
position in the first place. Plato should never have done this to
him. But he does do it, and we have to ask why.

NOTES

[1] Some recent interpretations of this term are reviewed below, n. 37, and its
previous history at cap. 3, n. 22.

[2] 392d5.

[3] 392d2 ὅσα ὑπὸ μυθολόγων ἢ ποιητῶν λέγεται.

[4] 394e1 πότερον μιμητικοὺς ἡμῖν δεῖ εἶναι τοὺς φύλακας ἢ οὔ.

[5] At 397a1, but the transition is supplied by the insertion of ῥήτορος 396e10.

[6] ἁπλῆ διήγησις 392d5, 393d7, 394b1.

[7] 394d5-9.

[8] 393c1-9.

[9] Adam Parry has pointed out to me that the gap in English syntax is wider
than in the Greek, where ὁμοιοῦν τὴν αὑτοῦ λέξιν leads naturally into ὁμοιοῦν
ἑαυτὸν κατὰ φωνήν.

[10] 397a1-398b5.

[11] 397c5.

[12] 398a1-2.

[13] Cap. I, n. 19.

[14] Above, n. 4.

[15] 394e3 ff.; cf. 395c2.

[16] 395c1.

[17] 395c3 ff.

[18] 394e3.

[19] 395d1-3.

[20] 396c5 μέτριος ἀνήρ.

[21] Below, n. 37.

[22] 396b10.

[23] 397d4-5, where however I have paraphrased τὸν τοῦ ἐπιεικοῦς μιμητήν ἄκρατον to express the inference that the quality of the agent here expresses the quality of the performance.

[24] Above, cap. I, n. 29.

[25] 595a6 ἐναργέστερον . . . φαίνεται.

[26] 595c7 μίμησιν ὅλως ἔχοις ἄν μοι εἰπεῖν ὅτι ποτ' ἐστίν; This would seem to dispose of the argument (below, n. 37) that there are two kinds of professional (i.e. artistic) mimesis, only one of which is dealt with in Book Ten.

[27] 596a5 ἐκ τῆς εἰωθυίας μεθόδου.

[28] It is the inclusion here of ζωγράφος (first at 596e6) as being also a μιμητής (597e2) which seems to have encouraged the inference that Plato is putting forward a 'Theory of Art' (below, n. 37). Thus Verdenius, p. 15: 'he expressly declares poetry and painting to be of a similar nature . . . so their characteristics are to a certain extent mutually applicable.' But the painter's presence in the present context is required for reasons which are purely ad hoc. He is a supposed δημιουργός (596e6) whose method is inferior to that of the 'true demiourgos', namely the κλινοποιός or τέκτων (597b9). Both work with their hands (cf. χειροτέχνης 596c5, 597a6). This enables Plato to construct a hierarchy of production in descending series (cf. Rosen, p. 142), that is, a hierarchy of 'producers' (ποιηταί 596d4). This in turn enables him to attach verbally to this series the poietes par excellence, namely the 'poet'. The need for constructing this series also explains the otherwise extraordinary suggestion that 'the god' must be the 'producer' of the Form. But the ultimate target remains not the 'artist' (in our sense) but exclusively the 'producer of words', that is, the 'poet' (597b6). He is (i) an indiscriminate copier of physical objects as in a reflection (596b12 ff.; this seems to presuppose the doctrine of εἰκασία as illustrated in the bottom section of the Line in Book 6; cf. Nettleship, p. 347, and Paton, p. 100) and (ii) a copier who also refracts and distorts and is therefore untruthful (598a7 ff., 602c7 ff.); this presupposes the doctrine of πλάνη in Book 5 (with 602c12 cf. 479d9, and below, cap 12, n. 37). In sum, then, the painter's technique is here made temporarily useful to Plato as (i) making possible the degradation of the poet below the craftsman, (ii) illustrating these two particular defects in poetry.

[29] 598c6-d5.

[30] 602c4-603b8.

[31] 598b6 ff.

[32] 603b10 ἐπ' αὐτὸ αὖ ἔλθωμεν τῆς διανοίας τοῦτο ᾧ προσομιλεῖ ἡ τῆς ποιήσεως μιμητική.

[33] Cf. especially 605b4 ἀπόλλυσι τὸ λογιστικόν.

[34] 605d3 ἐνδόντες ἡμᾶς αὐτοὺς ἑπόμεθα συμπάσχοντες.

[35] 598d7 ff., 599c6 ff., 600c2 ff.

[36] 606e1 ff., 607e4 ff.

[37] Among those who have denied any theory of art to Plato can be numbered Wilamowitz, Shorey, Cassirer (cf. Verdenius, p. 39, n. 9) and most lately Friedlaender (p. 119: 'the construction of which Plato never envisaged'). To their number can be added Paton, Sikes (cap. 3), and Rosen, who arguing in different contexts have concluded that Plato's final judgment on poetry is epistemological, so that its expulsion is determined by the premisses of his own system. A formidable roster of scholars (among them Greene, Tate, Grube, Collingwood, Webster, Cornford, Lodge, Verdenius) have in recent times sought to evade this conclusion, prompted by two understandable but mistaken assumptions (i) that 'art' must have meant to Plato much what it means to us, and consequently must be accommodated within the Platonic system, (ii) that Greek 'art' must include Greek poetry. These are held in defiance of the fact that neither 'art' nor 'artist', *as we use the words*, is translatable into archaic or high-classical Greek (cf. Collingwood, p. 6: 'If people have no word for a certain kind of thing it is because they are not aware of it as a distinct kind'). The possibility of a notion of aesthetic, as a distinct discipline, first dawns with Aristotle. It is improper to cite his theory of *mimesis* and its influence on the later 'classic' conception of artistic imitation (as e.g. does Verdenius, pp. 38, 41) as though it supported the proposition that Plato had already developed a theory of aesthetics. Support for a favourable Platonic estimate of 'art' must of course be extracted if possible from his text, and the methods of extraction have been various: (a) Plato it is argued believed in a 'good' *mimesis*, as well as the 'bad' variety discussed in *Republic*. The bad sort imitates realistically, but the good sort imitates ideally, so that while a 'bad' artist (and poet) deals with superficial appearances at two removes from reality, the 'good' artist (and poet) can imitate the Forms, or ideal beauty, at only one remove. To support the invention of a good *mimesis*, liberal use is made of such passages as *Rep.* 5.472d where the painter is cited for his construction of an 'ideal' man (dismissed by Wilamowitz, I p. 703, n. I, as 'meaningless idealisation incompatible with a true aesthetic') and *Rep.* 6 500b8–501d10 (admitted by Tate, who uses it, to be nevertheless only a 'sustained metaphor' C.Q. 1928, p. 21), and forced interpretations are placed upon the discussion of images and the use of the term *mimesis* in the *Sophist* (see below). This method was sponsored by Tate's two articles in 1928 and 1932, and has been adopted with some variations by Grube, Webster, Lodge, Cornford and Verdenius; cf. also Atkins, p. 68. Or else (b) it is argued that aside from mimetic art and poetry which is bad, and which is the variety discussed and dismissed in the *Republic*, Plato believed in a wholly non-mimetic variety, i.e. non-representational, which is good. This is philologically the converse of method (a), and in effect cancels it out, though it is forced to exploit many of the same available testimonies. The most vigorous exposition of this position has been Collingwood's: 'This Platonic attack on art is a myth whose vitality throws a lurid light on the scholarship of those who have invented and perpetuated it. The facts are that "Socrates" in Plato's *Republic* divided poetry into two

kinds, one representative and the other not . . . and banishes all representative poetry but retains certain specified kinds of poetry as not representative' (p. 46). Finally (c), fervent appeal is made (cf. Verdenius *passim*) to the many passages in the dialogues where the poet is described as inspired, inspiration being interpreted not in the pejorative sense of ignorance (cf. Atkins, p. 39; Rosen, 144-5) but as defining direct access to truth and reality. Of these various expedients for rescuing Plato from the consequences of his own words, it may be observed that (i) they all seek to correct the *explicit* discussion in Book 10 by resort to what can be extracted *implicitly* from his works elsewhere, (ii) they rely heavily on the metaphorical use of imitation, similitude, likeness, as exploited by Plato to describe the relationship of our lives (if we lived them aright) to the Forms (Tate, 1928, pp. 18-19, fails to note that at *Rep.* 401-2, a passage he exploits, it is 'we', i.e. philosophers, who know how to incorporate the ideal in the lives of pupils, while the poets remain under 'our' orders) or of particulars to the Forms. But nowhere does he suggest that poetry itself constitutes such a likeness, or ever could (on this metaphor in Platonism see below, cap. 14, n. 34). (iii) As it is erroneous to confine the sense, and hence the problem, of *mimesis* to 'imitation' (see my text), so also *poiesis* should not always be treated as though it were coterminous with 'poetry'. It covers both production and authorship (cf. *Sympos.* 205b8 ff.) and hence '*mimetic poiesis*' is a category of authorship; in *Rep.* 10 it defines that part of authorship which is 'poetic', (iv) in the *Sophist*, where *mimesis* may be said to be partly rehabilitated, poetry is not. As a term in the *diaeresis*, *poiesis* is still, as it was in *Rep.* 10, the symbol of production (265b), the 'images' which are considered are not the creations of what we call 'art', and are in any case never rescued from the stigma of deception and perhaps of falsehood (240a, 260c), and *mimesis* (with *mimema*) is used to describe a type of production or of statement in which truth is expressed only relatively or conditionally (264c12 ff.), as opposed to the absolute certainties of *episteme* derived from the world of Forms. This type of limited truth consciously attempted (267e) Plato now recognises to have its place in discourse, but it has nothing to do with 'art', or with poetry, which, so Plato (if he were asked the question) would reply, is that version of *mimesis* composed by a man who does not know what he is doing. (v) To assume that Plato would subscribe to the pretensions of the Hebrew prophets, or alternatively of the Romantic poets, is to stand Platonism on its head (on the inspirational controversy cf. below, cap. 9, notes 28, 29). Even in the *Phaedrus*, that supposed tribute to the superior insight of the inspired artist (Atkins, p. 53), the *poietikos* (248d-e), is relegated to sixth place from reality, below both *philosophos* and *politikos*. There is perhaps a fourth expedient which can be tried to convert Plato into an art-sympathiser, one which relies not on philology but on semantic manipulation. The words 'art' and 'artist' can be used to translate the metaphorical use in Plato of words like *techne* and *demiourgos* ('the art of living', 'the art of government', 'the artist of the universe'; cf. Lodge *passim*), and what is said in these metaphorical contexts is then interpreted as part of Plato's 'theory of art' in the professional sense. Hence even the Platonic philosopher can by this device be turned into an 'artist', and

Plato's text be reduced to a glutinous paste capable of adhering to any mental object in the critic's mind.

[38] 597e3 ff.

[39] Lodge, p. 96, *à propos* of Book 10, can write: 'The sculptor and the painter (and this is the essence of their arts) produce something whose proportions look "right" to the beholder and suggest the precise mathematical proportions of the original.' I take Plato's sense to be the exact opposite; such proportions, so far from being suggested, are falsified.

CHAPTER THREE

Poetry as Preserved Communication

IF we now look back over what has been said in the two
previous chapters it can be seen that in Plato's pages the Greek
poets play a series of roles which are hard to explain. Perhaps
Plato is trying to tell us something about them which is more
important than has been realised, but if so, what is it? Somehow
their presence seems to brood over his long argument as though
they were a persistent obstacle which might cut him off from contact with his public or pupils, and bar the way to Platonism.

However, our examination of what he says about them has not
really revealed the reason for this feeling. The problems it has
exposed are as follows:

First, why is it that poetry is treated as though it held a
monopoly in the present educational apparatus?

Second, why can the works of Homer and the tragedians be
treated not as though they were art but as though they were a vast
encyclopedia containing information and guidance for the
management of one's civic and personal life?

Third, why is Plato so absolutely determined to exclude poetry
altogether from higher education, rather than grant it at least
a minor role at this level?

Fourth, why as he applies the term *mimesis* to poetry and
examines its implications does he seem to assume that the artist's
'act' of creation, the performer's 'act' of imitation, the pupil's
'act' of learning, and the adult's 'act' of recreation all overlap
each other? Why are these situations so confused and jumbled up
together?

Fifth, why can he apply the term *mimesis* now to drama and

now to epic, and think that the genre distinction between them does not matter?

Sixth, why is he so frequently obsessed with the psychology of response as it is experienced by the audience? In his description of the emotional impact of poetry he seems often to be describing an almost pathological situation. At least he is exposing an intensity of response in Greek students and in Greek audiences which to us is unfamiliar.

These questions cannot all be answered at once, but they form a connected pattern and lead to a set of conclusions which as they are taken together illuminate the general character of the Greek cultural condition and begin to unlock some of the secrets of the Greek mind. Let us begin by noticing the rather obvious fact, implicit in problems five and six, that Plato finds it difficult to discuss poetry or make any statements about it without discussing also the conditions under which it is performed. This is strikingly true of the first exposition of *mimesis* in Book Three; it is equally true of the more advanced and drastic critique in Book Ten. The actual performance of poetry, we conclude, was far more central to the Greek cultural pattern than we would normally conceive to be the case. It is not just a matter of selected readings given in public or private nor of annual festivals in the theatre. On the contrary the fact that the situation of the learner on the one hand and of the adult on the other are treated without firm distinction implies that performance of poetry was fundamental in adult recreation: that the two situations in Plato's eyes were somehow serving the same end. The class who sat under the harpist and the audience who attended either an epic recital or a performance in the theatre were partners in a general and common practice.

The plain conclusion of this is that performance means oral performance. These people young and old did not habitually read books either for instruction or for amusement. They did not digest an item of information at a desk nor did they acquire their knowledge of Homer and of drama by buying the *Iliad* or a play and taking it home to read. The testimony of Plato already reviewed allows no other conclusion. And it is supported by that vocabulary in which he casually and repeatedly discusses the situation of the poet in his society. As we have seen, when the mighty argument opens in Book Two, the poets are discovered in the foreground of the discussion. After an interval they return to it and submit to censorship of matter and of style, in Books Two and Three. And then in Book Five their influence appears in the background as the opponent of philosophy, and in Book Ten they are dissected and damned. In all these discussions, over and over again, the relationship of the student or the public to poetry is assumed to be that of listeners, not readers, and the relationship of the poet to his public or his constituency is always that of a reciter and/or an actor, never of a writer.[1] The instances are too numerous to mention. One can be cited which happens to be striking. To open the polemic of Book Ten Plato charac- terises the offence of poetry as fundamental. Why is this? Because it 'cripples the intellect', but he adds 'the intellect of the listeners', and the addition, so unnecessary from our standpoint, bespeaks the unconscious assumption that even the intellectual influence of poetry, negative as it is, is mediated only in oral performance.[2]

It is fair to conclude that the cultural situation described by Plato is one in which oral communication still dominates all the im- portant relationshipsand valid transactions of life. Books of course there were, and the alphabet had been in use for over three cen- turies, but the question is: used by how many? and used for what purposes? Up to this point its introduction had made little practical difference to the educational system or to the intellectual life of adults. This is a hard conclusion to accept, not least in the eyes of scholars of the written word. For they themselves work with refer- ence books and documents and find it correspondingly difficult to imagine a culture worthy of the name which did not. And in fact when they turn their attention to the problem of written documen- tation they betray a consistent tendency to press the positive evidence for it as far[3] as they can and as far back[4] as they can. However, allowing for this unconscious prejudice, does it not still remain true that the Greeks had been using the alphabet since the eighth century? Are there not a wealth of inscriptions? What of the public decrees inscribed and put up in Athens in the fifth century? What of the references to the use of documents in Old Comedy? Did not the reform, fairly recent when Plato wrote, which converted the Attic alphabet to the Ionic model presuppose a widespread use of documentation? As to the educational curriculum, does not Plato himself in his *Protagoras*,[5] written presumably earlier than the *Republic*, supply the *locus classicus* which attests the teaching of letters in school? These are a sample of the objections which could be cited against the conclusion that Greek culture at the turn of the century was still essentially oral.

Yet the weight of Plato's testimony is there, impossible to shake off, and once one becomes ready to accept it, one becomes prepared also to notice how complicated may be the problem of the growth of Greek literacy and how slippery the evidence which bears on the subject.[6] It is in the first instance to be realised that the habit of public inscription does not necessarily imply popular literacy: it might imply its opposite; nor do the writing habits of Greek poets—for after Homer undoubtedly their works were composed in writing—prove it either. In each case we may be dealing with a situation best described as craft literacy, in which the public inscription is composed as a source of referral for officials and as a check upon arbitrary interpretations.[7] As for the poet, he can write for his own benefit and thereby can acquire increased compositional skill, but he composes for a public who he knows will not read what he is composing but will listen to it.[8] The clue to the whole problem lies not in the use of written characters and writing materials, on which scholarly attention has been concentrated, but upon the supply of readers, and this depended on a universalisation of letters. The reading trauma, to use a modern term, had to be imposed at the primary level of schooling, and not the secondary. As late as the first half of the fifth century the evidence, we suggest, points to the fact that Athenians learnt to read if at all, in adolescence.[9] The skill was imposed upon a previous oral training, and perhaps one learned to write little more than one's signature—the first thing one would want to write—and at that, spelling and orthography were erratic.[10] There is a passage in the *Clouds*,[11] dating from 423 B.C. or later, in which the boys' school presided over by the harpist is described. This omits any reference to letters and stresses oral recitation. It is written in nostalgic vein and, when compared with the statement of the *Protagoras* that children learned their letters in school, permits the inference that in Attic schools the introduction of letters at the primary level as a standardised practice had begun by the beginning of the last third of the fifth century.[12] Such a conclusion is consistent with the achievement of general literacy toward the end of the war, a condition to which the *Frogs*[13] in 405 called attention. Indeed, this last piece of testimony should remind us that Old Comedy not infrequently, if it introduces the use of written documents into some stage situation, tends to treat them as something novel and either comic or suspicious,[14] and there are passages in tragedy which betray the same overtones.[15]

In short, in considering the growing use of letters in Athenian practice, we presuppose a stage, characteristic of the first two-thirds of the fifth century, which we may call semi-literacy, in which writing skills were gradually but rather painfully being spread through the population without any corresponding increase in fluent reading. And if one stops to think about the situation as it existed till near the end of the Peloponnesian war, this was inevitable, for where was the ready and copious supply of books or journals which alone makes fluent reading possible?[16] One cannot build up a habit of popular literacy on a fund of inscriptions. All this makes the testimony of Plato, so inconvenient and yet so weighty, much easier to tolerate, and it becomes the easier if we add the presumption that up to his day the educational apparatus, as so often since, lagged behind technological advance, and preferred to adhere to traditional methods of oral instruction when other possibilities were becoming available. It is only too likely that Plato is describing a situation which was on the way to being changed as he wrote.[17] The testimony of the orators could probably[18] be used to show that by the middle of the fourth century the silent revolution had been accomplished, and that the cultivated Greek public had become a community of readers.

However, for Plato this is not the assumption, nor is he interested in noticing the possibility of change, and for a very fundamental reason. Once it is accepted that the oral situation had persisted through the fifth century, one faces the conclusion that there would also persist what one may call an oral state of mind as well; a mode of consciousness so to speak, and, as we shall see, a vocabulary and syntax, which were not that of a literate bookish culture. And once one admits this and admits that the oral state of mind would show a time lag so that it persisted into a new epoch when the technology of communication had changed, it becomes understandable that the oral state of mind is still for Plato the main enemy.

But we are anticipating what has not yet been demonstrated. Let us ask first the question: assuming a Hellenic social apparatus and a civilisation in which originally there had been no documentation, and then, for three centuries, a situation where documentation remained minimal, how is the apparatus of this civilisation preserved? We speak here of the public and private law of the group, its proprieties and its traditions, its historical sense and its technical skills.

The answer too often supplied to this question, if the question is ever asked, is that the preservation and transmission of the mores is left to the unconscious mind of the community and to the give and take between the generations without further assistance.[19] This in fact, we suggest, is never the case. The 'tradition', to use a convenient term, at least in a culture which deserves the name of civilised, always requires embodiment in some verbal archetype. It requires some kind of linguistic statement, a performative utterance on an ambitious scale which both describes and enforces the overall habit pattern, political and private, of the group. This pattern supplies the nexus of the group. It has to become standardised in order to allow the group to function as a group and to enjoy what we might call a common consciousness and a common set of values. To become and remain standardised it has to achieve preservation outside of the daily whim of men. And the preservation will take linguistic form; it will include repeated examples of correct procedure and also rough definitions of standard technical practices which are followed by the group in question, as for example the method of building a house or sailing a ship or cooking food. Furthermore, we suggest, this linguistic statement or paradigm, telling us what we are and how we should behave, is not developed by happy chance, but as a statement which is formed to be drilled into the successive generations as they grow up within the family or clan system. It provides the content of the educational apparatus of the group. This is as true today of literate societies in which the necessary conditioning is acquired through books or controlled by written documents as it was in preliterate society which lacked documents.

In a preliterate society, how is this statement preserved? The answer inescapably is: in the living memories of successive living people who are young and then old and then die. Somehow, a collective social memory, tenacious and reliable, is an absolute social prerequisite for maintaining the apparatus of any civilisation. But how can the living memory retain such an elaborate linguistic statement without suffering it to change in transmission from man to man and from generation to generation and so to lose all fixity and authority? One need only experiment today with the transmission of a single prosaic directive passed down by word of mouth from person to person in order to conclude that preservation in prose was impossible. The only possible verbal technology available to guarantee the preservation and fixity of transmission was that of the rhythmic word organised cunningly in verbal and metrical patterns which were unique enough to retain their shape. This is the historical genesis, the *fons et origo*, the moving cause of that phenomenon we still call 'poetry'. But when we consider how utterly the function of poetry has altered, how completely the cultural situation has changed, it becomes possible to understand that when Plato is talking about poetry he is not really talking about our kind of poetry.

The probable answers to two of our problems have now already been revealed. If Plato could deal with poetry as though it were a kind of reference library or as a vast tractate in ethics and politics and warfare and the like, he is reporting its immemorial function in an oral culture and testifying to the fact that this remained its function in Greek society down to his own day. It is first and last a didactic instrument for transmitting the tradition.[20] And if secondly he treats it throughout the *Republic* as though it enjoyed in current practice a complete monopoly over training in citizenship he likewise is describing with faithfulness the educational mechanisms of such a culture. The linguistic content had to be poetic or else it was nothing.

And the answers to several other puzzles become apparent if we consider precisely what in an oral culture the educational mechanisms amount to. They cannot be narrowly identified with schools and schoolmasters or with teachers, as though these represented a unique source of indoctrination, as they do in a literate society. All memorisation[21] of the poetised tradition depends on constant and reiterated recitation. You could not refer to a book or memorise from a book. Hence poetry exists and is effective as an educational instrument only as it is performed. Performance by a harpist for the benefit of a pupil is only part of the story. The pupil will grow up and perhaps forget. His living memory must at every turn be reinforced by social pressure. This is brought to bear in the adult context, when in private performance the poetic tradition is repeated at mess table and banquet and family ritual, and in public per-

formance in the theatre and market-place. The recital by parents
and elders, the repetition by children and adolescents, add themselves to the professional recitations given by poets, rhapsodists
and actors. The community has to enter into an unconscious
conspiracy with itself to keep the tradition alive, to reinforce it
in the collective memory of a society where collective memory is
only the sum of individuals' memories, and these have continually
to be recharged at all age levels. Hence Plato's *mimesis*, when it
confuses the poet's situation with the actor's, and both of these
with the situation of the student in class and the adult in recreation, is faithful to the facts.

    In short, Plato is describing a total technology of the preserved
word which has since his day in Europe ceased to exist. Nor
have we yet exhausted all the facets of that technology which
were peculiar to an oral culture. There remains to consider the
personal situation of an individual boy or man who is urgently
required to memorise and to keep green in his memory the
verbal tradition on which his culture depends. He originally
listens and then repeats and goes on repeating, adding to his
repertoire to the limits of his mental capacity which naturally
will vary from boy to boy and man to man. How is such a feat
of memory to be placed within the reach not only of the gifted
but of the average member of the group, for all have to retain a
minimal grasp of the tradition? Only, we suggest, by exploiting
psychological resources latent and available in the consciousness
of every individual, but which today are no longer necessary.
The pattern of this psychological mechanism will be examined
more closely in a later chapter. But its character can be summed
up if we describe it as a state of total personal involvement and
therefore of emotional identification with the substance of the
poetised statement that you are required to retain. A modern
student thinks he does well if he diverts a tiny fraction of his
psychic powers to memorise a single sonnet of Shakespeare. He
is not more lazy than his Greek counterpart. He simply pours his
energy into book reading and book learning through the use of

his eyes instead of his ears. His Greek counterpart had to mobilise
the psychic resources necessary to memorise Homer and the poets,
or enough of them to achieve the necessary educational effect.
To identify with the performance as an actor does with his lines
was the only way it could be done. You threw yourself into the
situation of Achilles, you identified with his grief or his anger.
You yourself became Achilles and so did the reciter to whom you
listened. Thirty years later you could automatically quote what
Achilles had said or what the poet had said about him. Such
enormous powers of poetic memorisation could be purchased
only at the cost of total loss of objectivity. Plato's target was
indeed an educational procedure and a whole way of life.

   This then is the master clue to Plato's choice of the word
mimesis[22] to describe the poetic experience. It focuses initially not
on the artist's creative act but on his power to make his audience
identify almost pathologically and certainly sympathetically
with the content of what he is saying. And hence also when
Plato seems to confuse the epic and dramatic genres, what he is
saying is that any poetised statement must be designed and
recited in such a way as to make it a kind of drama within the
soul both of the reciter and hence also of the audience. This kind
of drama, this way of reliving experience in memory instead of
analysing and understanding it, is for him 'the enemy'.

   In conclusion, if one applies these findings to the history of
Greek literature before Plato, one is caught up by the proposition
that to call it literature in our sense is a misnomer. Homer
roughly represents the terminus of a long period of non-literacy
in which Greek oral poetry was nursed to maturity and in which
only oral methods were available to educate the young and to
transmit the group mores. Alphabetic skill was available to a few
not later than 700 B.C. Precisely who these few were is a matter
of dispute. The circle of alphabet-users became wider as time
passed, but what more natural than that previous habits of instruction and of communication along with the corresponding states
of mind should persist long after the alphabet had theoretically

made a reading culture possible? This leads to the conclusion that all Greek poetry roughly down to the death of Euripides not only enjoyed an almost unchallenged monopoly of preserved communication but also that it was composed under conditions which have never since been duplicated in Europe and which hold some of the secret of its peculiar power. Homer may, for convenience, be taken as the last representative of the purely oral composition. Even this is dubious; it seems improbable that his poems have not benefited from some reorganisation made possible by alphabetic transcription. But this is a controversial point which does not affect the main perspective. It is certain that all his poet successors were writers. But it is equally certain that they always wrote for recitation and for listeners. They composed it can be said under audience control. The advantages of literacy were private to themselves and their peers. The words and sentences they shaped had to be such as were repeatable. They had to be 'musical' in a functional sense to which we will later return. And the content had still to be traditional. Bold invention is the prerogative of writers, in a book culture.

In short, Homer's successors still assumed that their works would be repeated and memorised. On this depended their fame and their hope of immortality. And so they also assumed, though in the main unconsciously, that what they should say would be appropriate for preservation in the living memory of audiences. This both restricted their range to the main stream of the Greek tradition and immensely strengthened what might be called the high seriousness of their compositions.

Our business here is not with literary criticism but with the origins of that abstract intellectualism styled by the Greeks 'philosophy'. We must realise that works of genius, composed within the semi-oral tradition, though a source of magnificent pleasure to the modern reader of ancient Greek, constituted or represented a total state of mind which is not our mind and which was not Plato's mind; and that just as poetry itself, as long as it reigned supreme, constituted the chief obstacle to the achievement of effective prose, so there was a state of mind which we shall conveniently label the 'poetic' or 'Homeric' or 'oral' state of mind, which constituted the chief obstacle to scientific rationalism, to the use of analysis, to the classification of experience, to its rearrangement in sequence of cause and effect. That is why the poetic state of mind is for Plato the arch-enemy and it is easy to see why he considered this enemy so formidable.[23] He is entering the lists against centuries of habituation in rhythmic memorised experience. He asks of men that instead they should examine this experience and rearrange it, that they should think about what they say, instead of just saying it. And they should separate themselves from it instead of identifying with it; they themselves should become the 'subject' who stands apart from the 'object' and reconsiders it and analyses it and evaluates it, instead of just 'imitating' it.

It follows that the history of Greek poetry is also the history of early Greek *paideia*. The poets supply successive supplements to the curriculum. Leadership in education is by Plato accorded successively to Homer, Hesiod, to the tragedians, to the Sophists, and to himself. In the light of the hypothesis that Greece was passing from non-literacy through craft literacy towards semi-literacy and then full literacy, this order makes sense. Epic had been *par excellence* the vehicle of the preserved word throughout the Dark Age. At that time it must also have been the main vehicle of instruction. Even in purely oral form the epic, assisted by the formulaic technique, assumed in part the guise of an authorised version. Once rendered into the alphabet, more rigidly standardised versions became possible for teaching purposes. Tradition associated some school reforms with the age of Solon and some recension of the Homeric text with Pisistratus. It is plausible to connect the two and conclude that what happened, perhaps over an extended period, was an accommodation of written versions to each other for school use. The rhapsodist was also the teacher. He, like the poet—and the two professions overlapped as the career of Tyrtaeus shows—responded to the traditions of craft literacy. He himself used his Homeric text as a reference to correct his memory, but taught it orally to the population at large who memorised but never read it. Like the poet, he also remained under audience control.

But at Athens, under Pisistratus, a second mode of oral composition was given formal status and state support. The Athenian stage plays, composed closer to the native vernacular, became the Attic supplement to Homer as a vehicle of preserved experience, of moral teaching and of historical memory. They were memorised, taught, quoted and consulted. You went to see a new play, but it was at the same time an old play full of the familiar clichés rearranged in new settings, with much aphorism and proverb and prescriptive example of how to behave, and warning examples of how not to behave; with continual recapitulation of bits of tribal and civic history, of ancestral memories for which the artist serves as the unconscious vehicle of repetition and record. The situations were always typical, not invented; they repeated endlessly the precedents and judgments, the learning and wisdom, which the Hellenic culture had accumulated and hoarded.

Plato casually identifies Homer as the archetypal figure for the fundamental reason that his epic was not only the prototype of all preserved communication and remained so; its compendious content and widespread performance provided a continuity within which Greek drama can be seen as imitating the content and adapting the method to a performance which, stylistically speaking, differed in degree rather than in kind, as Plato himself perceived. The Homeric background of tragedy is institutional and fundamental. It is a matter of the expanding technology of the shaped and preserved utterance, whether recited and mimed by an epic rhapsodist who himself 'does' all the characters, or split up into parts done by different reciters who become actors.[24] One may add that as this took place, the Attic intelligence was able to demonstrate its superiority over that of other Greek states by adding its own characteristic ingredient to the curriculum. Athenian children and adolescents of the fifth century who included the Greek drama or excerpts thereof in their memorised *paideia* could draw on larger resources than was possible in those communities where Homer may have retained a virtual monopoly.

But the main burden of Plato's attack is on Homer. He occupies the forefront of his mind and it is time to turn to test Plato's conception of Homer the encyclopedist; to test, that is, the hypothesis that this epic archetype of the orally preserved word was composed as a compendium of matters to be memorised, of tradition to be maintained, of a *paideia* to be transmitted.

NOTES

[1] Hence Cornford's translation of *poietes* as 'writer' (*Rep.* 397c8) and of *poiein* as 'write' (598e4) is unfortunate.

[2] 595b5-6. At *Rep.* 606e4 and *Apology* 22b Plato speaks of 'taking up' (ἀναλαμβάνειν) a poet, presumably in the hands, and therefore implying a reading from a MS., but these notices are I think exceptional, so far as the early dialogues are concerned.

[3] See n. 6.

[4] The tenth or ninth centuries B.C. had been the preferred period within which to place the introduction of the Greek alphabet, until Rhys Carpenter in 1933, after reviewing some previous 'authorities' in the field, argued that the historical and epigraphical evidence (possible contact with Phoenicians, comparative letter shapes, earliest dated *graffiti*, etc.) pointed inevitably to a date 'about 720-700' (p. 23). He was answered on behalf of the traditionalists by Ullman in 1934, who took him to task for ignoring other 'authorities' (as though the matter could be settled by counting learned noses) and produced a comparative table of characters in support of the contention 'that all the signs point not to the eighth but to the eleventh or twelfth centuries or even earlier as the time for the introduction of the alphabet into Greece'. This conclusion, aside from the weight placed on traditional opinions, patently relied on the proved antiquity of Phoenician letters, and on a disbelief that early Greek culture could have remained non-literate so long. Carpenter in turn replied in 1938, demolishing the early dating of a Greek inscription that had got into the controversy, but, more importantly, analysing the evidence of letter shapes from Ullman's own tables to conclude that 'the period of transmission from Semitic to Greek must therefore fall between circa 825 . . . and the seventh century'. It is instructive to

observe how scholars have responded to this controversy. Lorimer in 1948 once more reviewed (pp. 11-19) the 'authorities' for the traditional dating, down to Rehm who as late as 1939 posited a tenth-century date (p. 19) and herself proposed to move it down as far as 780-50, but ignored Carpenter to whom it was due that the whole question had been reopened, and who had set the overall limits within which her own dating secured itself. Moreover she added 'at no point do specialists examine the conditions in which the borrowing according to the date selected must be supposed to have been made' although Carpenter had in fact attempted a reconstruction of these very conditions (*AJA* 37, pp. 20, 28). In 1950 she repeated this dating, but now supported it by acknowledging only Ullman and by reprinting his table of characters, a procedure which meant that the sponsor of the corrected (and now accepted) dating was ignored in favour of the authority whose dating had been corrected (and rejected). The notes supplied by Ullman to his tables, and also Lorimer's own text (p. 129) ignored likewise the recently corrected dating of the Dipylon vase (see below) on which so much has been made to depend. Meanwhile, Albright (1949, p. 196), taking note of the Carpenter-Ullman dispute, but again ignoring the corrected dating of this vase, admonished Carpenter for placing it too late, and preferred to state 'in the author's *long-held* opinion (italics mine) the Greek alphabet was borrowed from the Phoenician either in the late ninth or more probably in the early eighth centuries B.C.'. The sense of this *ex cathedra* pronouncement, founded one feels at bottom on the accepted antiquity of Phoenician letters, is then reaffirmed by the same author in 1950 and 1956 (cf. notes 1 and 66 of the latter article), and is then (1958) used by Webster (p. 272) to posit a date 850-750 as 'the most recent statement' of the problem. Dunbabin a year earlier had pronounced in favour of the same period (p. 60), adding 'the extreme view of Rhys Carpenter and other scholars that the origin of the Greek alphabet is not older or not much older than 700 B.C. can hardly be maintained'. In 1959, Page (p. 157) reduced these limits by saying the Phoenician was not adapted to the Greek 'much if at all earlier than the middle of the 8th century' and then added 'the *much later* date (italics mine; the actual minimum difference being 30 years) supported by Rhys Carpenter now seems untenable'. He likewise, *more* Lorimer, added 'this conclusion (viz. adoption from Phoenician during ninth to eighth centuries) has always seemed to me to follow from the very full evidence set out by Ullman'. So once more, while a date in the eighth is admitted as probable, the authority preferred is one who had put the alphabet in the thirteenth to eleventh. The reasons why Carpenter's dates 720-700 are stated to be 'untenable' (rather than at least disputable) are to a non-specialist not immediately clear. That group of objects so far discovered which carry the earliest examples of alphabetic inscription numbers about a dozen. These are distributed over the Mediterranean world from east to west (Athens, Boeotia, Aegina, Argolid, Rhodes, Gordion, Ithaca, Pithecusa, Cumae, Etruria). Not one of them, so it appears from the various professional descriptions, can be placed *with absolute consensus* in the eighth century. The earliest discovered remains the oldest: this is the Dipylon vase of Athens, dated by Young (pp. 225-9) 'on the evidence of the shape at the end of the 8th century or later' (and in any case the inscription was incised after firing). Or there is the 'Nestor cup' which Buchner (Atti del Accad. Naz. dei Lincei Ser. 8 Vol. 10 (1955), pp. 215-22) would like to place in the eighth century, but 'perhaps in the last quarter', and he who reads between the lines of the article can see that a seventh-century date is not excluded. Or again (ranging from west to east) there are the Gordion examples, the latest to be found. Of these Young says (1960, pp. 385-7) that 'they are fully as early as any Greek examples we possess'. Precisely where this leaves us is not clear, but it is crystal clear that the epigraphic foundations of Carpenter's argument have not yet been overthrown: 'The earliest surviving specimens are of the 7th or even of the late 8th century' is the conclusion of Cook and Woodhead (175 ff.). 'Authorities' who would still move the date back have to rely heavily on the 'development' hypothesis (Page, Lorimer, Dunbabin *et al.*), viz., that behind *any* surviving alphabetic inscription from Greece, Magna Graecia or A. Minor must lie a period of experiment of unspecified character and uncertain length ('a few decades long'— Page, p. 157; Young, *loc. cit.*, speculates that *if* a Phrygian alphabet developed from Greek—not a clear conclusion, one gathers—the latter must have been formed anterior to the eighth century to give it time to penetrate. But then he adds 'he who travels overland carrying only an alphabet travels light and fast', which seems to leave the problem where it was. This is after he has already described long distance communication between Phrygia and Carchemish in the late eighth century 'probably in cuneiform or clay tablets'). Carpenter's persuasive reasoning pointing to the unlikelihood of any such lengthy period of development (1933, p. 20) has once more been ignored, though Young himself stresses the fact that the vowels, the essential factor in the invention, do not vary. Lorimer's preferred dating is patently inspired by the hope that the earliest Olympian victor lists (starting from 776 B.C.) rest on an original alphabetised version ('the higher date would allow of its use to record the Olympic victors from Coroebus onwards', she said in 1948 (p. 20), and again, in 1950 (p. 129) proposed that the alphabet came 'early enough perhaps to record the name of Koroibos as victor at Olympia'). This point had also been attended to by Carpenter (1933, p. 24), but again he is ignored. It is clear that a date as late as the last quarter of the eighth century has proved unpalatable to scholars on grounds which have little connection with the evidence so far revealed and discussed, and that they find it hard to forgive the scholar originally responsible for destroying the traditional dating, which is now reluctantly judged to be impossible, but which fosters the desire for compromise achieved by pushing the date as far back into the eighth century as possible, and even into the early ninth. The excuse for this long note, an intrusion by a non-specialist into a field of highly specialised findings, is not to settle a question beyond my competence—and indeed a somewhat earlier date than Carpenter's may in the end be substantiated, especially in the light of Wade-Gery's not unreasonable hypothesis (pp. 11-13) that the invention was the work of the minstrels—but to expose how controversial datings are still in part controlled by extrinsic motives which spring from preconceptions about the character of early Greek culture. It is precisely to those preconceptions that my own text, in a different context, is addressed. One piece of indirect evidence bearing on the question of alphabetic writing has long lain under our noses. If either Hesiod, or, as Wilamowitz said, Archilochus emerges as the first personality in Greek literature, the question arises Why? if not because the memory of an individual poet was likely to survive only as autobiography in his own verse, and this particular kind of verse (as against the epic) would not survive to become literature until alphabetised (cf. also below, cap. 15, n. 35). Epigraphy has so far only tended to confirm a conclusion to which the known history of Greek literature has been pointing for a long time.

Addendum: it must be gratefully acknowledged that Miss Jeffery's prefatory review (pp. 1-21) of the origin of the Greek alphabet, which became available to me only after the above note was written, makes, it would seem, handsome amends for the previous bias of others in this matter. 'Nothing', she says (p. 16), 'needs to be added to Carpenter's succinct comment "The argument ex silentio grows every year more formidable and more conclusive".' She assumes that the Dipylon oinochoe furnishes the earliest inscription, so that its dating still remains crucial (the possibility of subsequent incision is not pursued): at p. 16, n. 1, this is given as 'the end of the 8th' (citing from Young, who had however not excluded the early seventh), but at p. 68, n. 4, 'the 2nd half of the 8th' (citing Dunbabin), a judgment which may reflect some residual unwillingness to envisage the arrival of the alphabet as late as 700. For this event her preferred date is 'somewhere about the middle of the 8th'. On the face of it, and so far as a non-specialist may judge, we still lack any *incontrovertible* evidence that would *insist* it was earlier than 700. She disposes effectively of what I have called the 'development' hypothesis, and argues moreover that the early portions of the Olympic and ephor lists may plausibly rest on oral tradition, citing in support not only examples of memorisation, but also the early titles of certain officials which imply the memorising function—a small but significant piece of evidence which I feel well accords with that portrait of the conditions surrounding 'preserved communication' in archaic Greece which I have tried to draw in later chapters. Since a 'sub-geometric' date for the alphabet, even as late as 700, might conjure up the spectacle (or nightmare? Albright, 1950, would place the Greek epics in the tenth century) of a Homer dictating the *Iliad* to a scribe *after* 700, it will obviously remain unpalatable to many scholars on grounds other than epigraphical.

⁵ 325e, where however note that the pupil after learning letters (γράμματα) is set reading the poets (ἀναγιγνώσκειν) in order to learn them by heart (ἐκμανθάνειν). This is presumably the stage at which he now learns κιθάρισις (325e1 and 326a4); cf. below, n. 12.

⁶ Turner's valuable review of the testimonies bearing on the use of books 'in the fifth and fourth centuries' has the disadvantage, suggested in the title, that the situations of the two centuries are not distinguished. What is supplied by tragedy, old comedy, and fifth-century vase paintings and inscriptions is amalgamated with evidences of a very different colour supplied by fourth-century authors (Isocrates, Plato's *Laws*, etc.) to support such affirmations as

that 'reading and writing *is* a normal part of everyday Athenian education . . . The ordinary Athenian *is* a literate person . . . the stories which have been supposed to prove the contrary carry no weight . . . What I take as *axiomatic* is this: widespread ability to read and write *is* a basic assumption of the Athenian democracy.' I have supplied the italics to bring out the fact (a) that this perspective on the problem is indeed an 'axiom' of the modern literate mind rather than a conclusion enforced by the evidence (cf. the parallel situation in scholarship discussed above n. 4), (b) that in this perspective the Athenian experiences of the fifth and fourth centuries are treated as a single homogeneous phenomenon in which the data (as symbolised in Turner's present tenses) are constants, so that for example conclusions based on Plato's notice of calligraphy in the *Laws* can be transferred backward to the age of Pericles, or that the situation which prompted the use of costly marble engravings in the fifth century can be identified with that which prompted Isocrates' practice of circulating his written works in the fourth. Yet one is grateful to Turner for defining the target of inquiry as 'the part played by the written word in the revolution which took place in the technique of thought'; he adds 'during the 5th century'. It is simply my contention that this anticipates the date, and that if it had indeed occurred in the fifth, there would have been no need for Plato's polemic.

⁷ Even a papyrus document could be treated as a unique archetype and placed in storage rather than put into general circulation; cf. Aesch. *Supp.* 947 ff. especially ἐν πτυχαῖς βίβλων κατεσφραγισμένα, interpreted by Turner as referring to a sheet of papyrus folded and sealed carrying version of decree for preservation in Metroon. Similarly Heraclitus (D.L. 9.6) deposited his MS in a temple (or else a collection of his sayings composed by disciples was so treated?). Hence the invention of 'letters' is explained by the need to preserve memoranda (Aesch. *P.V.* 459 ff., cf. 789; Eur. *frag.* 578; Gorg. *Palamedes* 30; cf. also Plato *Phaedrus* 275a) not to compose, still less to read, 'literature'. It is as memoranda that written documentation is so often exploited in old comedy (*Clouds* 19 ff., *Birds*, as below, n. 14, *Wasps* 538 ff., *Thesm.* 769 ff.).

⁸ The Muse is represented on a *pyxis* in Athens, c. 445, giving recital with book in hand (cited by Turner). Contrast the silent reader in a grave relief dated at the end of the century (Birt, *Die Buchrolle in der Kunst*, fig. 90). Plato when making a formal distinction between painting and poetry still does so in terms of *opsis* versus *akoe* (*Rep.* 603b6-7). The first prose writers had no choice but to adopt the same methods. In their connection, Turner says 'According to the angle of approach, it may be said that speeches or lectures are first written down and then learnt by heart by the speaker, or that books are designed to be read aloud to a large audience'. If so, such habits bespeak that culture of oral communication and memorisation which Plato assumes; the publication and dissemination of the prose word conformed at first to the previous rules set by the poetic. There is no immediate break in habits, no sudden emergence of a reading public. The term *apodexis* in the proem to Herodotus surely implies oral publication (Pearson, *Early Ionian Historians*, p. 8, assumes otherwise) in the traditional epic manner, serving the epic purposes defined in the remainder of the sentence

(for even the last clause, introducing the *aitia*, paraphrases *Iliad* 1.8). *Per contra*, the self-conscious contrast drawn by Thucydides (1.22.4) between his own κτῆμα ἐς ἀεί and the ἀγώνισμα ἐς τὸ παραχρῆμα ἀκούειν of predecessors surely identifies the permanent influence of a MS stylistically composed for readers, as against the more ephemeral effects of a composition designed for recitation at an oral 'competition', an interpretation strengthened by the previous sentence but one: καὶ ἐς μὲν ἀκρόασιν ἴσως τὸ μὴ μυθῶδες αὐτῶν ἀτερπέστερον φανεῖται. But contrast Turner's discussion of the same matter, which seems to me to reverse the historical logic: Herodotus he says adopts the 'new publicist technique' while Thucydides' conception of his own worth is more 'archaic'. Protagoras published orally (D. L. 9.54) and the practice is continued by Isocrates (cf. *Antid.* init.).

9 Cf. the so-called 'school scene' on the Duris vase, *c.* 480–470? (references in Richter, *Attic Red Figure Vases*, p. 84 and note), and the 'Linos-Mousaios' school scene (?) on red-figured cup (Louvre G, 457, cited by Turner).

10 The Abou Simbel inscriptions and signatures (Jeffery, pp. 354–5) must be dated *c.* 591; they include 8 names (and others illegible), are written in 'mixed' script, and the inscription is in Doric dialect. Jeffery infers presence, in the 'Ionian' (Herod. 2.53) contingent, of mercenaries from the 'area' of Doric hexapolis, some perhaps born in Egypt. Equal Attic competence at this date should not be assumed. For Attica, cf. the anecdote of the rustic who wanted the name Aristides scratched for him on a sherd (Plut. *Arist.* 7) and the scene exploited by Euripides, Agathon and Theodectas in which an illiterate rustic describes the marks which mean 'Theseus' (Athen. 454b–e). As for the ostraka, they exhibit varieties of letter-shape and spelling (Beazley, *AJA* 64 (1960), refers to 'so many mistakes in spelling' on the inscription on the Duris cup; in the absence of socialised literacy, orthography would be fluid) and groups of them were incised severally by the same hands (explained as 'ballot stuffing', which may have been the case, but this would have been all the easier if many voters had to ask for a sherd with the name they wanted already on it; either they could not read it and so were deceived, or their oral votes were solicited previously against this or that candidate and then they were brought to the poll in a group and given the sherds as they went in).

11 11. 961 ff.

12 But even so, the 'secondary' curriculum, i.e. the preparation for adult life, remained oral; you learnt letters in order to compose and read memoranda (above, n.7), but not 'literature'; cf. *Knights* 188 ff.: the sausage-seller has no 'skill of music except writing, and poor stuff at that poorly managed', to which Demosthenes replies with partial consolation that the poor standard to be sure is a disadvantage, but the absence of music does not matter: political leadership is no longer in the hands of a 'musical' man with proper instincts; it has devolved on an uneducated scoundrel—where the hallmark of the uneducated (*amathés*) is not illiteracy but lack of music. That is, the educational situation is still (424 B.C.) not too different from that implied in Plutarch's story (*Them.* 3) of the retort of the 'uneducated' Themistocles to the cultivated gentry of his time. Strepsiades in the *Clouds*, init. a man equally innocent of 'music', can read and annotate his

account book. Figures indeed may represent in purest form the earliest *popular* use to which the alphabet was put, namely memoranda. The ability to handle simple numerical notation may precede the capacity to read speech fluently, for it calls for a more economical mental apparatus of recognition.

[13] 1114 βιβλίον τ᾽ἔχων ἕκαστος μανθάνει τὰ δεξιά and below, n. 16.

[14] Cf. the exx. gathered by Denniston, pp. 117-19 (more particularly from *Birds* and *Frogs*), who infers that 'books were rare enough to be the hallmark of a type'. I would conjecture that the attacks on Euripides as a 'book poet' (esp. *Frogs* 1409 'get into the scale pan, and take . . . your book collection with you') supplied the excuse for the Hellenistic biographers to credit him with the first 'library' (Athen. 3A). A stage bonfire (cf. present conclusion of *Clouds*) of documents could have similarly inspired an item in the 'life' of Protagoras, who we know was pilloried in Old Comedy (FVS Protagoras A1).

[15] Cf. the king's statement in Aeschylus *Supplices* (above, n. 7) strongly implying that an oral promise and the oral memory that preserves it are more reliable than tricky documentation; also Eur. *Hipp.* 954. The prejudice lasted into the fourth century: Plato *Phaedrus* 274e; cf. also Xen. *Mem.* 4.2.10. A Spartan *rhetra* forbade inscription of laws (Plut. *Lyc.* 13), presumably a piece of post-Lycurgan tradition reflecting the same prejudice, for the educational reasons given in Plutarch for the prohibition are the familiar Platonic and Peripatetic ones.

[16] In the vase paintings, only poetical texts are represented (so Turner) and these I would argue are only the 'archetypes'. The populace relied on oral memorisation. Thus, Turner interprets the Sappho vase as meaning 'the poetess is reminding herself of the words she is to sing'. To illustrate the first Attic prose, Turner appropriately cites the 'manuals' ascribed to Sophocles, Agatharchus, Ictinus, Polyclitus, Meton, Hippodamus, which he says ignored style. The 'book' of Anaxagoras purchasable in the 'orchestra' 'for a drachma at most' (*Apol.* 26d) is often cited to argue a widespread reading habit, on grounds of both procurability and price. But the clue lies in 'book' which is a mistranslation. Turner points out that βίβλος in Aesch. *Supp.* (above, n. 7) and βιβλίον in the phrase βιβλίον τοῦ ψηφίσματος (as in Tod G.H.I. II. 97; date 403 B.C.) mean not 'book' but 'document', which in the former case is interpreted as a (single) piece of folded papyrus; he also notes the later βιβλιοφόρος meaning 'postman'. I would conclude that a written *biblion* purchasable for a drachma was a single (folded?) sheet, a leaflet or pamphlet, and that the great majority of 'books' available for circulation in the last quarter of the fifth century were precisely of this character, including the 'manuals'. This invites the further conclusion that they contained not the full 'text' whether of play or of treatise or speech, but only a collection of extracts. The 'Theognis' corpus testifies to the habit of anthologising. In the case of drama, the extracts would consist of telling lines and paragraphs felt to be especially memorable (and memorisable). These anthologies are described at *Laws* 7.811a: either you learn 'whole poets' by heart or else you select κεφάλαια καί τινας ὅλας ῥήσεις and put them in collections for memorisation. (From this passage it is a fair inference that new reading habits were already impairing the traditional capacity to memorise 'whole poets'.)

56 PREFACE TO PLATO

Such a pamphlet of quotations or 'turns of speech' (called τά δεξιά at *Frogs* 1114; cf. *Clouds* parabasis 547-8) is put into the hands of the audience so that they can con and follow (μανθάνει above n. 13) the *agon* of quotations as it is conducted between the two protagonists. The context is quite specific and cannot be explained away in general terms as though it meant 'we are all readers nowadays' (so Turner), nor need such a conclusion 'go against the grain'; the *Frogs* relies on exploiting the memories of the audience supplemented by aid of an anthology (or anthologies). As for prose pamphlets, their content would consist of definitions, summary statements (cf. *Laws*, above), telling paragraphs and aphorisms, which summed up the author's position or his main points. These might be couched in memorisable form (e.g. with some degree of parallelism and antithesis), but full doctrinal exposition was still oral. This would account for lack of 'style' in early handbooks, and is consistent with what survives of Anaxagoras, Diogenes of Apollonia, and Democritus. Thus a single *logos* or *biblion* would contain a string of such *logoi*, so that Socrates can say of Anaxagoras' *biblion* that it γέμει τούτων τῶν λόγων, indicating the compression of the composition and perhaps the autonomous character of the separate paragraphs. It was in fact in this respect not unlike a poetic manual of τὰ δεξιά. Where 'orality' prevailed in the prose of rhetoric, length of written exposition and continuity of written argument came easier, as in Antiphon's 'tetralogies' (which however is still a manual). Thucydides was the first Attic author to extrapolate written memoranda into continuous written discourse, just as Plato and Isocrates were the first to adapt sustained oral teaching to the same end.

¹⁷ Turner well says of *Phaedrus* 274 that Plato is fighting 'a rearguard action'. In fact, his preference for oral methods was not only conservative but illogical, since the Platonic *episteme* which was to supplant *doxa* (below, cap. 13) was being nursed to birth by the literate revolution.

¹⁸ It depends upon what inferences one chooses to draw from quite a variety of indirect testimonies: e.g. Demosthenes *De Corona* 258, sneering at Aeschines' humble beginnings, refers to fact that he had attended to the inkpots in his father's school; Isocrates several times mentions the circulation (apparently private) of his MSS; and orators begin to refer to marks in margins of MSS (instances in Turner) which may argue increased habit of silent reading. There are of course abundant citations from written documents in the speeches, but these after all are being recited by readers to listeners. However, if public orations as we have them are edited versions, as is usually assumed, this is eloquent proof of a reading public. Turner cites interesting evidence of a papyrus showing *paragraphus* to indicate alternation of speakers (hence for silent readers?) but this is *c.* 300-280.

¹⁹ Cf. Sabine, *History of Political Theory*, p. 320: 'the society that by its own spontaneous approval generates binding practices for its members, that makes law half-consciously and gives its assent through the voice of its natural magnates'.

²⁰ Testimonies that indirectly corroborate this are very widespread (e.g. quoting the *Iliad* to back a political claim as at Herod. 7.161; the need, felt very early, to allegorise epic, by Theagenes, Stesimbrotus, Ion; the urgency and detail with which Plato pursues his own programme of censorship). The *Frogs* (e.g.

at 1009, 1030 ff., 1464) makes explicit what had been implicit from time immemorial, which is to be expected at a time when new methods of *paideia* were forcing overt recognition of the old.

²¹ On poetic memorisation as basic to *paideia* cf. Xen. *Sympos.* 3.5-6 (this would not have called for comment 50 years earlier), Plato *Laws* 7.810e. The 'Simonides interlude' in the *Protagoras* relies on the memories of the participants. When at *Rep.* 7.518b8 Plato corrects the theory that education is 'putting some-thing into the psyche' he may be referring to a view which grew out of the necessity of oral memorisation; cf. also Notopoulos, 'Mnemosyne', p. 469— 'the poet is the incarnate book of oral peoples'.

²² I understand the choice to be Plato's, in that he first comprehended the basic psychology of the oral-poetic relationship between reciter and listener or between reciter and the material recited, and the corresponding characteristics of the oral-poetic 'statement' (see below, cap. 10), and first articulated these into a single system of human experience which he labelled *mimesis*. What of the pre-Platonic status of this term? Does previous usage shed light on Plato's? A lengthy foot-note seems preferable to an interruption in our text. G. F. Else, effectively re-butting the restriction which Koller had sought to place on the early meanings of μῖμος, μιμεῖσθαι, μίμημα, μίμησις which would have confined the terms to the dance, and to musical accompaniment as employed in 'cult drama', has placed scholarship in his debt by reviewing the pre-Platonic occurrence of the words, that is, as they were employed by authors 'who wrote or at least began to write before 425 B.C.' (Else n. 65). However, it seems to me that the full significance of this usage can be elucidated only by combining in some measure the views of Koller and Else. The former correctly saw the element of 'expres-sionism' implied in the words, which flows from the basic sense of 're-enactment'; the latter saw they were applied to the manipulation of the living voice, gesture, dress and action generally, and not narrowly to dancing and music. Down to 450 B.C. it is Else's conclusion that all usage (with one very doubtful exception) of μῖμος and μιμεῖσθαι is concentrated upon actual miming 'of looks actions and / or utterances of animals or men through speech song and/or dancing (dramatic or protodramatic sense)' (p. 79). To call this however 'direct representation' (*loc. cit.*) is to adopt the terminology and viewpoint of Plato in *Rep.* 10, which abstractly separate the original from the copy, so that an idea of 'imitation' in the sense of 'representation' or 'reproduction' of an 'original' becomes possible. This meaning does not seem to me explicit in any of the pre-Platonic usages cited. A great many of them, even after 450, continue to describe actual miming (so often in Ar.). The remainder (with a few exceptions to be noted) refer not to the Platonic and Aristotelian 'ethical imitation' of a type, but to 'doing what some-body else does' or in effect 'becoming like him'. This is conspicuously true of all remaining Aristophanic instances (as Else says 'They seem to bring a whiff from the world of the mime'). It is equally true of those usages in Euripides, Herodotus, Thucydides, Democritus which Else would classify as 'ethical imitation'. To give a few instances: when Cleisthenes (Herod. 5.67.1) in attack-ing Attica 'mimes' his maternal grandfather, he is 'doing something like what

he did'. When we render this as 'following the *example* of Cleisthenes', by inserting the term italicised, we import into the Greek the Platonic abstract reduction of this process to a relationship between original and copy. When Helen says to Theonoe (Eur. *Helen* 940) μιμοῦ τρόπους of your father, this means 'reenact his behaviour' rather than 'imitate his ways'. When Clytemnestra (*El.* 1037) referring to her husband's adultery adds that in that case a wife wants to 'mime' her husband, she means 'do as he does' (and so identify with him), where, if we explain this as 'justifying her adultery by the *example* of Agamemnon', we once more reduce the equation to abstract terms. Therefore, to say that there is a pre-Platonic progress which moves away 'from the live imitation in the style of the mime towards a more abstract and colourless range of meaning' (Else, p. 82) is to distort the semantic situation. One would better say that all usage refers to 'sympathetic behaviour', not to abstract copying or imitation, and in a great many cases this behaviour is physical, a matter of speech, gesture, gait, pose, dress and the like. Likewise when Else assigns a pejorative colour to three instances (from Aeschylus, Aristophanes and Democritus) implying 'deliberate deception' 'inadequacy of imitation' and 'the contrast between being and becoming', this seems too explicit: imitation is assigned that inferior status required by the Platonic analysis, where it was suitable to the Platonic epistemology, and this is then read backwards into pre-Platonic usage. In this connection, two sayings of Democritus, himself a sophisticated source, are instructive: frag. 39 says 'one must either be good or mime (a) good (man)'. If this referred to the contrast between being and seeming (Else, p. 83) then the two alternatives would be treated as mutually exclusive. In fact, the apothegm advises: 'either be good or at least do what a good man does'; frag. 79 adds: 'It is a difficult case if you mime bad men while not even wishing to mime good men' where the apothegm defines that rather hopeless moral condition where 'to do as the bad do' is instinctive, and even the contrary volition (let alone the act) is absent. Hence 'miming' here defines a pattern of behaviour, whether good or bad, by its correspondence to some 'live' standard. One must therefore agree with Koller as against Else that the pejorative sense of *mimesis* was invented by Plato in *Rep.* 10 (and in the *Sophist*, in an altered context, *mimesis* recovers its status cf. cap. 2, n. 37). To this conclusion, a speculative comment can be added: Gorgias, true to the pragmatism of the sophists, had rationalised the effects of illusionism in tragedy as a contrived *apate* which it is the business of the artist to achieve and equally of the audience to submit to (Rosenmeyer, pp. 227, 232). This essentially corresponds to one modern conception of the artist's task and of the proper frame of mind with which an audience should approach a work of art (cf. Collingwood who however would reject the formula as characteristic only of 'amusement art'). No doubt the second of these principles in particular, which seems to encourage the 'lie in the soul' in human beings, gave deep offence to Plato's idealism, but he could not reject the facts from which it was deduced. He therefore in *Rep.* Book 10 accepts the Gorgian rationalisation, but at the same time attempts a more inclusive description of the whole poetic situation, which he calls *mimesis*, and which is now defined and damned as systematic *apate*, something too frivolous and immoral to merit serious inclusion in an educational curriculum. The sense of *mimesis* as 'ethical imitation of an original' is built up in the course of this polemic, and is wholly a Platonic creation. I agree that it is quite unnecessary to invent a pre-Platonic *mimesis* theory put forward as a counter-blast to Gorgias (cf. Else, n. 64, who discerns a connection between Gorgias and Plato). So far then the earlier usage has justified the link which Plato established between *mimesis* and psychological identification. There is also another early coloration equally congenial to Plato's intention, even though at first sight, to modern preconceptions, it seems incompatible with the first. To 'mime sympathetically' might seem to be an act both spontaneous and intuitive. Yet Greek usage constantly tends to identify this act as a skill or craft and hence employed in *mousike* (in the generic sense described below cap. 9). The earliest instance of all is decisive. In the *Delian Hymn to Apollo* the girls in the chorus 'know how to (ἴσασιν, where a later composer might have used ἐπίστανται: cf. below, cap. 15, n. 22) mime the accents (or dialects) of all men'. Theognis 370 refers to the inability of the ἄσοφοι (cf. ibid. on *soph-* words) to 'mime me', and a glance at the instances of the same verb as they are culled by Else from Aeschylus, Pindar, Aristophanes will reveal the constant colour of 'skilled re-enactment' by voice, musical instrument, studied gesture and the like. Hence μιμεῖσθαι from the beginning enjoyed an intimate connection with the processes of *mousike* whether in epic, hymn, dithyramb or drama. This brings us to the nouns *mimema* and *mimesis*. In Euripides, the former can, like the verb, be applied to musical and vocal miming (*Iph. Aul.* 378; *I.T.* 294), but it also occurs in Aeschylus in the senses of (a) garment and (b) an 'image' (prob. not a 'painting', as Else, but an animated doll) and once in Euripides as (c) 'embroidered figures'. These are all artifacts, the products of *techne* (actually called '*mimema* of Daedalus' in example (b), with which we can compare the sole instance of *mimesis* in Herodotus, applied to a statue, 3.37.2). These four pre-Platonic instances show that the notion of miming could be extended to skilled production of an inanimate object which unlike voice and gesture was related to a *visible* original. For this extension, we suggest, the notion of skilled performance inherent in the verb supplied the bridge. As a 'contrivance', *mimema* then appears in Euripides' *Helen* to denote either the pseudo-Helen that went to Troy or the real Helen (but which was real?) who is taken for pseudo (lines 875, 74). Thus the use by Plato of the analogy of graphic art in *Rep.* 10 to illustrate poetic *mimesis* has some pre-Platonic support. But (except for the one Herodotean example) *mimesis* as opposed to *mimema* is regularly applied to the process of skilled but sympathetic identification which is carried on in the various branches of *mousike* (below, cap. 9). Thus it occurs twice in Aristophanes of contriving a dramatic role, and in Thucydides, Pausanias' generalship (1.95.3) is 'cast in the role of a tyranny' (note emphasis on royal style and dress, cited by Else); and Nicias appeals to the aliens in the fleet (7.63.3) 'who command our dialect and have identified with our ways' where the reference, linked with skill of speech, is to the adoption of the Athenian *paideusis*. Finally in Democritus' anthropology (cf. Havelock *Liberal Temper*, p. 116) men 'become pupils of swan and nightingale in melodious utterance (ᾠδή) in the course of miming' where the mimicry is the foundation of one of the *technae* of civilisation, viz. *mousike* itself. One concludes that when Plato chose *mimesis* as his all-inclusive term for 'poetry', his readers would have little difficulty in following him, but would have been shocked indeed when in Book 10 he demoted poetry to a status *below* that of a skilled craft.

²³ Commentators baffled by Plato's vehemence have resorted to the artificial expedient of suggesting an internal conflict—'When he ejects Homer . . . he is ejecting part of himself'—Ferguson, p. 139; cf. Grube, 'Plato's Theory of Beauty'.

²⁴ *Rep.* 10. 595b10 ἔοικε μὲν γὰρ τῶν καλῶν ἁπάντων τούτων τῶν τραγικῶν πρῶτος διδάσκαλός τε καὶ ἡγεμὼν γενέσθαι, cf. 598d8, 607a3. Such statements are usually explained as referring to borrowing of plots from epic tales. But Plato's target is not limited to plot structure. The problem of the 'origins' of drama is of course usually viewed through the medium of Aristotle's *Poetics*.

CHAPTER FOUR

The Homeric Encyclopedia[1]

TO approach Homer in the first instance as a didactic author
is asking a good deal from any reader and is not likely to
win his early sympathy. The very overtones of the word
'epic', implying as they do the grandiose sweep of large conceptions, vivid action, and lively portraiture, seem to preclude such an
estimate of Europe's first poet. Surely for Homer the tale is the
thing. Didactic or encyclopedic elements that may be there—one
thinks for example of the famous Catalogue of the Ships—are
incidental to the epic purpose and likely to weigh as a drag on the
narrative. However, we are going to explore the argument that
the precise opposite may be the case; that the warp and woof of
Homer is didactic,[2] and that the tale is made subservient to the
task of accommodating the weight of educational materials which
lie within it.

Let us prepare the way if we can for such an approach, and
perhaps soften up some of the immediate opposition to it, by
first noticing a very early Greek document which has something
to say about the purpose and content of epic poetry, even though
it is not often considered from this point of view. The preface
to Hesiod's *Theogony*, of 103 lines, can be assumed to date from
a period not later than the end of the seventh century. It is cast
in the shape of a *Hymn to the Muses*, comparable in form and
substance to the *Homeric Hymns* properly so called. That is, the
deity is celebrated by describing its birth, prerogatives, powers
and functions in human society. To be sure, the structure of this
Hymn is loose and not very logical. There are overlappings and
repetitions which may betray the use of more than one original,
but this can be characteristic of Hesiod's style elsewhere.[3] One

reason for this looseness of composition lies in the fact that at times he seems to be addressing the Muses as mouthpieces of the particular poem he is going to sing, namely a poem about gods, and at other times he seeks to delineate them in more general terms as the representatives of all oral poetry. As we shall argue later, these two aspects of their performance are not incompatible.

At any rate, when at lines 53 and following the poet turns to describe their birth from Zeus and their present dwelling-place near Zeus' Olympian home, he surely celebrates them in their general aspect as embodying the universal power of poetry, and in this context he proceeds to define the content of what they sing as:

> the custom-laws of all and folk-ways of the immortals.[4]

There is an ambiguity in the syntax of these words that seems to reflect the bifocal character of the *Hymn* as a whole, which, we have said, addresses itself to the Muses in part as authors of the *Theogony*, and in part as patrons of all minstrelsy. According to the most likely interpretation, the poet began in his first line with a general statement:

> They sing the laws and ways of all

and then added a second line, associatively linked with the first,

> even of the immortals do they celebrate (these).

This solution means in effect that in Hesiod's mind there was no rigid distinction between the ways of men and the ways of gods. As we shall see later, this blending of the two does represent the world-view which lies behind the *Theogony*, and it also represents the blend which is found in Homer, where the divine society mirrors the human.

What is meant by the two words *nomoi* and *ethea* which we have translated as *custom-laws* and *folk-ways*? *Nomos*[5] becomes familiar in later Greek as the normal term for 'law', even though two and a half centuries later, in that treatise of Plato which carried the title *Nomoi* or *Laws*, the sense of solemn custom often prevails over that of statute. *Nomos* in fact represents both the force of usage and custom before it was written down, and also the statutory law of advanced Greek societies which was written down. But the word in this sense is not Homeric. Hesiod was the first to use it and was perhaps responsible for bringing it into currency. In so early a poet the word cannot mean statute but it might cover usage which was promulgated orally. What then are the *ethea*? Originally the word may have signified the 'lair' or 'haunt' of an animal;[6] in later Greek it develops into the meaning of personal behaviour-pattern or even personal character and so in Aristotle supplied the basis for the term 'ethics'. That is to say, between Hesiod and Aristotle both *nomos* and *ethos* passed through a similar evolution out of the concrete towards the abstract. The poet here, we suggest, may be using both of them to describe the social and moral behaviour pattern which is approved and therefore proper and 'goodly'. Perhaps his conception or rather his image of this code of behaviour is roughly polarised between what we would call the public law of the group and its private instincts and family usage, and this is why he uses the two words. *Ethea* are not less binding than *nomoi* but are more personal; the word may originally have denoted the way a human being lived in his 'haunts'. If so, it could be easily extended to cover the mores of the human haunt which is the household and family, whereas the *nomoi*, which may be connected with the distribution of pasture, would look at custom and usage from a rather larger and more social point of view. *Nomos* has a wider field of vision. Thus *ethos* would cover a man's proper feelings and reactions to intimates and to enemies. *Nomos* would describe, as it does in Hesiod, the universal law of hard work or the prohibition instinctively observed by mankind against cannibalism.[7]

Here then is a rather comprehensive definition of what oral poetry (we say oral, because of Hesiod's obvious proximity to the non-literate condition of Greek culture) is all about. Is it however meant to apply to the epic? We shall argue below that it does; that in fact, when Hesiod somewhat later in the *Hymn* says of the bard that:

> As servant of the Muses, he chants the mighty deeds of former men
> And the blessed gods[8]

he intends no distinction between this kind of service to the Muses and that performed by a singer who celebrates 'customs and ways'.

At any rate, the two terms of the definition, corresponding as they do to what we might roughly term the public and the private, or the political and the familial law of Hellenic society, can be applied rather aptly to describe the encyclopedic contents of Homeric epic, as we shall proceed to discover them in Homer's narrative. But first let us pay tribute to that narrative, as we find it exemplified in the first book of the *Iliad*.

The Greeks at Troy have sacked a neighbouring city and in the division of the spoils Agamemnon has appropriated as his property the daughter of a priest of Apollo. Despite the appeal of the girl's father he decides to keep her. The god thus outraged through the indignity done to his representative sends disastrous plague on the Greek host and an assembly has to be convened to deal with the emergency. Chalcas the seer, prodded by Achilles, chief fighting man, reluctantly reveals the truth: the commander-in-chief must give the girl back to avert the plague. This proposal enrages Agamemnon; he took her as his portion of the booty; he at least requires a substitute. Achilles points out there is at present no substitute available unless the previous distribution of spoil is cancelled. Agamemnon only gets angrier and threatens to compensate himself by taking from Achilles his own prize, Briseis. At this point the wrath of Achilles boils over in an explosion which matches Agamemnon's own. He almost kills him and then vows total abstention from the war. He will make not only the commander but all the Greeks pay for the insult to his prowess. The aged and revered Nestor intervenes with an attempt to conciliate the quarrel. Both sides, he implies, are somewhat at fault. But the two powerful men ignore his plea. Achilles retires to his tent and watches while Agamemnon's heralds take away Briseis. He then takes his grievance to his mother, the mermaid Thetis, who by the seashore promises to intercede with Zeus. The father of gods and men will arrange matters so that the withdrawal of Achilles will prove effective. Victory is to pass to the Trojans. Ceremonious arrangements meanwhile are concluded for the restoration of the priest's daughter. She is sent back in charge of a deputation headed by the politic Odysseus, and Apollo is duly appeased with prayer and sacrifice. The scene then shifts to Olympus, as Thetis makes her appeal. Zeus assents, though reluctantly, for he knows his own wife Hera does not wish the Trojans to win, even temporarily; and in fact, Hera finds out what he has promised, which provokes a bitter quarrel between the two on Olympus. This however is promptly resolved in Zeus's favour: he threatens to thrash her if she does not mind her own business. One of her sons advises her to submit and the tension is relieved. The rest of the divine family who have been spectators of this tense scene then sit down and relax at a banquet. Evening draws on, and so to bed.

Plato argues in the tenth book of his *Republic* that when this kind of story is reduced to prose it does not amount to very much.[9] Modern readers are not likely to agree. The poet's narrative, even when stripped of its verse, still reveals an economy of treatment and a degree of dramatic power and a controlled pattern of shifting moods and scenes which, taken together, are remarkable. Homer's command of the art of dramatic story-telling with its characterisation and sustained tension is so conspicuous that this book if any is likely to appeal to us as the work of personal genius; so much so that we will be reluctant to look at the composition from any other standpoint. The poet, we feel, has his initial conception of a grand quarrel, a major feud which is to provide the controlling theme for his whole story, and he then proceeds to carry out this conception with all the powers of a creative imagination and of a forceful style. Whatever traditional materials he has inherited, he moulds them to suit his own powerful design.

So far, so good. Yet we propose now to look at the poem, so to speak, from the reverse end of the telescope, not as a piece of creative fiction, but as a compilation of inherited lore. Consider then the Muse of the first book of the *Iliad* as though, while celebrating 'the mighty deeds of former men', she were recording what Hesiod also says she records, namely 'public usage and private habit of all', whether men or gods: as though in fact her utterance did conform to Plato's conception of Homer as a sort of tribal encyclopedia. We shall deliberately adopt the hypothesis that the tale itself is designed as a kind of convenience, that it is put to use as a kind of literary portmanteau which is to contain a collection of assorted usages, conventions, prescriptions, and procedures.

Her tale is of a conflict between two men of power, in whose passions and decisions the fate of the whole group is involved. While we tend to focus our attention on the heroes as autonomous personalities, we are never allowed to forget that they are not in fact autonomous. Their acts and thoughts disturb the conduct and affect the fate of the society in which they move. Yet at the same time they are controlled by the conventions of that society. This kind of poetry is public or political, and so the tale of the quarrel becomes in the first instance a vehicle for illustrating the public law, what we might call the governing apparatus of the Achaean society.

The quarrel would not have arisen in the first place were it not for the strict conventions governing the division of spoils. These pose a dilemma for the commander-in-chief and for the army at large. Agamemnon had committed a form of sacrilege which in itself could have been expiated by returning the girl in exchange for a ransom. But he turned down the father's offer, and Apollo's terms for expiation then stiffened. The offer of ransom is withdrawn. The penalty of plague can now be lifted only if the girl is restored without compensation.[10] He might still do this without loss of face, were it not for the fact that she represented the commander's share of the spoils of a sacked city, and the distribution of these shares was governed by strict convention which accorded preferential choice to men of superior station. Agamemnon therefore justly required a substitute. Where was it to come from? The sole recourse would be to cancel the entire previous distribution and start again. The complications would be enormous, and indeed this solution was impossible. It is left to Achilles to point out the fact, and incidentally put on record the convention governing the distribution:

> How shall the great-hearted Achaeans give you a prize?
> We are not aware of any large common store lying available anywhere.
> What things we took from cities when we sacked them have been distributed.
> It is not proper that the people should reverse this and collect them back
>   and amass them again.[11]

Hard experience of the wrangling and social disorder that would result had produced this *nomos*; hence the descriptive formula 'It is not proper . . . '. This piece of preserved usage is well concealed because of its close relevance to the context; the narrative scarcely pauses at all.

But there is a later and parallel example which is more conspicuous. As the quarrel between the two heroes becomes exacerbated Achilles vows withdrawal from the fight:

> Verily by this staff—it never will leaves and shoots
> Put forth again when once it has left its stump in the mountains
> Nor will it ever bloom again. Round about it the bronze has peeled off
> The leaves and the bark. And now the sons of the Achaeans
> Bear it in their hand grip, even the arbitrators of rights who the precedents
> Do guard under the eye of Zeus. This shall be to thee a great oath;
> Verily one day will desire of Achilles come upon the Achaeans.[12]

The sweep of his anger is interrupted by an excursus on the staff as symbol of authority; how you go into the woods and cut it, what it looks like, and who is entitled to hold it. The essential function of the holder is then briefly memorialised. His pronouncements conserve the legal precedents. The interruption in the narrative might sound rather quaint, were it not that the imagery employed is also relevant to the critical solemnity of the occasion, the irrevocable intensity of the hero's mood.

A little later Nestor attempts the role of peacemaker and addresses Achilles, admonishing him as follows:

> Son of Peleus, venture not to contend with a prince
> Forcefully, for he never has a portion of things on a par with that of others,
> Even a prince who holds the staff and to whom Zeus has given glory.
> If you are stronger in force, being the son of a divine mother,
> Yet Agamemnon is the superior, since he rules over greater numbers.[13]

Relationships which are basic to the stability of the social structure are here recapitulated. The authority of a prince must be maintained because he is a prince, not because he may be physically more powerful, and he often is not. The sanction of the divine apparatus stands behind this arrangement. The staff which he carries constitutes the outward symbol of his authority.

Thetis on behalf of her son Achilles repairs to Zeus' palace requesting that Zeus aid her cause. Her behaviour and that of Zeus is a complete paradigm of how a petitioner presents his petition in audience and how the prince receives it. Zeus finally consents and nods his head up and down, adding this comment:

> This that I have done is among the immortals the biggest
> Sign of all. For what is mine is not recallable nor to be falsified
> Nor to be unaccomplished; I mean whatever with my head I confirm.[14]

The concluding words define an age-old convention, for a formal nod was subject to public witness by all members of the audience. Therefore the divine apparatus is a projection of the human.

Calchas, voicing his fears that he will offend Agamemnon, describes him as

> He who mightily over all
> The Argives does exercise power, yea and the Achaeans hearken unto him.[15]

which is a fair definition preserved in the epic line of the political status of Agamemnon in Achaean history. And the seer continues by voicing the following sentiment:

> A king is greater in power whenever he is angry with an inferior.
> Suppose that for the present day he swallows down his choler
> Yet later on he keeps the grudge till he accomplish it
> In his breast.[16]

This can be cited as an example either of *nomos* or of *ethos*, the code of public law or the pattern of private behaviour. This is the way kings can behave; this is one of the hard facts of power. A prince may find it politic to postpone his anger; he can afford to, provided his opponent is a subject. Psychological is combined with social observation; there is no moral judgment passed. The minstrel is simply reporting and describing, and this gives to the epic idiom its curiously dispassionate quality, elevating it in the grand manner. But it is in the grand manner because the poetised speech is devoted to framing a 'pedagogic' observation in preserved and permanent form.

The above examples are statements of the kind of political relationship by which this kind of society expected to be governed. They are composed summarily and formulaically, and are not offered systematically, but only as the story prompts their intrusion. They are a small sample of the hundreds of such statements which occur in the course of the *Iliad* and *Odyssey*. Being political, confined that is, to the legal and social relationships between human beings as such, they are comparatively easy to identify. But the public law embraced much more. In the epic tale the human apparatus is counterpointed against the religious. Both alike were conducted in formulas which lent a ceremonial quality to anything that was done or said. But the religious apparatus can make demands of its own with which human pride and passion can conflict. Human political arrangements must conform to these demands, but situations may arise where the requirements of the one are incompatible with those of the other. The purely political needs of the army would have been better served if Agamemnon had been allowed to keep his girl. The religious apparatus under which they all lived, and the premises of which they all accepted, made this impossible. The story of the *Iliad* thus is impelled to describe this conflict, and as it does this the poet is prompted to repeat for the record a great deal of ritual prescription and procedure (and belief) which equally form part of the tribal encyclopedia.

His brief preface is designed as a forecast of the course of his tale: disaster awaits the Greeks because of a feud between their leaders. To this he adds almost parenthetically the following comment: 'and the counsel of Zeus was accomplished'.[17] Brief as it is, this half line performs two different functions at once. On the one hand it is designed to summarise specific events which are to occur in this particular tale. Zeus, as we are told before the first book ends, will in fact reluctantly assist Achilles and arrange events so as to satisfy his anger. By the end of the eighth book, and still more by the end of the fifteenth, this divine counsel has indeed been accomplished. But the ancient audience, when they first heard the sentiment, would automatically interpret it in a larger context. The counsels of Zeus have a habit of prevailing in all circumstances. This truth might apply not just to the immediate satisfaction of Achilles, but to that later ironic reversal of his hopes and desires which follows once his prayer has been granted. The total tragedy of the *Iliad* has a kind of universal logic in which the counsel of Zeus was indeed accomplished on a grand scale. These reflections far exceed the bounds of Homer's conscious or contrived thought. They are phrased in terms of a sophisticated critique. But we offer them in order to illustrate how, as the formulas can yield these sophisticated results to the modern reader, they also to the Homeric reader became the utterance of rules, the expressions of standards, in aphorism or proverb, which the syntax of the tale might require to be cast in the past tense,[18] but which are really concealed aphorisms. The counsel of Zeus was accomplished and it always is.

How, asks the poet rhetorically, did this feud begin?

The son of Leto and Zeus was angry with the king
And had aroused an evil plague throughout the army, and the people were
  perishing.

Here on the one hand is a specific statement essential to the plot.
But it also follows the accepted formula for all plagues: this is
how they arise; this is why divine anger is dangerous.
  But why was Apollo angry in the first place?

The priest Chryses had been dishonoured by the son of Atreus.[19]

Here is another specific statement narrated in the past tense; at the
same time it implies a timeless statement of a general directive.
Here is what always causes divine anger. The listener is insensibly
reminded that it is dangerous to deny priests their proper prerogatives. The rule is recalled in the description of its abrogation.
The implicit aphorism is given its own explicit formulation a few
lines later. The army, on hearing the priest's account of his
grievance,

Cried aloud 'Well said!' Priests must receive respect[20]

where the Greek idiom does not distinguish between this priest
and any priest. This priest had approached the Greek camp:

To get his daughter free, and bearing countless ransom.

Here is a standard performance of a custom law which governed
one aspect of human relationships in time of war. It is itself
secular, though a priest happens here to be the agent. The same
performance will recur again and again throughout the tale.
This particular one is memorialised three more times in the first
hundred lines. It is incidentally interesting to observe that
the order of statement is paratactic, in the sense that the two
'actions', or the decision plus the action, are narrated in order
of their occurrence 'in nature':

He intended to free her
And he carried ransom.

where a sophisticated but post-Homeric logic could use the reverse order:

> He was carrying a ransom
> In order to free her.

So far the priest's performance is secular, but as a priest he carries equipment proper to his special status:

> Holding in his hand the fillets of Apollo the far-shooter
> Upon a staff of gold.

This is a formula which prescribes efficacy to him who has the right to carry such equipment. The fact is memorialised again when Agamemnon warns the priest to depart,

> Lest staff and fillets of the god avail thee not.[21]

Agamemnon in the story is going to break the rules which are expressed in these ceremonious trappings. But the story is told in such a way that the rules themselves are continually recalled. The record is indirect but it is a record.

The priest offers his request and after repeating the formula for ransom, he concludes his address to the sons of Atreus and the Greeks as follows:

> As ye do reverence to the son of Zeus even Apollo the far-darter.[22]

Once more the specific appeal contains also a general prescription observed in this kind of society. Apollo must always be reverenced; his proper title is son of Zeus. And when the priest withdraws after rebuff to invoke his god, the poet repeats the definition of this god's parentage, this time from the mother's side:

> He prayed many things
> To Apollo the lord whom fair-tressed Leto bore.

His prayer is then given in *oratio recta*. It sounds like a paradigm of all such addresses:

Hearken unto me, O thou of the silver bow, who dost encompass Chryse
And Cilla the holy place, and over Tenedos with might dost rule
O Sminthean . . .

The god that is selected for address receives his proper definition.
He is the one localised at given cult-centres, and he has specific
functions—as here he controls the arrows of death—and his
worship is located at and off the north shore of Anatolia. The
prayer continues:

If ever I have roofed over a dwelling-place for you
If ever I have consumed fat thighs of cattle for you
Even of bulls or goats, then accomplish for me this my desire.[23]

The lines run in a refrain which commemorates the simple but
standard practice required for setting up and maintaining a cult.
While specific to this particular crisis, the priest's appeal also
serves as a reminder of regular procedure. Here is a fragment of
the religious code of behaviour.

The plague follows and the army is decimated. Achilles
summons an assembly and proposes that they listen to what a
soothsayer may have to say. The actual situation, were Homer
keeping his eye on it exclusively, would call for Achilles to nominate Calchas promptly for this role. He is the obvious choice. But
the saga in fact reverts once more to the idiom of record, not
invention, and substitutes the general formula in place of the
specific:

But come let us ask of some seer or holy man
Or yet a dream interpreter—for indeed a dream is of Zeus—
Who will tell us

The aphorism about the divine source of dreams is by natural
association included in the generalised list of the three principal
sources to which one looks for inspired guidance. And the
speech continues with an equally formulaic statement covering
the performances required for maintaining friendly relations
with the deity:

> Or be it for an offering does he find us sinful, or be it for a hecatomb,
> Or if perchance the savour of sheep or yet of goats unblemished
> He may desire to obtain and so ward off the plague.[24]

The Greek in both passages goes with an acoustic jingle which can be rendered only imperfectly in English. These jingles characteristically creep into the formulas of religious ceremony, revealing their character as familiar and popular definitions but ones for which, however familiar, there was the felt need of constant recall. Indeed, the formula which combines offering and hecatomb with the mention of divine resentment is repeated 28 lines later, when it is incorporated into the reply of Calchas with that minimum verbal alteration necessary for the changed context.

Achilles had couched his first speech in a framework of general rules. The specific response is for Calchas to get up. But this event once more sets in motion in the poet's mind the mechanism of the generalised utterance rather than that of the specific narrative:

> Calchas son of Thestor of dream interpreters by far the best
> Who knew the things that be, and the things that are to be, and the things that be before,
> And he directed the ships of the Achaeans as far as Ilium
> Because of his prophecy that Phoebus Apollo conferred on him.
> And he before them with goodly thought spake and made utterance among them.[25]

Of these five lines only the third is immune from any influence of the typical or general. In the first is concealed a reminder that soothsayers are a prized institution of this society. The second defines the bounds of possible intelligence: the formula is repeated by Hesiod in the *Theogony* to describe the minstrel's poetic powers conferred by the Muses. Here it appears under the aspect of prophecy, conferred by Apollo, who is the proper source of such powers, and we are reminded that he is. The reminder is repeated in a variant formula by Achilles when he replies. Thus equipped, a man may properly 'speak well with goodly thought'. The poet recalls one of the social 'moralities' even as he describes an event. The 'morality' is secular no less than sacred. The usages prescribed by religion are at the same time the usages of the political apparatus. And if the status of priest or seer as formulated above can be classified as part of the public law of this society, the practice of that intelligence which is expected of him becomes part of the same society's *ethos*, its personal code. The one passes imperceptibly into the other. Both alike are recalled in language which tends to be couched in terms of standardised procedures or situations.

The poet's description of Calchas is then followed by the seer's own speech which is framed within the same generic limits. He turns to Achilles with these words:

> Therefore will I speak and do thou utter and swear to me
> In very sooth to stand with me in word and deed most ready.

The formal appeal describes the relationship of two allies whose alliance is confirmed by formal agreement—the spoken oath characteristic of an oral culture. The situation is specific, yet as expressed it becomes a general paradigm of such a treaty and the loyalty which it both affirms and on which it depends. Its echo remains in the mind as the proper formula of comradely association in such a society. It is both *nomos* and *ethos*.

Then the reason for the appeal is given: 'Agamemnon may be dangerous to me.' But this specific danger is at once translated into general terms which become a formalised description of the status proper to a commander-in-chief:

> For indeed do I think that a man there is who will be angry, he who over all
> Does mightily rule, and the Achaeans hearken to his word.

It is characteristic of this stylised type of statement that Achilles when he replies and gives assurance repeats the reminder of Agamemnon's status:

> No man shall lay hands on you, not even should you name Agamemnon
> Him who now far the best of the Achaeans does claim to be.[26]

These words make the specific point that Achilles is not afraid of challenging his rival in the army. But they also convey the generic affirmation that aristocratic status is a fact. Here is a line which as hoarded in the memory becomes prescriptive no less than descriptive, an encouragement to the learner himself to admire the status which is 'best' and perhaps to aspire to it. It is another fragment of society's *ethos* preserved and hoarded in the epic idiom.

As one examines Homer's text in search of items of the public law, one is continually led on to discern also items of the personal code as these are interwoven with the public. The epic idiom becomes a preservative at once of familiar and proper customs and of acceptable and worthy habits and attitudes. Our present search for religious custom-law as it is embedded in the first book of the *Iliad* has illustrated this effect. This preserved *ethos* is so penetrative and pervasive in Homer's lines that its analysis could proceed almost indefinitely. Let us here leave it and return to the more conspicuous items of hoarded usage which tend to reveal themselves more obviously as they deal with customs which in the first instance are public rather than private. We have looked at political custom and then turned to religious custom as found in the procedures of prayer and cult worship. These latter occur at a later stage in the story when the girl is restored to her father and to the shrine from which she had originally been taken. The Greek deputation deposits her at Chryse, the priest is consequently reconciled with the Greeks, Apollo's anger is appeased, and the plague averted. This reversal of the original plot mechanism is then duly marked as the priest turns once more to his god and repeats the same prayer formula which we have already noted, but now reverses the request:

> Now yet again accomplish for me this my desire.
> Now ward off from the Greeks most grievous pestilence.[27]

In terms of the narrative this specific appeal tidies things up and disposes of the issue. But it has also a generic ring: it enshrines the prayerful idiom anyone shall use when confronted by such an affliction.

The performance of the Greek deputation provides a conspicuous example of Greek ceremonious behaviour formulaically preserved. They carry out for Apollo, as part of the expiatory process, a ritual sacrifice, the description of which in nine lines[28] sounds like a guide to all similar ceremonies, with the operations of slaughtering, slaying, dividing, dressing, and cooking the meat itemised in series. The ritual is then rounded off with the equally ceremonious description of a banquet and a musical performance, and so to bed.[29] The minstrel has reported the conclusion of a day in the life of a group of men in a paradigm which, as we shall have reason to notice, is essentially repeated later when he describes the end of a day in the life of the gods. The whole forms a little idyll, a tableau of religious but also of social usage, hardened and preserved in the epic verse.

After this fashion the verse composes itself so that the specific situations which are necessary to make a story are put together out of behaviour patterns which are typical. They are all bits and pieces of the life and thought of the day as it is lived in this kind of society. Continually therefore the characters as they speak or act reveal the public apparatus of political government and also the private code of intimate relations between friends and enemies, men and women, within the family, and between families. Thus Agamemnon in his desire to keep Chryseis provides a natural occasion for the insertion of two descriptions which bear upon domestic mores. His original refusal to restore her is amplified as follows:

> Her I will not let go. Ere that shall old age overtake her
> In our home in Argos, far from her country,
> Going to and fro before the loom and going up to my bed.[30]

The accepted lot of the concubine is here summarised. She can be acquired as a prize, she does her share of the weaving and child bearing, and she becomes in time the aged servant of the household. The lines are almost equally pertinent to the accepted role of a wife, and as Agamemnon warms to his congenial theme, the formula for wifehood is developed further. Warned by Calchas to give the girl back, he is provoked to expressing his growing desire to keep her. He now goes further in his thoughts, and considers her as a possible consort. Whereupon, the poet through his mouth frames the proper requirements, the criteria which should govern male choice:

> Indeed I have formed a preference for Chryseis above Clytemnestra,
> My original bed-fellow. For Chryseis is not inferior to her
> In looks nor in build, nor in wits nor in the work she can do.[31]

Since, however, so much of the human plot of the *Iliad* takes place on or near the battlefield, the domestic mores are more conspicuously put on record when the poet shifts his perspective to Olympus. Thus Zeus after giving audience to Thetis in his counsel chamber returns to the dining hall and:

> All the gods stood up together
> From their seats in the presence of their father. Nor did any venture
> To stay in his place before Zeus's arrival. Yea, they all stood up before him.
> And then he sat down in his tall chair.[32]

The paradigm of table manners conserves the mores of a patriarchal household system where the adult children are still subordinate. Such a social system requires from its men and women, husbands and wives, an *ethos* appropriate to each sex which shall also conform to the system as a whole. So, as Hera proceeds to needle her spouse about his recent audience with Thetis, his reply is couched in terms of a typical paradigm:

> Do not expect that all communications I may have made
> You will know. They would be over your head, bed-fellow though you are.
> Any communication that is proper to tell you, you will learn
> Before any other of gods or men.
> But any that it is my decision to think over in private
> I must ask you not to pursue in detail nor inquire after.[33]

The passage in specific context may be amusingly pompous, especially when it turns out that what Zeus thought he had guarded as a top secret is no secret at all. But it is also a generalised statement of the proper male role in the patriarchal family, not the less formally shaped for being personally appropriate. The first three lines of Hera's reply, with equal formality, express an acceptance of this convention that Zeus has stated. But this acceptance is then cancelled as she reveals her knowledge of his interview with Thetis and taxes him with making a decision she profoundly dislikes. The course of the story thus allows the domestic code to be broken. But its breaking can offer a fresh occasion for affirming it. As tempers rise dangerously, one of the younger sons intervenes with advice to his mother:

I my mother would induce—and she herself does attend—
That to our own father she confer what is fitting, even to Zeus, that no longer
May father be enraged.[34]

In this phraseology the realities of the familial situation are summed up and accepted. The formula 'what is fitting' is characteristically both descriptive and yet prescriptive. Nor need we wonder that a society like that of Athens which at a later epoch preserved Homer's poems as a vehicle of education should have also preserved the patriarchal *ethos* even when new conditions and circumstances might work against it.

The whole domestic scene is then concluded on a more relaxed note as the poet makes the gods sit down to dinner and entertainment. The proceedings are memorialised as though they were a ritual; a day in the life of Olympus ends very much like that day which had seen the heroes restore Chryseis and then celebrate with banquet and song:

So they the whole day long to the sun's setting
Banqueted, and they sated their spirit partaking of the symmetrical board
And of the ever-lovely lyre which Apollo held
And of the Muses singing antiphonally with fair utterance.[35]

Plato, describing those fields of human activity over which
Homer was claimed to preside as instructor, had twice used the
word *dioikesis*.[36] This overall 'management' of life, social and personal, proceeding outwards from the family into the sphere of
political and religious obligations, is what we have so far been
disentangling from the text of the first book of the *Iliad*. Plato
had also mentioned Homer's claim to command instruction at
the technical level.[37] However surprising and indeed irrelevant to
the poet's proper role this may seem to modern taste, even the
first book of the *Iliad* can furnish examples of what Plato might
mean. We should first notice how usage as it is recorded in the
political, religious, or family sphere can itself often turn into a
kind of technique. The boundary between moral behaviour and
skilled behaviour in an oral culture is rather thin.[38] This is inherent
in the fact that so much of social behaviour and deportment had
to be ceremonial, or had to be recorded ceremonially, which may
amount to very much the same thing.

Procedures have to be observed, and are recorded as operations
made up of distinct acts precisely defined, which must follow each
other in a certain order. Thus, when Achilles digresses in order to
describe the staff of authority which he dashes on the ground, the
digression furnishes a piece of tribal law but it also illustrates an
item of tribal technique, simple to be sure, but precise for all that.
The staff must be properly prepared and ceremoniously handled.
A more evident example of the way in which *nomos* and *techne*
overlap is seen in a description of that sacrifice which the Achaeans
offered to Apollo when the girl was restored. The ritual is an
operation made up of distinct acts, precisely defined, which must
follow each other in the order stated.[39] The narrative requires that
these be put into the past tense. But the series conveys the effect of
a procedure carefully generalised so as to be easily imitable. It is
a piece of preserved know-how. An oral culture felt the need of
a ritual conservation of such procedures. Their memorisation
and observance might be the province of specialists—the priests
and holy men—but a general knowledge of such was likewise

diffused through the whole society and taught through the whole epic. It is therefore not very surprising if the Greeks who wrote the first histories of the origins of their culture should have included religious practice among the invented crafts.[40] Concretely speaking, Greek religion was a matter not of belief but of cult practice, and cult practice was composed of an accumulated mass of procedures which had to be performed skilfully in order to be performed dutifully and properly and piously.

To repeat then: in an oral culture the hoarded usages of society tend also to assume the guise of hoarded techniques. This tendency was inherent in the virtuosity with which these operations were invested. This is true of the practice and still more true of the record of practice. The most striking example as furnished in the first book of the *Iliad* is that of the practices of seamanship, a craft central to Greek civilisation at all periods. The poet's narrative is so composed that opportunity is afforded for a sea voyage. The girl, if she is to be restored to her father's shrine, must be transported on shipboard. This becomes the occasion for recapitulating some standardised operational procedures, which are spelled out in four distinct passages forming a progressive pattern, as follows:

Agamemnon is speaking; he has reluctantly assented to the demand that he restore her:

> As for now a black ship let us draw down to the great salt sea
> And therein oarsmen let us advisedly gather and thereupon a hecatomb
> Let us set and upon the deck Chryseis of fair cheeks
> Let us embark. And one man as captain, a man of counsel, there must be.[41]

The word 'advisedly' here recalls the attention that Achilles and Hephaestus gave to what was 'proper' and 'fitting', in previous examples. Such prescriptive terms are often included in epic summaries of procedure. They might seem to express the bard's own consciousness of his didactic function.[42]

So far we have the proposal of a procedure. Over two hundred lines later there follows its execution, described in words which repeat the items of the proposal:

The son of Atreus a swift ship to the salt sea drew down
And therein oarsmen he selected twenty and thereupon a hecatomb
He embarked for the god and on the deck Chryseis of the fair cheeks
He set having brought her. And therein a captain went, even Odysseus of
    many counsels.[43]

The two formulaic passages elucidate several important facts
about the character of preserved communication when the
method of preservation is oral. The order of events, of acts, and
of objects in the two passages is identical: first the launching of
the ship, second the mustering of the crew, third the cargo is
shipped, fourth the passenger is embarked, fifth the captain is
appointed. The order of operations in sacrifice can be compared.
But the actual verbal formulae used—those building blocks made
up of rhythmic units of two or more words recurring in identical
order and in identical place in the line—show considerable
variation. The first lines for example in each passage have unique
verbal structure. The three words common to both do not occur
in the same rhythmic position. This demonstrates the fact that
the real and essential 'formula' in orally preserved speech consists of a total 'situation' in the poet's mind. It is made up of a
series of standardised images which follow each other in his
memory in a fixed order. The verbal formulae serve as the
instrument by which these images are deployed. But their syntax
can vary, provided the essential images are preserved. One also
notices that when mechanical procedures are reported, the rhythmic devices used to assist memorisation themselves can become
mechanical. The repeated *therein* and *thereupon* have a nursery-
rhyme quality.

However, even in reporting mechanical procedures, an entry
of this kind does not contain such detailed instruction as you
would expect to find in a modern text book. Rather, what is
preserved is a simplified portrait of what goes on. The record is
a synthesis of experience, not an analysis. A thousand specific
details of the navigator's skill were left to be communicated by
example and habituation and imitation and never got into the

epic formulas. The epic idiom in fact is used to preserve techniques only as part of a general education. Hence the descriptions
are always typical rather than detailed. It was no doubt part of
Plato's objection that this was so: the poet was not an expert.

When the girl is actually transported back to her home, the
arrival of the ship at Chryse is described:

> And they, when within the harbour of many depths they came,
> The sails did furl and set them in the black ship,
> And the mast to the crutch they lowered, releasing it by the stays
> With speed, and the ship to anchorage they rowed forward with oars.
> And out they cast the mooring stones and made fast the stern ropes
> And out themselves they went upon the foreshore of the sea
> And out the hecatomb they took for far-darting Apollo
> And out Chryseis went from the seafaring ship.[44]

The verbal and rhythmic mechanisms reminiscent of nursery-
rhyme are here quite evident, the more so as in the original Greek
the words for 'sail' and 'mast' are assonant. The steps in the
regular procedure are itemised with sharp clarity. First you
reach harbour, second furl sail, third lower the mast, fourth row
to the beach, fifth anchor the stern in deep water, sixth get out
(by the bow), seventh get the cargo out, eighth disembark the
passenger. This is how you dealt with any ship under given
circumstances, not just Chryseis' ship. We cannot call it a
digression, for it is wholly relevant to its context, but it constitutes
nevertheless a leisured pause in the tale. It spells out and tallies
the required procedure with a kind of relish. The bard is not
governed by the economies of dramatic art as we understand the
term. He is at once a storyteller and also a tribal encyclopedist.

Still another example of navigational report occurs when they
return back to camp:

> And they the mast set up and upon it the white sails they spread
> And into the middle of the sail the wind puffed, and the wave
> All-flashing around the stem hissed loud as the ship passed
> And the ship ran over the waves accomplishing her path.
> And when they came into the wide camp of the Achaeans

The black ship they drew up upon the dry land
High up on the sand and under it extended long props
And themselves scattered.[45]

The mechanical and repetitive use of adverbs at the beginning of clauses ('up', 'into', 'around', etc.) here once more marks the nursery-rhyme style.

Taking the four passages on ships together, we can say that the first book of the *Iliad* preserves a complete and formulaic report on loading, embarking, disembarking, and unloading. In short, here is a complete example of Homeric 'technology', if that word is used to describe definitions of skilled procedures which are quite popular and general, but which are also definite. If we now recall Plato's statement, that the poets, according to popular estimate, 'possessed the know-how of all techniques',[46] we can begin to see what he meant.

NOTES

[1] For the qualifications with which this term should be used cf. below, p. 92.

[2] This adjective may mislead, if it suggests an emphatically conscious purpose on the part of the oral poet, yet it is difficult to choose a better. He is didactic by necessity, but also in large part unconsciously. In chapter six it will be noted how Hesiod, voicing a conscious didacticism, speaks for oral epic and not just for himself; and in chapter nine, how nevertheless, in the poet's awareness of himself, his power to please has priority over his duty to instruct.

[3] Jacoby (p. 138) is forced to resort to multiple ingenuities of marginal notation to distinguish what he thinks are various types of unauthentic verse in Hesiod, as for example early interpolations, late interpolations, and edited passages. But if Hesiod's material is 'the Achaean heritage of oral poetry' (Notopoulos, *Hesperia* 29, 177 ff.), then literate standards of consistency cannot be applied to it; cf. below, cap. 7, n. 7.

[4] Line 66; its 'authenticity' (see previous note) is irrelevant to our purpose.

[5] Van Groningen, p. 11 (and notes 3 and 6): '*nomos* . . . means the "custom" which became law and ordinance' (in contrast to *thesmos*, which, so he argues following Ehrenberg, exhibits reverse development).

⁶ Animal haunts *WD* 525; human haunts *WD* 222; human haunts or habits (ambiguous) *WD* 137, 167.

⁷ *WD* 388, 276.

⁸ *Theog.* 100-101.

⁹ Cf. above, cap. 1, n. 30.

¹⁰ Line 99.

¹¹ 123 ff.

¹² 234 ff.

¹³ 277 ff.

¹⁴ 525 ff.

¹⁵ 78 ff.

¹⁶ 80 ff.

¹⁷ 5.

¹⁸ Hence the 'gnomic' aorist; a narrative context is required for mnemonic purposes (below, cap. 10) and narrative by definition is 'past'; cf. Van Groningen, p. 19, who argues that for the Greeks 'objective certainty can be found only there' (*sc.*, in the past). I would argue however that this preference for the past is at bottom a preference for the concrete, and that therefore to call the aorist 'more abstract' (ibid.) is to reverse the proper priorities.

¹⁹ Lines 9-11.

²⁰ 22.

²¹ 13-14 and 28.

²² 21.

²³ 35-41.

²⁴ 62-67.

²⁵ 69 ff.

²⁶ 76-9, 89-90.

²⁷ 455-6.

²⁸ 459 ff.; cf. below, n. 39.

²⁹ 467 ff.

³⁰ 29-31.

³¹ 113-15; cf. 9.341-2.

³² 533 ff.

³³ 545 ff.

³⁴ 577 ff.

³⁵ 601 ff., and above, n. 29.

³⁶ *Rep.* 10 599c8, 606e3.

³⁷ 598e1, 599c1 ff.

³⁸ Cf. *Od.* 3.21 ff.

³⁹ Richardson's suggestive article observes (pp. 52-4) how this rule applies not only to the passage in question, but to its counterparts at *Il.* 2.421 and *Od.* 12.359, and also to the 'arming scenes' at *Il.* 3.328 ff., 11.17 ff., 16.131 ff., 19.369 ff. (on arming as a Homeric 'technology' cf. Ar. *Frogs* 1036). The navigation directives (below) exhibit similar organisation. Cf. also cap. 8, n. 6, and cap. 15, n. 44.

⁴⁰ Aesch. *P.V.* 484 ff.

⁴¹ 141 ff.; the passage is noted by Richardson *loc. cit.*, but not the three others which complement it.

⁴² Cf. also the formula (ἦν) θέμις ἐστιν.

⁴³ 308 ff.

⁴⁴ 432 ff.

⁴⁵ 480 ff.

⁴⁶ *Rep.* 598e1.

CHAPTER FIVE

Epic as Record versus Epic as Narrative

THE reader will remember our appeal to him to suspend judgment while the *Iliad* was, so to speak, turned upside down and looked at in the first instance not as a work of poetic invention, that is as a work of art, but as a kind of metrical text book. The results if we examine the first book as a sample are now before us. Taking the first hundred lines alone, we have separated out a total of about fifty and identified their content as didactic in the sense that they recall or memorialise acts, attitudes, judgments, and procedures which are typical. As they accumulate, they begin to read like a running report of that society to which the bard addresses his tale, but a report drafted also as a series of recommendations. This is the way in which the society does normally behave (or does not) and at the same time the way in which we, its members, who form the poet's audience, are encouraged to behave. There is no admonition: the tale remains dispassionate. But the paradigm of what is accepted practice or proper feeling is continually offered in contrast to what may be unusual or improper and excessive or rash. So far as the bard's own invention is concerned, this is more likely to show itself when his characters depart from the accepted *nomos* and *ethos* than when they conform. In sum, when Hesiod describes the content of the Muses' song as *nomoi* and *ethe*, he is describing epic, and Plato's conception of Homer's function as it was claimed by Homer and for Homer makes sense. He is indeed an encyclopedia of Greek or at least Homeric *paideia*. This is a poetry of preserved communication and what is preserved has to be typical.

Let us in Homeric fashion attempt three different similes to illustrate how the substance of this kind of oral poetry is composed. We can speak of the epic as a mighty river of song. Caught up and borne along in this flood there is a vast mass of contained materials which as they colour the waters are also sustained by them. This simile is imperfect so far as it suggests a qualitative distinction between the river with its power of narrative description and the gross body of information and prescription and catalogue which depends on the power of the stream for its movement but is not itself part of that movement. Let us therefore suggest a second simile of an architectural complex designed, proportioned, and built, which yet depends for its effect upon the quality of the stones and the wood, the brick and the marble which have been used in building it. The colours and shapes of these materials enter into and inform the whole geometric design. This simile is superior so far as it indicates that Homer's running report is not something he has worked artificially into his narrative, but is essentially and inherently part of his style. It is difficult for him to say anything without infusing it with some colour of the typical.

Yet we need a third simile which shall describe the sharpness of vision with which these typical elements are framed. They are not as undifferentiated as bricks and mortar and stone. And yet the vision is not unique so much as typical. Homer did not personally invent these ways of recollecting custom and usage. His report of his society must have been shared by all bards, though no doubt at different levels of virtuosity. He did not create this code, nor can he alter its general colour by imposing upon it a personal vision, except within narrow limits. Let us think of him therefore as a man living in a large house crowded with furniture, both necessary and elaborate. His task is to thread his way through the house, touching and feeling the furniture as he goes and reporting its shape and texture. He chooses a winding and leisurely route which shall in the course of a day's recital allow him to touch and handle most of what is in the house. The route that he picks will have its own design. This becomes his story, and represents the nearest that he can approach to sheer invention. This house, these rooms, and the furniture he did not himself fashion: he must continually and affectionately recall them to us. But as he touches or handles he may do a little refurbishing, a little dusting off, and perhaps make small rearrangements of his own, though never major ones. Only in the route he chooses does he exercise decisive choice. Such is the art of the encyclopedic minstrel, who as he reports also maintains the social and moral apparatus of an oral culture.[1]

In this, we suggest, lies the clue to that peculiar elevation which critics continually recognise in Homeric poetry. For some translators the only possible response has been to attempt versions in the idiom of the King James rendering of the Old Testament. Others with their fingers on the pulse of modernity have felt equally impelled to get away from the grand style as far as possible in order to render Homer in the idiom of modern speech. Both types of version represent some inevitable compromise between failure and success, but the former at least reveals an awareness of the thing in Homer which is unique, namely, an encyclopedic vision, with which goes a total acceptance of the mores of society, and a familiarity with and an affection for its thought-forms. Homer is about as close as poetry can ever come to a report on the normal juxtaposed over against the abnormal. To describe his manner as elevated is to use a poor metaphor. His power derives from his function, and his function does not carry him vertically upward above the spirits of men but extends him horizontally outward to the confines of the society for which he sings. He profoundly accepts this society, not by personal choice but because of his functional role as its recorder and pre- server. He is therefore dispassionate, he can have no personal axe to grind, no vision wholly private to himself. The furniture in the house may undergo some rearrangement but there cannot be a manufacture of new furniture. If we ask: Why then is he not dull? we should reply perhaps that he would be dull if he per- formed these functions as would a literate poet composing for readers. But he is an oral poet composing according to certain psychological laws which were unique, which have literally ceased to exist, at least in Europe and in the West. Plato showed keen awareness of this psychology even as he sought to eliminate it. A little later we must revert to it and consider the psychic mechanisms which this kind of poetry was forced to exploit, and the type of consciousness which it fostered.

Among such poets, superior genius would belong to him who had superior command of the art of relevance. With one part of his attention focused on his tale, itself in part traditional, though amenable to invention, the larger and more unconscious part of his energy would be engaged in bringing the tale into continual contact with the general social apparatus. The more of the apparatus that gets in, the more enriched the narrative mixture becomes. The more aptly and easily the apparatus is controlled by the context of the narrative, the smoother seems the result and the more dramatic the effect. Continually therefore a poet's superior talent can employ the apparatus at two levels, both as a general report and also to gain a specific effect, some heightened parallel or contrast in some specific narrative situation. We have described Achilles' description of the staff of authority as an excursus which interrupts the sweep of his anger. Yet it is also true that as the listener hears him describe this piece of a tree which will never burgeon again, for it has become something else, he would catch a note of relevance: the separation of the wood from its tree is irrevocable and so is to be the separation of Achilles from his own parent body the army. A piece of reporting turns into a dramatic device.

It is, however, characteristic of the whole bent of modern criticism that the element of reporting is ignored and the element of artifice is exaggerated. Our conception of poetry does not find room for the oral act of reporting and so does not allow for the complexities of Homer's task. Artistic creation as we understand the term is a much simpler thing than the epic performance and it is one which implies the separation of the artist from political and social action. If this were an essay in Homeric criticism alone one should not perhaps choose to take sides between his encyclopedic functions on the one hand and that artistry on the other with which he weaves his report into his story. These may stand as coeval aspects of his united genius.[2] But the quest we are pursuing here is for a goal which is not Homeric and which grows larger and more oppressive, if that is the word, as Homer is left progressively farther behind. It is the Platonic quest for a non-Homeric mind and language, and in the context of this quest the overwhelmingly important thing about Homer is the thing that Plato said about Homer: in his day and for many days later he was the chief claimant for the role of educator of Greece. Plato did not himself analyse the historical reasons why this was so. We have sought to supply them by considering Homer as the representative of that kind of poetry which has to exist in a culture of oral communication, where if any 'useful' statement, historical, technical, or moral, is to survive, in more or less standardised form, this can be done only in the living memories of the members who make up the culture group. The epic therefore is from the standpoint of our present quest to be considered in the first instance not as an act of creation but as an act of reminder and recall. Its patron muse is indeed *Mnemosune*[3] in whom is symbolised not just the memory considered as a mental phenomenon but rather the total act of reminding, recalling, memorialising, and memorising, which is achieved in epic verse. For a Roman writer the Muse might represent invention applied to content[4] as also to form. But in the antique accounts of her skill in the archaic and high classical period of Greek civilisation this is not stressed. The story of invention belongs properly to the sphere of *logos*, not *mythos*: it was set in motion by the prosaic quest for a non-poetic language and a non-Homeric definition of truth.

Now if the framed word and the important communication could survive only in the living memory, the poet's task was not simply to report and recall, but to repeat. Within the confines of repetition, variety would occur. The typical can be restated within a fairly wide range of verbal formulas. A written encyclopedia on the contrary separates its material into topics and treats each exhaustively with a minimum of repetition. Varying versions of what is 'knowledgeable'[5] are pruned down and reduced to monotypes. Oral record demands exactly the reverse procedure and literate interpreters who have not schooled their imaginations to understand the psychology of oral preservation will accordingly divide and prune and excise the repetitions and variants in a text of Homer or Hesiod to make the text conform to literate procedures where the requirements of the living memory are no longer in question.[6] The metaphor which describes Homer as a tribal encyclopedia is in fact loose if we use the term encyclopedia in that bookish sense which is proper to it. For Homer continually restates and rehandles the *nomos* and *ethos* of his society as though from a modern standpoint he were not quite sure of the correct version. What he in fact is quite sure of is the overall code of behaviour, portions of which he keeps bringing up in a hundred contexts and with a hundred verbal variants.

This habit of 'variation within the same' is fundamental to Homer's poetry and betrays that root principle of its manufacture as it was analysed by the late Milman Parry. The oral technique of verse composition can be viewed as built up out of the following devices: there is a purely metrical pattern which allows successive lines of poetry of standard time length to be made up of interchangeable metrical parts:[7] second, a vast supply of word-combinations or formulas of varying length and syntax rhythmically shaped so as to fit portions of the metrical line but themselves also made up of interchangeable verbal parts so disposed that either by combining different formulas or combining pieces of different formulas the poet can alter his syntax while maintaining his meter. His overall artistry thus consists of an endless distribution of variables where, however, variation is held within strict limits and the verbal possibilities, while extensive, are in the last resort finite. Or putting it semantically, we can say that the possibilities of variation in meaning, of alteration of statement, are also in the long run finite. This finitude corresponds to the finitude of that pattern of *nomos* and *ethos* which the poet continually recalls.

The virtuosity of this technique in Homer is astonishing and to explore it further can be an esthetic delight. But in our present context, the technique comes into consideration for only one very elementary reason. What was the psychological motive which prompted its development on the part of the Greek minstrels? Homeric criticism has sought to answer this question within the limits of our modern conception of poetry as an act of invention. Ignoring the furniture in the house, we tend to concentrate attention wholly on the narrative path which the poet takes as he threads his way through it. Consequently the epic formulaic technique has been considered almost exclusively as an aid to poetic improvisation, a device to allow the poet to get on easily with his tale.[8] But in fact it came into existence as a device of memorisation and of record; the element of improvisation is wholly secondary, just as the minstrel's personal invention is secondary to the culture and folkways which he reports and preserves.[9]

The notion that Greek epic is to be considered as an act of improvisation, that is of limited but speedy invention, has been assisted not only by modern notions of what we expect of a poet, but by modern analogies drawn from the surviving oral poetry of the Balkans and Eastern Europe.[10] The comparative method used here, which seems so assured and scientific, has in fact been guided by an assumption which is not scientific. It has lumped together two poetic situations which are entirely different, that of the Balkan peasantry and that of the Homeric governing class. It was of the essence of Homeric poetry that it represented in its epoch the sole vehicle of important and significant communication. It therefore was called upon to memorialise and preserve the social apparatus, the governing mechanism, and the education

for leadership and social management, to use Plato's word. It is
not only that Agamemnon, for example, if he had to muster a
fleet at Aulis might be compelled to get his directives organised
in rhythmic verse so that they could remain unaltered in transmission.[11] This same verse was essential to the educational
system on which the entire society depended for its continuity
and coherence. All public business depended on it, all transactions which were guided by general norms. The poet was in the
first instance society's scribe and scholar and jurist and only in a
secondary sense its artist and showman.

But in countries where the oral technique has survived, it is no
longer central to their culture. Modern analogies drawn from
these pocket survivals, as exemplified in Yugoslavia or Russia,
ignore the vital fact that the central business of government and
of social leadership in European countries has for centuries been
transacted in letters.[12] Either the governing class has been
literate, or it has commanded a literate apparatus centred in the
capital cities. The singer therefore becomes primarily an entertainer, and correspondingly his formulas are designed for easy
improvisation, not for the preservation of a magisterial tradition.
But Homer's were quite otherwise. In them were framed both
law and history and religion and technology as these were known
in his society. His art therefore was central and functional as
never since. It enjoyed a command over education and government, which was lost as soon as alphabetic literacy was placed at
the disposal of political power. The role of the Balkan singer
shrank and dwindled long ago to the status of a teller of tales. In
time of trouble and social dislocation his patriotic themes might
briefly revive some of his old prestige as society's leader and
teacher. But this is a temporary phenomenon. Leadership
normally resides elsewhere.

The Hellenic experience in short cannot be duplicated in
modern Europe. That experience had been of a poetry which as
it was functional was also magisterial and encyclopedic. The
arrival of literacy changed things slowly. The drama even down

to Euripides took over for Athens some of the functions of epic and retained some basic elements of what we can call the functional (rather than the merely formulaic) style. The political and moral relations considered proper in society continue to be stated and repeated in aphorisms, proverbs and paragraphs, and in typical situations. The characters themselves are still typical so far as they still have to serve as preserved paradigms of proper and improper behaviour. As criticism of society emerges and the artist begins slowly and imperceptibly to separate himself from his report, even the criticism has still to take the form of juxta-posing what appear to be contradictions within the *nomoi* and *ethe*. These antitheses are themselves still stated as alternative patterns of behaviour and are framed in conventional terms. The artist cannot yet voice some specific and personal creed of his own.[13] The power to do this is post-Platonic.

Thus even the language of Euripides is still woven to a sur-prising degree out of the conventions of oral utterance. With the advance of literacy, the ceremonial style lost its functional purpose and hence its popular appeal, but to the end of the fifth century the role of the poet as society's encyclopedist, and the function of his formulaic speech as the vehicle of the cultural tradition, remain discernible and important.

NOTES

[1] Cf. Adam Parry (p. 3): 'The formulaic character of Homer's language means that everything in the world is regularly presented as all men . . . commonly perceive it. The style of Homer emphasizes constantly the accepted attitude toward each thing in the world and this makes for a great unity of experience.'

[2] Once remove the strictly functional role of oral poetry from the centre of critical perspective, and the temptation grows to distinguish in Homer 'certain elements originating from the workaday terminology of craftsmen soldiers sailors farmers storekeepers and the like' from 'matter which *came from the poets themselves*, the inspired product of imagination and art'—Richardson, p. 56. I have italicised the words which expose the basis of this fallacy.

[3] Below, cap. 6, n. 6.

4 Below cap. 7, n. 19.

5 But not yet 'knowable' or 'known' in the Platonic sense; cf. below, cap. 12.

6 Below, cap. 7, n. 19.

7 Below cap. 9, notes 2, 3.

8 Notopoulos 'Mnemosyne' while noting that the powers of Hesiod's Goddess of Memory have relevance to 'utility' (p. 468) nevertheless adds (p. 469) 'of far greater importance in oral poetry is the use of memory as a means in the process of creation'.

9 *Od.* 1.351-2 has been cited to prove the contrary: τὴν γὰρ ἀοιδὴν μᾶλλον ἐπικλείουσ᾽ ἄνθρωποι, ἥ τις ἀκουόντεσσι νεωτάτη ἀμφιπέληται cf. Alcman I μέλος νεοχμὸν ἄρχε παρθένος ἀείδην (Smyth, p. 174). νεωτάτη however refers to 'most recent' in theme (viz., the *nostoi*, as opposed to the war which preceded, lines 326-7) not to 'new in invention'. Lyric on the other hand, which in oral society enjoyed an ephemeral life, and did not carry the same didactic burden, was less inhibited from invention.

10 This is not to discount the fundamental benefit for Homeric studies that has accrued from Milman Parry's researches, as they have been continued and fulfilled by Albert Lord. Moreover, Lord, working with the Balkan materials, is able to elucidate that 'stability of essential story which is the goal of oral tradition' (p. 138), a stability which is thematic, and which he proceeds to demonstrate within Homer (cf. pp. 146-52).

11 Below, cap. 6, and cap. 7, notes 19, 20.

12 Myres, p. 23: 'In mediaeval and modern history this kind of folk memory for events does not count for much, all the principal occurrences being established by contemporary documents, official and otherwise . . .' Lord (pp. 154-5) cites the instructive example of the modern Greek poet Makriyannis, whose written work (as opposed to his oral) was evoked by the response to a literate élite, and the wish to ascend from a lower social stratum to a higher. He adds 'The gulf between the oral singer and "the creative artist" was both broad and deep in Makriyannis' time. In Homer's, on the contrary, the oral singer was a creative artist.'

13 Adam Parry (p. 6): 'Neither Homer then in his own person as narrator nor the characters he dramatises can speak any language other than the one which reflects the assumptions of heroic society.'

CHAPTER SIX

Hesiod on Poetry

P LATO's estimate of Homer and the poets as a vehicle of
Greek education is governed by his own situation. He is
wholly preoccupied with a contemporary crisis, and properly so, for he proposes to supplant the poets himself. In the context of current needs he was content to identify the previous
functional role of poetry with clarity and vehemence in order to
reject it as a dangerous obstacle to intellectual progress. He did
not ask the historical question: Did circumstances once exist in
which these claims were proper and relevant? To be sure, he had
some intuitive sense of history or he would hardly have insisted
so sharply on Homer's didactic role in Greek society nor would
he otherwise have recognised correctly that this claim was not
confined to epic.

Despite these qualifications, Plato's account remains the first
and indeed the only Greek attempt to articulate consciously and
with clarity the central fact of poetry's control over Greek culture. This is not to say that the earlier poets—one thinks of
Pindar especially—had not expressed their own didactic claims.
Plato, one can say, was the first to define the fact that these claims
had a general significance.

Yet he had been anticipated far back in time by one of the poets.
This was Hesiod, who, coming so soon after Homer, was the
first to attempt a statement of how the minstrel viewed himself
and what his profession meant. His portrait, as we may call it, of
the profession, drawn with a certain virtuosity, has an outline
which corresponds to those claims for poetry reported by Plato.
Indeed, Hesiod near the beginning and Plato near the end of the
great transition from oral to literate habits of communication

provide accounts of the poetic situation which supplement each other. The philosopher looking back adopts a view of the bard's relation to society which is sophisticated and also hostile. The poet of Ascra equally desires for reasons of his own to express this relation, but for him the relationship is contemporary and the only resources available for expressing it are themselves poetic and symbolic and the only possible attitude is one of partisanship. Hesiod defends and describes a profession which was his own profession, and with a pride which was wholly appropriate at a time when its performance was not yet an anachronism.

The allegorical vehicle chosen for this purpose is that *Hymn to the Muses* which has already been cited in an earlier chapter, and which appears as the preface to his *Theogony*. We call it a hymn, for it is much more than an invocation, and its elaboration permits the assumption that this poem of 103 lines[1] is conceived in the spirit of the *Homeric Hymns*, which as they celebrate the birth, career, and prerogatives of a deity also in effect provide a definition of the function of that deity in the world of men.

Here, the deity in question is the Muses themselves. This permits an inference as to the poet's design and purpose in composing the poem. Homer, and, by inference, the epic poets who had preceded him, had been content merely to invoke the Muse as the presumed source of their song. But if Hesiod wishes also to commemorate the Muses at length, as he might have commemorated Apollo or Aphrodite, this marks him off as a rather special kind of poet, and a more self-conscious one. He has chosen as his theme the source or patron of poetry itself. If he is committed to defining the prerogatives and functions of this patron his design in effect is to attempt a definition of his own profession. This is why his *Hymn to the Muses* becomes the first documentation we have of the Greek minstrel's conception of himself and his role in society; of the kind of thing he was expected to say and the kind of performance he was to employ in saying it. The Muses as they sing and dance in his lines are the eponymous representatives of the poets themselves. If they teach history and prophecy, if they prescribe morality, issue orders and give judgments, this also betrays the poet's own function in the contemporary scene.

But is it true that the Muses of Hesiod represent a general poetry? Or are they not a projection of his own personal kind of verse? Are they not simply his own muses, the representatives of a Boeotian school of didactic epic which he either joined or had founded? This conception is widely shared by scholars,[2] and it uses the Hellenistic habit of classifying early literature in genres, just as early philosophy was classified in schools. It is a conception which lacks historical perspective. For one thing, it ignores the pan-Hellenic character of the epic technique in the eighth and seventh centuries.[3] For the present it will be sufficient to test the hypothesis that the Muses of Hesiod are the Muses[4] of all epic poets, and to test the proposition that Hesiod's account of poetry's place in the society of his day corresponds with some exactitude to the suppositions about poetry which Plato still entertained over two hundred and fifty years later.

Homer simply invoked[5] the Muse who is figuratively responsible for anything he says. Hesiod in effect asks, Who is the Muse? What precisely does she do, and how does she do it? which means, What am I doing, and how do I do it? As he asks and answers this question he begins himself to transcend the epic purpose and conception. He marks the beginning of a great transition. He has moved to define that content and purpose of poetry which for the wholly oral minstrel had been unconscious. So it is a mark of his slight conceptual advance beyond Homer that his own verse, though framed wholly within the verbal and formulaic conventions of oral epic, starts to cut down narrative to a minimum. Hesiod is not primarily a story-teller, but a recollector and describer. He does not invent a journey through the crowded furniture of the house in the course of which he continually but incidentally handles the furniture. He tries to dispense with the journey altogether in order to put together a kind of catalogue of the furniture. He is looking much more directly at the furniture, that is, at the apparatus of his society, both historical, political, and moral. This non-Homeric purpose, which might seem to demand a professional effort at a new level, can be viewed as a concomitant of his new impulse to define the content of the Muse's song, instead of merely assuming her inspiration. If the epic tale functioned as the record of a culture, it was Hesiod who may be said to have become aware of the fact, and this made him reflect upon what the role of the poet really was.

Oral verse was the instrument of a cultural indoctrination, the ultimate purpose of which was the preservation of group identity. It was selected for this role because, in the absence of the written record, its rhythms and formulas provided the sole mechanism of recall and of re-use. This fact of technology, to which Plato is indifferent, is in Hesiod's allegory intuitively perceived. His hymn, like all hymns to the gods, must commemorate the birth of the god. The birth itself is a device for naming the gods' parentage, that through his parentage can be symbolised the god's relationship to the rest of the Olympic system. Hesiod accordingly, as he hymns the Muses, commemorates their birth and identifies them as the daughters of *Mnemosune*.[6] As we have said, the Greek word means more than just memory. It includes or implies the notions of recall and of record and of memorisation. Through this allegorical parentage Hesiod identifies the technological reasons for poetry's existence: it describes the Muses' function. They are not the daughters of inspiration or invention, but basically of memorisation. Their central role is not to create but to preserve.

Their other parent is Zeus. In Hesiod's allegorical system this is of equal importance. It symbolises the fact that the province of the Muses is that political and moral order which under Zeus has come to be established. It is this that they commemorate. It is this that poetry itself commemorates. To confirm this interpretation we may turn to the main body of the *Theogony* and consider the scheme of the poem. It narrates the successive stages in the history of the world under the guise of successive generations in the families of the gods. First comes a series of deities, most of

whom symbolise without disguise some of the fundamental fea-
tures of the present physical world; they include Earth, Heaven,
Night, Day, Hills, and Seas.[7] From the union of Earth and
Heaven spring the 'Ouranids',[8] a more miscellaneous collection
of primeval forces and monsters, but among them are numbered
two goddesses symbolic of the human cultural condition. These
are Precedent (*Themis*) and Memory (*Mnemosune*).[9] They occur
together and the coincidence may not be accidental. Was it not
in Memory, the future mother of minstrelsy, that Precedent was
hoarded? if by Precedent is symbolised that fund of legal decisions, orally promulgated and preserved, which was guarded, says
Achilles, by the *dikaspoloi* who held the sceptre in their hands.[10]

The reign of *Ouranos* (Heaven) was superseded by that of his
son Kronos, and Kronos in his turn yielded to his son, Zeus.
Under Ouranos and Kronos the scores of deities who come to
birth symbolise in the main (though not exclusively) a great
many phenomena of the present physical environment—thunder,
lightning, rivers, springs, volcanoes, earthquakes, storms, winds,
and the like. There is much conflict between these elements,
much violence and disorder, until under Zeus,[11] once his power
has been established, there supervenes a reign of peace and comparative harmony. This is prefigured in the successive matings of
Zeus, and the consequent progeny. One group[12] of these serves to
codify, though not completely, the Olympic system of personalities found in Homer. Leto bears him Apollo and Artemis,
Hera bears him Hebe, Ares, Eileithyia and Hephestus, Athena is
born from himself.

But there is another series of alliances contracted by Zeus which,
as they are antecedent in the poem to the Olympian system, also
have priority in the poet's mind. It runs as follows:

First Zeus weds Counsel (Metis)
The Progeny is to be Athena but her birth is postponed.
Second he weds Precedent (Themis)
The progeny become the Hours, Good-Law, Right, and Peace, and the
   three Destinies or Portions (Moirai).

Third he weds Wide-Law
The progeny become the three Graces, namely Brilliance and Good-Cheer
    and Enjoyment (Aglaia, Thalia, and Euphrosyne).
Fourth he weds Demeter
Their daughter Persephone is given by Zeus to Hades as bride.
Fifth he weds Mnemosune
Their progeny become the Muses.[13]

In this list the allegory of death and rebirth, of Hades and Persephone, is an intrusion, but an understandable one. It memorialises
a central fact of the human condition. That same condition is in
its political, social, and moral aspect symbolised in the four other
marriages with four wives. Two of these, as we have seen, are
daughters of Earth and Heaven: the two others are grand-
daughters. These and their progeny commemorate in Greek
terms the elements of the civilised life: the use of the human
intelligence to create a settled political order so as to enjoy its
fruits in recreation and the pursuit of beauty and in the elegance
of adornment and graciousness. Death can, for the individual,
terminate these things. But even as the season is born again and
yields without fail the annual grain, so in poetry (the Muses) does
the record and recall (Mnemosune) of man's life survive. The
content of this record is precisely that political and moral order
which has just emerged in the first three marriages. This, we
suggest, is the poet's intention in thus constructing his list. For
poetry can compass also the cycle of death and birth itself, of
Hades and Persephone.

In short, the allegory may suggest for poetry precisely that
central role in the maintenance of Greek culture which Plato
would reject. The content of the Muses' song is encyclopedic
and magisterial, embracing the order which emanates from Zeus
himself. We have drawn this inference less from the poet's explicit statements than from the way he has arranged these statements so as to suggest interconnection. The passage is placed near
the poem's conclusion. A similar pattern of suggestion is traceable
in a passage[14] which comes near the beginning of the poem. In

fact the two passages, one near the end, the other near the beginning of the *Theogony*, employ a common reference, for both celebrate the Muses' birth, and in the earlier one, which occurs in the
Hymn, this is done with some elaboration. Then, being born,
they are described, and also their home and their theme, which
is to celebrate 'the custom-laws and folk-ways of all (gods and
men)'. Then they repair to Olympus to sing before Zeus. The
manner of their performance is described with some virtuosity.
'Now Zeus', continues the poet, 'reigns in heaven'

> With personal power over the thunder and lightning
> Having forcefully overcome his father Kronos.
> And in goodly fashion did he severally
> Assign (matters) to the immortals and devise their prerogatives.[15]

The pattern of suggestion, as we call it, is as follows: at the end
of the poem Zeus had established his reign, superseding previous
disordered epochs; he then begot the modes of civilisation, and
next the Muses, daughters of Memory (who conserve them). In
this earlier passage, the Muses are born of Zeus and Memory, and
then sing the modes of civilisation, and then repair to Zeus who is
discovered reigning over that civilised order which he disposes.
The modes of civilisation and the dispensation of Zeus are both
linked with the Muses' existence and performance. This we infer
is because they constitute the content of that performance. The
Muses singing before Zeus are describing the conditions of his
reign, and these are summed up in the *nomoi* and *ethe* of Greek
society.

This is why it is natural that Hesiod's hymn as it celebrates the
Muses can turn also into a celebration of Zeus himself. Their song
is coextensive with the mind of Zeus;[16] it comprehends the social
and political order. Poetic record pervades and controls every
sphere of the human condition. This may be the allegorical
reason for multiplying the Muse by nine: they form an Olympian
system of their own. They have, indeed, their own little Olympus, namely Helicon, a remote habitation on a mountain top
whence they 'fare forth through the night'; or alternatively they

are born 'just a little below Olympus' and are themselves styled 'Olympian'.[17] Hesiod did not himself invent this mythological apparatus, or at least not all of it, but he exploits its allegorical possibilities.

He can also describe the content of the Muses' song in terms which are quite specific. Here one must make allowance for his own conception of himself and the poet's task which he sets himself in the *Theogony*. This is nothing less than a kind of rationalisation of world history and the present civilised order. His intention is to dismiss the epic tale altogether and concentrate on the furniture in the house. He has a technique for doing this, whether it be called a verbal device or more properly an intellectual invention, which is semi-conceptual, a device framed by a mind which needs categories to think in and has not yet got them. He arranges both world history and human moralities under the guise of an immense divine genealogy. Gods, demons, nymphs, and demi-gods, disposed in appropriate family trees, gather up the 'facts' of life into an encyclopedia of information which is now no longer to be discovered by implication in the saga, but is gathered together and exists *per se*. The divine apparatus is for him not just a convenience. It is the way he visualises the realities he wishes to organise and describe. It is therefore natural that when he thinks most directly about the content of the Muses' song, he defines it six times over[18] as the celebration of the gods in their generations.

There are, however, a few other references to this song which are couched in different terms. Describing his own moment of instruction (itself probably figurative) he represents the Muses saying to him:

We know the speech of many deceptions in the likeness of truth
And we know also if we choose the declaration of what things are true.[19]

The two lines are framed in a verbal parallelism, the design of which is symbolic of a general definition. He is offering a formula: all poetry is of these two kinds. The suggestion has been made that the two kinds symbolise the fictions of the epic story-teller versus the 'facts' as related in Hesiod's didactic verse. But the formula is fitted also to describe not merely a contrast between Homer and Hesiod but a contrast which occurs within Homer himself. It is a general description of the double role of the epic minstrel as on the one hand the tribal encyclopedist and on the other the story-teller who delights by his command of the art of relevance.

The Muses, so Hesiod continues, then placed in the poet's hand the staff of his office and breathed into him their inspiration

> That I might celebrate the things to be and the things that were before.

And then invoking them, he describes their own songs sung on Olympus to Zeus:

> Speaking the things that are and those to be and those that were before.[20]

It was in these terms that Homer had described the intelligence of Calchas.[21] Strictly speaking, what minstrelsy preserves is 'the things that are'—the *nomoi* and *ethe*. But it addresses itself also to the group-sense of history; these things 'were before' also with our ancestors, and became what they are now because of our ancestors; the future is added as a further extension of the present, not to prophesy change but to affirm continuity.

After this fashion Hesiod delineates the seriousness of the poetic function and what he feels to be the constructive content of poetry. This is the truth (as opposed to mere deception) of which the Muses command the knowledge. This is not in any sense poetic truth as opposed to prosaic or expository statement. On the contrary, if anything is to be equated with 'poetic' truth, in the modern non-functional sense of that word, it would be the deception practised by the bard, the narrative fictions, the plots, dramas, and characters. These are part of the stuff of poetry but not the main reason for its existence.

So far, Hesiod's testimonies have been symbolic and general. He has been considering the oral poet as the priest, prophet, and

teacher of his community and has sought to express a conception
of oral poetry as an overall source book of history and morality.
He views it as a general model, the source and support of the group
tradition. Such typification was characteristic of the material
contained in the first book of the *Iliad*. It is to this generalising
moral function of poetry that Plato's strictures were addressed.
That is why he had assigned to poetry the traditional claim to
control the general education of Greece.

There was, however, another kind of operation which the
daughters of record and recall might be called upon to perform.
The preserved word as a vehicle of general education acquired a
survival power of many generations. This was the voice of history
and tradition. But there were other types of preserved word
which might require a shorter life, enough to survive as a military
directive or a legal decision effective for today and tomorrow but
not necessarily to become part of the tradition, though they might.
The content of tradition was completely typical. The longer the
material was required to survive in unchanged form, the more
typical it became. To give the simplest examples, the group could
not lightly change its theology or its political habits or its family
customs governing marriage, children, property, and the like.
But such a society also had constant need to frame short-term
directives and legal formulas which, though designed to suit
specific occasions, were nevertheless required to have a life of
their own in the memories of the parties concerned for varying
periods of time, or else the directive failed through lack of fixity
in transmission, or the legal formula became unenforceable
because the parties concerned had forgotten what it was or were
in dispute because of variant versions. Such directives could
therefore remain effective only as they were themselves framed in
rhythmic speech of which the metrical shape and formulaic style
gave some guarantee that the words would be both transmitted
and remembered without distortion. The colloquial word-of-
mouth which in our own culture is able to serve the uses of even
important human transactions remains effective only because

there exists in the background, often unacknowledged, some written frame of reference or court of appeal, a memorandum or document or book. The memoranda of a culture of wholly oral communication are inscribed in the rhythms and formulas imprinted on the living memory.

Here is the *fons et origo* of the poetic process,[22] the poetic act applied at its simplest primary level. The voice may be that of a professional who assists the agent or that of the agent himself speaking in rhythms in which he has been schooled and which are effective for their purpose. Was Hesiod, whose allegory could express his awareness of the partnership between poetry and memory, aware also that the matter to be memorised might include not only theology and law, tradition and custom, but also specific directives issued from day to day by the governing apparatus? He lists the nine Muses by name; the last of them being Calliope, or 'Fair-utterance', and he then continues:

> She is most pre-eminent of them all
> She it is who even with revered princes does consort
> For whomsoever the daughters of great Zeus do honour
> And mark him at his birth, even (a scion) of Zeus-nurtured princes,
> On him do they pour sweet utterance, even upon his tongue
> And from him do *epe* (epic formulae?) flow honeyed, even from his mouth.
> And the people
> All look to him as he disposes (*diakrinonta*) precedents
> With rights (*dikais*) that are straight. Yea, speaking forth reliably
> Straightway with skill does he stop even a great feud.
> For this reason are princes sagacious, that for their people
> Bewildered (*blaptomenois*) in the speaking-place they accomplish works that convert
> With ease, as they divert with *epe* that soothe.
> When a prince goes up unto contest, they adore him as a god
> With honey-sweet reverence. He is pre-eminent among the gathering throng.
> Such indeed is the quality of the Muses' sacred gift to men.[23]

This vignette compresses into a few lines material for social and historical commentary upon the life of Greece in the so-called dark ages. Here is a prince, a local lord of the manor, no unregu-

lated autocrat, but the father of his people. His leadership resides
in his *arete*; not brute force but the power of persuasion is his
weapon. The society is aristocratic in the sense that such qualities
of mind and heart are instinctively admired. The people, however, are Greek freemen arguing aloud the merits of a case.
Whether the case be legal or political makes at this stage of evolution little difference. The terminology of precedents and rights
might imply a legal issue. There is a famous description in the
Iliad, a scene on the shield of Achilles, of two litigants who argue
their case before assessors who then declare judgment.[24] It forms
a companion-piece to the present passage as also does that description of the staff of office which Achilles had dashed to the
ground, for it was normally held in the hands of the sons of the
Achaeans

> Even the arbitrators of rights
> Who do guard the precedents under the eye of Zeus.[25]

But in such a society where oral debate and decision is the sole
vehicle for the transaction of public business, the line between
political and legal decision, between political direction and legal
judgment, would be thin, and Hesiod's description of the people
bewildered in the agora would apply as aptly to an issue of war
versus peace as to a legal dispute over blood-price or the like.

Our present business, however, is not with the actual apparatus
of the society, whether legal or political, but with that technology
of communication which sustains it. And here Hesiod's testimony
is decisive. The prince who is the source of decision in the community is himself to be found in company with the Muse. He was,
perhaps, born with her gift, and if so, the gift is itself to be a source
to him of honour and esteem. Does this simply mean that a
prince enjoys some extra pull if he happens to be something of a
singer and entertainer? No, Hesiod's language affirms that his
political power has its source in his command of effective utterance, which utterance is to be in the strictly technological sense
'musical'. That is to say, the transactions of this society are not

merely oral; they do not merely imply that the relationship between governor and governed is that between speaker and audience. They affirm also that the speech of transaction must be metrical and formulaic, otherwise the utterance would not be the voice of the Muse. The speech thus shaped by the prince's poetic power is not a song or a tale; it is a legal or political decision but framed so as to persuade and win over the disputants. Thus cunningly does the use of meter also imply the art of seduction so that, as 'art' in our modern sense of the term, it cajoles through pleasure the ear which however must also conserve the judgment and remember it. In short, while in modern conception the prince's honeyed powers would be merely an extra talent which he may be gifted enough to exercise, we must urge that for Hesiod this talent was an inherent part of his job. He had to be able to frame executive orders and judgments in verse; at least his effectiveness increased as he was able to do this, for in this way his authority and his word carried further and was remembered better.

Through this power, exercised in a society which relied on the oral preservation of communication, a man might find a ladder to political leadership. The career achieved by the minstrel David in Hebrew society may provide an analogy. Technological conditions of communication among the Hebrews of his epoch bore some similarity to the Greek; in fact they were a little more advanced in so far as the Phoenician syllabary was already in use. At any rate, Homer testifies that even for an Achilles, a man in whom leadership rested on immense physical strength and courage, a princely education was designed to make him 'a speaker of tales' as well as 'a doer of deeds'.[26] In adult life he is indeed discovered in his tent

> Rejoicing his heart with a clear-toned lyre
> Even with this did he rejoice his spirit, and he was chanting the glories of
> heroes.[27]

The passage, which goes on to describe Patroclus waiting to 'take over' from his master when he stopped chanting, unmistakably delineates the epic technique of a narrative minstrel. Achilles and his squire then, we naturally conclude, were amateurs of the contemporary art. But the functional and the aesthetic aspects of oral poetry were simply obverse and reverse of a single method. Homer does not say Achilles used verse to announce his decisions to summon the Myrmidons to battle and the like. And yet, why should he? Is not every word put into Achilles' mouth a metrical utterance? The modern reader replies Yes, but Homer is a poet and he poetises the deeds and words of men who were not poets: one must not confuse art and act. To which we may be allowed to reply that this particular period of Greek culture, for technological reasons, was precisely one in which art and act, poet and politician, overlapped each other's roles.

The passage in Hesiod about the Muses' relationship to the prince continues as follows:

> For from the Muses and Apollo are there chanters and harpists over the
> earth
> And from Zeus are princes. Prosperous is that man whomsoever the Muse
> May love. And sweet is the speech that flows from his mouth.[28]

There is a teasing ambiguity about these lines. The poet is employing a bifocal vision upon his subject. He has delineated the prince as if he were himself a kind of poet. But now he recognises perhaps that many princes are not poets. At any rate, the social performances of prince and of poet are distinguishable. The prince wields political power; he is therefore Zeus's child. The minstrel wields power over words; he therefore is the child of Apollo and the Muses. But the two kinds of power are somehow coeval, linked together. In practical terms a prince might formulate his own edicts and if he could and did, the greater might be his influence. More likely his poet did it for him. Hence, earlier in this passage, and with the same bifocal vision, Hesiod had spoken of the Muse 'consorting' with the prince: this symbolises the minstrel standing by his side attendant to his words which he is to reframe in *epe* for the audience: and in the same breath he speaks of her as 'presiding over his birth';[29] this would apply to a prince with enough poetic gift to dispense with poetic assistance. Either prince or minstrel are 'prospered' by this art, for it is the source of political as well as social prestige.

It may perhaps be significant and of some consequence to this argument that as Hesiod catalogues the nine Muses the one he holds in reserve, so to speak, in order to link her powers with those of princes, is 'Fair-utterance'.[30] Of the other eight, three variously symbolise what might be called the psychological effects of minstrelsy: it 'delights', it 'gives enjoyment', it is 'lovely'.[31] Three perhaps suggest its themes, for it 'celebrates' (that is, heroes) and it 'hymns' (that is, the gods) whence also it is 'heavenly'.[32] Two are more technical, symbolising the Song and Dance respectively that accompany a performance.[33] But only Calliope carries the name that identifies the verbal shapes which poetry commands. She is pre-eminently the symbol of its operational command of the formulas. She therefore is reserved for the princely function. And yet in this guise is she not the prototype of all her sisters? Hence the poet, while still engrossed in his portrait of a political transaction, makes easy transition from the singular 'Fair-utterance' back to the plural again.[34] It is the Muses generically who are patrons of this verbal technique.

NOTES

[1] I concur with Solmsen (p. 4, n. 13) as against Jacoby in refusing to excise lines 80-103, and would argue further that the 101 lines as they stand, admitting that they include variants and overlapping, represent fairly faithfully Hesiod's method of composition, on which see above, cap. 4, n. 3; cf. von Fritz 'Prooemium.'

[2] The 'Boeotian School' hypothesis had become enshrined in classical scholarship at least as early as the middle of the nineteenth century: vid. W. Mure (vol. 2, p. 377 ff), K. O. Mueller (Eng. edn., pp. 111, 116, 126, 128, etc.), Paley (Preface, pp. V, XIII). Much recent English scholarship has continued to build on a 'Farmer George' conception of Hesiod (Evelyn-White introd., pp. X-XII, Bowra O.C.D. sub. nom. Page Homeric Odyssey, p. 36, HHI, p. 152) in defiance of the Theogony (which the agriculturalists would like to disown) and of the

non-rural aspects of the *WD*. The hypothesis has been encouraged by the habit (ancient as well as modern) of ascribing to Hesiod a corpus of genealogical and didactic works now lost which treat Boeotian and Thessalian myths, cf. Schwartz, p. 629, and also Lesky, p. 97, who, apparently indifferent to the claims of a 'Boeotian School', points out that the catalogue format is an inheritance of the old epos.

³ Cf. Lorimer's very perceptive remark (p. 461): 'His (sc. Hesiod's) education included the composition and recitation of hexameters; if he went abroad to acquire it, he can only have gone to Attica . . .' and Webster's comment (p. 178): 'Homer and Hesiod inherited a common poetic tradition . . .'; *vid.* also cap. 15, n. 42.

⁴ They are 'Olympian' at *Iliad* 2.491, and remain so at *Theog.* 25, 52; 'from Pieria' at *WD* I, which at *Theog.* 62 is interpreted as born near Olympus. They are 'Heliconian' at *Theog.* I and *WD* 658. They perform on Olympus *Theog.* 36 ff., 68 ff., and to gladden the *noos* of Olympian Zeus (*Theog.* 51, cf. below, n. 16) or to celebrate his purposes (*WD* proem). They perform also on Helicon, at *Theog.* 2 ff., which they use as a base for more widespread performance *Theog.* 8 ff. Hesiod himself when he was 'taught' (ἐδίδαξαν) minstrelsy resided below Helicon (*Theog.* 22-23, cf. *WD* 639-40) and dedicated his prize to the Heliconian muses (*WD* 658), but also claims his function is to declare the *noos* of Zeus in minstrelsy 'taught' (ἐδίδαξαν) by the Muses, this *noos* being in the present instance the rules of seafaring (*WD* 661-2), and that minstrels and harpists are of Muses and Apollo 'over the earth' (*Theog.* 94-5); presumably a larger acreage than Boeotia is intended. The only obvious conclusion to draw from this amalgam of notices, so it seems to me, is that Hesiod himself, while putting his local origin on record, is determined to identify himself as a member of a pan-Hellenic profession and to define his message as pan-Hellenic ('Panhellenes' occurs *WD* 528, in the calendar). The symbolism of his verse, by decentralising the Muses and giving them so to speak a 'chapter' on Helicon, may suggest the existence of a local Boeotian guild of singers, but their technique and themes remain as pan-Hellenic as the Zeus who likewise had an altar there (*Theog.* 4). The headquarters remain Olympian. The two aspects, central and local, remain interwoven in both poems, though the Heliconian receives emphasis only in the *Theogony*, while the 'Boeotian hypothesis' would require it in the *WD*; cf. Marot, p. 99 nn. 1, 2.

⁵ On the invocation at *Iliad* 2.484 ff., see below, cap. 10, n. 15.

⁶ *Theog.* 53 ff. and 915. Her presence here is well expounded by Notopoulos, 'Mnemosyne', pp. 466 ff. (who cites also *Hymn to Hermes* 429, Terpander 3, Solon 13, and Plato *Euthyd.* 275d *Theaet.* 191d, Pausanias 9.29.2). He also adduces the etymology *Monsai (the Reminders) behind Mousai.

⁷ *Theog.* 117 ff.
⁸ 133 ff.
⁹ 135.
¹⁰ Above, cap. 4, n. 12.
¹¹ 881 ff.
¹² 918 ff.
¹³ 886 ff.

14 53 ff.

15 72 ff.

16 *Theog.* 37; cf. *WD* 661, 483.

17 Above, n. 4.

18 *Theog.* 11 ff., 21, 33, 44, 101, 105.

19 27-28: the lines have been frequently discussed and variously interpreted. Their possible effect upon Parmenides B 1.11-12 and on the Gorgian theory of *apate* will be noticed in a later volume.

20 Lines 32, 38.

21 *Iliad* II. 1.70.

22 And recognised in effect in the aphorism preserved at *WD* 719-20 γλώσσης τοι θησαυρὸς ἐν ἀνθρώποισιν ἄριστος φειδωλῆς, πλείστη δὲ χάρις κατὰ μέτρον ἰούσης which identifies not only the rhythm and its spell, but the economy of vocabulary characteristic of the oral technique of preserved utterance.

23 Solmsen has drawn attention to the importance of this passage, but his discussion is predicated on the assumption that 'gift of speech', or eloquence, on the one hand, and the poetic gift on the other, are in the Homeric and Hesiodic period quite distinct faculties, so that the respective roles of prince and poet are mutually exclusive. Once this dichotomy, derived from post-Homeric experiences (even Demodocus in Homer is a 'hero', *Od.* 8.483), is accepted, the clues to the pertinence of *Iliad* 13.730 ff. are lost, as they were probably lost in later antiquity, which wished to sacrifice line 731: ἄλλῳ μὲν γὰρ ἔδωκε θεὸς πολεμήια ἔργα ἄλλῳ δ'ὀρχηστύν, ἑτέρῳ κίθαριν καὶ ἀοιδήν κτλ. Solmsen would join Leaf in describing the second line as a 'tasteless interpolation'. The Hesiodic passage repeats, and in part expands, *Od.* 8.170-3, describing how the god can confer various gifts on various men, among them 'shaped utterance' (μορφὴν ἔπεσιστέφει, perhaps an allusion to the formulaic character of rhythmic *epe*? cf. below, cap. 9, n. 9). Hesiod's dependence on the *Odyssey* formulae Solmsen seems to accept (pp 11-13) rather than the reverse order as argued by Wilamowitz. *Iliad* 1.249 (Nestor's eloquence) and 16.387-8 (men who deal crooked judgments in speaking place) have also contributed formulae to Hesiod's paragraph, which is thus a résumé of the role of Homeric 'political poetry'. The assumed dichotomy between eloquence and poetry compels Solmsen in exegesis to assume (a) that Hesiod speaks of 'the two gifts of the Muses' (p. 5) and also (b) that 'this implies that his (sc. the king's) relation to the Muses cannot be expressed in the same terms as Hesiod's own'. Neither of these statements seems to me justified by the text, and indeed are in effect contradicted by ll. 94-7. Many of the interesting points in the passage to which Solmsen calls attention—e.g. the role of Calliope— are more readily clarified if this dichotomy is removed from the mind: with διακρίνοντα θέμιστας (l. 85) cf. *Rep.* 10 599.a6 ff., especially νομοθέτην ἀγαθόν.

24 *Il.* 18.497 ff.

25 1.238, with which compare 9.63, 98.

26 9.443.

27 9.186.

28 *Theog.* 94 ff.

²⁹ 11.80, 82.
³⁰ *Καλλιόπη* 79; cf. above, n. 23.
³¹ 77–8 *Εὐτέρπη, Θάλεια, Ἐρατώ.*
³² Ibid. *Κλειώ, Πολύμνια, Οὐρανίη.*
³³ Ibid. *Μελπομενή, Τερψιχόρη.*
³⁴ Line 81.

CHAPTER SEVEN

The Oral Sources of the Hellenic Intelligence

THE so-called Dark Age of Greece is that epoch which perhaps about 1175 B.C. or later supervenes upon the fall of Mycenae. The word 'Dark' used in this context is ambiguous. Does it refer to the Greek condition itself as constituting a substandard level of culture, or does it simply refer to our own state of mind about the Greeks in this period? In the latter sense the Dark Age is terminated by the appearance of Homer and Hesiod, or more correctly, by the appearance of four documents we know as the *Iliad*, the *Odyssey*, the *Theogony*, and the *Works and Days*. Regardless of the date of their original composition—which in Homer's case at least was oral—they were the first compositions to achieve alphabetisation,[1] an event or process which can be placed approximately between 700 and 650 B.C. This appears to have ensured their canonisation, and certainly has given them an effective monopoly as representing the preliterate condition. This has usually been recognised for Homer. It is equally true, though in a more sophisticated sense, for Hesiod.

It is tempting to see Homer as looking back at a past which for him is already remote in time. This is misleading. He, like Hesiod, is better thought of as embedded in that social system and that state of mind and morality which he indexes, so to speak, in his encyclopedia.[2] The vanished era of which his tale preserves the memory is Mycenaean. At first both the *Iliad* and to a lesser extent the *Odyssey* seem as though they were a report on this era. This is not in fact really true, but the degree to which it is true casts some light on the methodology by which a *paideia* (we will use Plato's word for it), was conserved and transmitted when conservation depended on the living memory and relied exclusively upon the spoken and repeated word.

Thanks to archaeology and epigraphy we have lately learned a good deal more than we used to know both about the Mycenaean civilisation and about its relation to the obscure period which followed it.[3] We can speculate also with less uncertainty about the probable development of Greek institutions within this obscure period itself. As to Mycenae, we visualise a type of society analogous to those in the Near East which had preceded it or were contemporary with it—Sumerian, Assyrian, Hittite, Palestinian. Government is centralised under autocrats who live in palace complexes, the architectural remains of which are impressive and testify to the easy command of serf labour. The artistic remains bespeak for the most part a desire to decorate and embellish a courtly society. We get a feeling that the arts of leisure were not widely distributed and that the possibility of power was restricted to dynasties.

So far, the picture is not Hellenic, if we mean by Hellenic the *nomos* and *ethos* of the *polis*. But yet, the autocrats of the Greek mainland appear to have been Hellenes. Their script has been deciphered by applying the hypothesis that the language it expresses was Greek. The hypothesis seems to work.[4] This at once establishes the fact that the Dark Age was linked to Mycenae by the fundamental continuities carried in a common speech. To be sure, when the Greeks emerge after Homer and Hesiod into historical daylight, their institutions have changed drastically and so presumably has the pattern of their manners and mores. But their oral memory of Agamemnon and company has been handed down without translation.[5] Translation is impossible within an oral medium which is alive and is kept alive in the living memory. If it occurs, the medium has been broken. In short, the decipherment of Linear B establishes a fact which could have been deduced otherwise from two related facts about Homer: (*a*) that he is a living encyclopedia in Plato's sense, and (*b*) that he nevertheless talks a great deal about Mycenae and is familiar with her history.

The fact, however, that the Mycenaeans, like the Assyrians and Hittites, had a script which they employed for recording catalogues of men, material, and the like, and perhaps could have used for more elaborate types of communication, has tended to obscure the vital importance of the oral technology both in the Mycenaean age and after. Once it is ascertained that the Mycenaeans used 'writing'—the word writing being used without qualification—it is conveniently assumed that they were conditioned to those literate habits with which alphabetisation has made us familiar. It is of vital importance to recognise that the Near Eastern scripts of all shapes and sizes shared two common limitations: (a) they employed a large number of signs and (b) the signs used left a wide range of ambiguity in interpretation. These two factors combined to make them elaborate but also very clumsy weapons of communication,[6] as is amply testified in the records of the Egyptian, Assyrian, and Hittite empires. Only scribes specially trained could handle the script. The governor or executive dictated: the scribe translated his words into script; another scribe on receipt of the script retranslated it back into acceptable speech and read it out to the recipient.

Our present concern is with the Greek experience in these matters after Mycenae, and initially with that state of language and of consciousness which in Homer and Hesiod[7] is demonstrably oral. There is the less need therefore to engage in controversy over the degree of 'orality', if the word may be allowed, which reigned in the communication systems of the Near East generally. Since a majority of scholars would concede that in any case, among the Greek-speaking peoples, the Mycenaean or Linear B script perished,[8] one can propose with assurance that the pre-Homeric epoch—the Dark Age—yields for the historian what might be called a controlled experiment in absolute non-literacy. Here, if anywhere—and it has already been argued why Balkan and other analogies should be excluded—we can study those conditions in which a total culture, and a very complex one, relied for its preservation upon oral tradition alone. If there are those who would argue that in fact the use of Linear B must have survived through the Dark Ages—the Greeks being too intelligent to forget it—it can safely be replied: So what? The use of the script in Mycenaean times could never have superseded the oral technique of preserved communication, for it was too specialised to serve general social needs: it could never have been used to transmit and teach the *nomoi* and the *ethe* of the society.

Starting about 1200 B.C. the Mycenaeans confronted a fresh incursion of fellow Greeks who had to be accommodated in the Greek peninsula. The political apparatus which had held the confederacy of Agamemnon together proved too frail to survive the shock of defeat and the shift in population. The castle palaces were abandoned. Their cyclopean architecture became obsolete; their arts of courtly decoration no longer found customers. The peninsula was now over-populated and large-scale displacements were bound to occur. One begins to gain a picture of refugees, who may not all have been displaced Mycenaeans, funnelling into Attica where the Mycenaean dynasty and its institutions survived longer than elsewhere; settling under the shadow of the acropolis of Athens,[9] and then building ships to take them overseas. The migrations that followed populated the islands and the coast of Anatolia with Greek-speaking peoples. Some to be sure had preceded in the Mycenaean age itself, perhaps rather as traders than as settlers.[10] But the later migrants of the Dark Age took everything with them. They were not drawn abroad by the temptations of commerce but forced abroad to find and found new homes.

It is usually said that they carried with them memories of Mycenae which their minstrels found it profitable to keep alive when overseas. This is true, but only part of the truth. The conservation of Mycenaean memories in Homer is not a symptom of romantic nostalgia. Rather it provided a setting in which to preserve the group identity of the Greek-speaking peoples.[11] It was a matrix within which orally to contain and preserve their *nomoi* and *ethe*. Homer's stories of Mycenaean heroes are often interpreted as designed for the amusement of a small group of Greek aristocrats whose political power was buttressed by claims to descent from the Homeric heroes. And his ceremonial style is sometimes explained as reflecting the manners and modes of address pertaining to courts and to aristocracies. But Homer's is essentially not court poetry nor is it nobles' poetry in the sense that his style is moulded to suit the specific customs and mannerisms and pleasures of a restricted élite. If it were, then the universal hold of Homer upon the *polis*-civilisation of Classic Greece would be inexplicable and incredible.[12] It is better to go to the other extreme and assess the heroic tradition in his poetry as though it were a technical convenience. The problem faced by the migrating Greeks who left the mainland in mass formation and placed water barriers between themselves and their previous homes and institutions was in the first place to resist absorption by their new neighbours and conserve their group consciousness as Greeks. Political institutions were in fact destined to change during these obscure centuries. The answer to *diaspora* and decentralisation was to invent the *polis*, an adaptation and enlargement of the Mycenaean palace complex which converted it into something new. But the tradition, the continuity of law, custom and usage must be maintained, or the scattered groups would disintegrate and their common tongue be lost. The essential vehicle of continuity was supplied by a fresh and elaborate development of the oral style,[13] whereby a whole way of life, and not simply the deeds of heroes, was to be held together and so rendered transmissible between the generations. The fact that this task was more urgent at the circumference than at the centre may explain the prevailing Ionic colour which the epic technique acquired. But it was developed in this period essentially as the encyclopedic and moral instruction of Greece. Its purpose was pan-Hellenic. Homer's style represents therefore the Greek international style just as his content provides the tribal encyclopedia for all the Hellenes.

It need not therefore surprise us if, as some scholars have discerned,[14] the epic tale occasionally even goes so far as to dramatise the educational process itself. The ninth book of the *Iliad*, crucial for the movement of the tragic plot, is an epic essay in the education of Achilles: his early training is described by Phoenix; his present instruction (which fails) is narrated by Homer as it is received at the hands of his peers. In the phrases and formulas of their exhortations we hear the preserved voice of the community affirming its manners and mores and imperatives.[15] The career of Telemachus in the *Odyssey* is more conspicuously that of a youth who, as he faces manhood, is instructed in the procedures necessary to meet his responsibilities. A divine mentor supplies the paradigm of what is essentially a piece of preserved *paideia*, not poetic invention. As for his heroic father, beginning with the opening lines of the poem, is he not continually presented to the audience as the prototype of the learner[16] who thus indirectly but effectively expresses the minstrel's own conception of himself as the educator of his people?

We have described the Greek Dark Age as affording a controlled experiment in the maintenance of a fairly complex culture in a rather difficult situation under conditions of total non-literacy. Of course, the very fact that this is true automatically robs us of any documentary evidence as to how it was done. One must reconstruct by use of inference, intuition, and even imagination, and draw on what seem to be principles of human psychology and behaviour. With the help of these one is free to postulate a situation in which orally preserved communication was operating at three levels or in three different areas. There would be the area of current legal and political transactions; the issuance of directives which would accumulate as precedents. Here the governing class bore the main responsibility for oral formulation of what was necessary. Then there would be the continual re-telling of the tribal history, the tale of the ancestors and how they behaved as models for the present. This historical task would be the special province of the minstrels. And finally there would be the continual indoctrination of the young in both tale and precedent through recital. They would be required to listen and to repeat and their memories would be trained to do this. These three areas overlapped and interpenetrated each other. Thus the prince or judge as he issued rescripts and made decisions cast his performative utterance into the idiom of epic recital in which he had been trained from youth. The same formulas could recur, and the precedents he set would in fact be variations on time-worn procedures. He would cite the ancestors whom epic poetry celebrated. Finally, if he were a notable prince or judge, his influence might work the other way and some of his more notable directives and pronouncements could be picked up by the minstrel and put into his story. The picture drawn in Homer and Hesiod of the arbitrators holding the staff of office and giving judgment in the speaking place, of the prince who commands the speech which will resolve a quarrel and control a throng, is not Mycenaean but contemporary.[17] It is a picture of the oral technique at the service of government in a non-literate community. And these habits of communication long survived in Greek culture. They are in fact essentially part of the secret of Greek culture and the Greek way of life down to the Periclean age. Solon provides the surviving classic example of Hesiod's 'prince' on whom Calliope has breathed her inspiration and so given him effective functional control over the preserved word. He was not a politician by profession and a poet by accident. His superior command of metrical composition gave him his efficacy as a policy-maker. His policies became inscribed upon the memory of his audience so that they knew what they were and were able to carry them out.[18]

The inhibition against new invention, to avoid placing any possible strain upon the memory, continually encouraged contemporary decisions to be framed as though they were also the acts and words of the ancestors. Thus the minstrel was automatically drawn to compose and nourish tales about the ancestors of the group. The historical framework, in short, itself constituted an element in the mnemonic apparatus. Mycenaean ancestors are not thought of strictly in historical perspective as they would be if history-making were a literate process. They are part of the present consciousness. The Ionic Greeks are still Mycenaeans, or re-enact the Mycenaean past. This does not insure that the past is accurately recorded and preserved. On the contrary, the confusion between past and present time guarantees that the past is slowly but continuously contaminated with the present as folkways slowly change. The living memory preserves what is necessary for present life. It slowly discards what has become wholly irrelevant. Yet it prefers to remodel rather than discard. New information and new experience are continually grafted on to inherited models.

The famous catalogue in the second book of the *Iliad* can be cited to illustrate this process.[19] Here lying concealed and embedded, let us say, is an original directive of Mycenaean kings to muster for war. The king in this case was famous; the war was famous; this particular rescript, itself issued in formulaic verse, transmissible through Greece without alteration, was recollected and incorporated in a minstrel's tale. The directive to muster must have used a muster list itemising the effectives that each principality was expected to contribute for war, and the names of the local chieftains who, as the king's agents, were responsible for collecting and heading up their contingents. Such a list would also constitute a rough description of the Mycenaean confederacy. Was it set down in Linear B script and kept in the Mycenaean archives? Such is not improbable, but if we were able to recover it from surviving tablets we would expect to find a version showing wide differences from that which Homer preserves. Nevertheless, it need not surprise us if such a list, even when written down, proved to have been composed formulaically and rhythmically. This would have been its original operational form.[20]

So far, the hypothetical raw material behind the Homeric catalogue is specific. But it is of the genius of the oral memory that as it picks up the material of specific directives it converts them out of the specific into the shape of the typical. The language, be it remembered, is typical already. Thus, in the epic tale, such incorporated material is remembered and repeated as a kind of rough paradigm of the Hellenic peoples. It becomes suitable for *paideia*, for teaching to the young as history and as geography. Its conservation in verse-form lasts some centuries during which the Greek experience changes. The Mycenaean tradition has become remote, though the figure of Agamemnon and his empire stays alive in a living memory. The Hellenes are no longer concentrated in the peninsula but dispersed in settlements all over the Aegean islands and coasts and engaged in maritime commerce. Nay, they are even penetrating westward to Sicily and Italy and finally northeastward into the Black Sea. Their changing situation influences the catalogue. It becomes remoulded in fact to suit contemporary conditions. The addition of the Trojan list of allies is consistent with this tendency for it enlarges the geographic perspective. The ships and the harbours and the river mouths, whether or not they were originally there, become intrusive and emphatic. The summons to war and the Mycenaean muster list turn partly into a sailors' guide to the Aegean as it was perhaps about 700 B.C.: a guide centred on Rhodes, a piece of encyclopedic information, or a rough portrait of how the Hellenes of 700 visualised themselves in relation to the Aegean context.[21]

After some such fashion past and present interpenetrate when the vehicle of record is the formulaic word carried in the living memory. Strictly speaking, an historical time sense is impossible.[22] All present encyclopedic guidance is also of the past: this was the way of it in the times of our ancestors. In actual fact, the ways of the ancestors may have been quite different, but the approximation is worked out instinctively in the verses which are repeated and remodelled, and what was at one time or occasion specific turns into what is typical.

The formulaic technique in this typical aspect was employed as the instrument of education. Here it must have enjoyed a monopoly over the sources of instruction and indoctrination, that is, of all instruction that could properly be verbalised in typical form. To be sure, skills and procedures of all kinds must also have been transmitted empirically, by practical imitation and word of mouth, as indeed they were in the Periclean age. The navigational directives in the first book of the *Iliad* are only typical and general, not detailed enough to cover an actual operation. But they provide a paradigm for any Greek boy who will have to deal with the sea as a way of life. It is possible that during the Dark Age the epic education did not assume a specific institutional form; that is, it did not require a system of organised schooling. The school master, even in the days of Aristophanes, is still styled the 'harpist', as though he were not a professional teacher but somehow a scion of the 'harpists' whom Hesiod had designated as 'sons of Apollo'.[23] Herodotus[24] is the earliest author who identifies the educational process as such under the name *paideusis*. The youth were active during the day performing practical tasks in company with their elders. When these were concluded, old and young sat down at common mess tables and perhaps spent considerable time there. Homer himself supplies one reference to this kind of situation, which could provide daily opportunity for epic indoctrination.[25] A purely poetic *paideia*, to be effectively transmitted, requires only regular occasions for performance, whether professional or amateur. The youth would be required to repeat and to match their memories against each other and against their elders. Everything that was to be absorbed and remembered was communicated to them as the deeds and thoughts of their great ancestors. The minstrel's creativity, ready with a new song on his lips, was here less in demand than his copious and accurate memory. Since the materials stored in his memory were continually being repeated and memorised though with less facility by his audience, since in short minstrel and audience continually found themselves as partners in a common performance, it was difficult to identify minstrelsy as a distinct profession and difficult to distinguish between the creative composer and the mere repeater of compositions. This may explain both the meagreness of reference to the minstrels as a college and the obscurity which envelops the early relationship between the minstrel and the rhapsodist.[26] The activities of both were contemporary and also overlapped.

The contests of singing which the overseas Greek communities organised could afford occasion for the publication of a new song but also for the performance of an old one. The Homeric poem, it has been plausibly argued, was recited in relays at protracted festivals held at regular times and places by the Panionion.[27] The member cities of the federation attended these from considerable distances. Here perhaps is represented the first stage of that canonisation of the *Iliad* and *Odyssey* which displaced all other oral epics and removed them from memory. The festival version would be the first to get into written circulation among minstrels and rhapsodes. But our present argument is not concerned with these poems or their predecessors as 'literature'. They were the sole verbal vehicle of the group *paideia* and the Hellenic way of life. They carried its materials within their tale. It was the instinctive recognition of this fact which must have prompted these communities, equipped as they were with meagre economic resources, to give a financial and organisational support to these contests and festivals which is otherwise inexplicable. Functional importance came first, this is what they were willing to pay for, and indeed, had to pay for. Only as the epic word was continually performed could the governing class learn the technique of effective direction and only so could the loyalty of the general body of the community to the ancestral *paideia* be re-enforced and as it were, solemnised.

In sum then, Plato's conception of poetry, if we apply it to that pre-literate epoch in which the Greek institutions of the Classical age first crystallised in characteristic form, was basically correct. Poetry was not 'literature' but a political and social necessity. It was not an art form, nor a creation of the private imagination, but an encyclopedia maintained by co-operative effort on the part of the 'best Greek polities'.

This same technological situation was at least in part responsible for an interesting result: it tended to throw political power into the hands of the more cultivated members of the community— 'cultivated', that is, in terms of an oral culture. That type of directive had more influence and carried further which was more effectively, that is poetically, composed. Hence, within limits, the community's leadership lay with those who had a superior ear and rhythmic aptitude, which would be demonstrable in epic hexameter. It would also however show itself in the ability to compose *rhemata*—effective sayings which used other devices besides the metrical, such as assonance and parallelism. Again, the good performer at a banquet would be estimated not exclusively as an entertainer but as a natural leader of men, for he, like Achilles, was a superior 'speaker of tales'. Since new directives and judgments were always to be framed in terms of the old—since oral precedents held such firm sway—the effective judge or even general tended to be the man with the superior oral memory. Likewise, such a memory kept a man in close psychological rapport with the ancestral tales in which the tribal encyclopedia was carried. He would be in this sense a more cultivated man even though not a creative minstrel. The general effect was to put a great premium upon the intelligence in Greek social transactions and to identify intelligence with power. By intelligence we specifically mean a superior memory and a superior sense of verbal rhythm. It has already been said, and is here to be repeated, that the portraits in Hesiod of the prince controlling a confused mob by the effectiveness of his epic decisions, and in Homer of the judges giving oral judgments in the speaking place, and of Achilles who as a future prince had been trained to be an effective speaker, are drawn from conditions of the so-called Dark Age and apply also to the epoch which immediately followed it.

This natural union of force with a certain kind of oral acoustic intelligence can be set in contrast against the situation in later Europe of the feudal baron, himself unlettered and sometimes coarse and brutal, but an effective governor so far as he has at his side the monk or clerk who commands the essential technology by which his power is made effective in transmission. A similar situation had existed in the Near Eastern autocracies, which the Mycenaean must in this respect have resembled. The king understood the raw mechanisms of power. The Cyclopean masonry with which he surrounded himself symbolised at once his isolation from his community and the crudeness of his material concepts. The missing link is the scribe to whom he dictated and whom perhaps he despised. But he cannot do without him. The mechanisms of power, in short, are split and divided between the men of physical brawn or crude cunning and the men of skill, trained to use the clumsy elaborate script system.

In the early *polis* communities of Greece, because of the total 'orality' of communication, this split did not exist. You cannot flourish a document to command a crowd: it is symptomatic that as late as Aristophanes the use of the document for this purpose is regarded as funny and inept.[28] But you can give an epic speech. Even this will only sweep them temporarily off their feet unless it is easily memorisable or carries phrases which are repeatable and which will be repeated from mouth to mouth. This is what Homer calls 'leadership in counsel'.

We can hazard the guess, in short, that that specific and unique Hellenic intelligence, the source or cause of which has baffled all historians, received its original nurture in communities in which the oral technique of preserved communication threw power and so prestige into the hands of the orally more gifted. It made the competition for power, endemic among all human beings, identifiable with the competition for intelligence. The total nonliteracy of Homeric Greece, so far from being a drawback, was the necessary medium in which the Greek genius could be nursed to its maturity.

The condition of communication had an effect which, so it could be argued, showed itself in the field of the visual arts, not *vice versa*. Was the protogeometric style in painting initially a psychological reflex of that severe training in acoustic patterns

which the business of daily living and listening required? The
patterns of the *Iliad* have been treated as though they were a visual
arrangement, contrary to the premise that the composition was
oral, and have then been compared to the visual arrangements in
geometric pottery.[29] Is it not more proper to view them as
patterns built on acoustic principles, which exploit the technique
of the echo as a mnemonic device? If so, then the visual geometry
of the plastic artist might be a reflex in himself of that acoustic
instinct now transferred to the sphere of vision, and not *vice
versa.*

This explanation can stand as debatable, but it conforms to the
established fact that in the Classical Age the specific genius of the
Greeks was rhythmic. What we call the Greek sense of beauty, in
architecture, sculpture, painting and poetry, was more than anything else a sense of elastic and fluid proportion. This faculty,
presumably shared to a degree by all races, was, we suggest, in the
special Greek case perfected by an unusual degree of exercise in
acoustic, verbal, and musical rhythms during the Dark Age. It
was the popular mastery of the shaped word, enforced by the
needs of cultural memory, which brought the Greeks to a mastery
of other kinds of rhythm also. Their supposed disadvantage in the
competition for culture, namely their non-literacy, was in fact
their prime advantage.

NOTES

[1] Lord argues for the probability, not that 'Homer' was literate, but that his
poems were taken down by a scribe (or scribes) in a text which then assumed
fixity.

[2] Cf. M. I. Finley, cap. 1.

[3] Cf. Webster, caps. 1–6, Page, cap. 5, Kirk 'Dark Age', Phillips 'A Suggestion'.

[4] Ventris and Chadwick furnish basic texts.

[5] Webster, pp. 94-7, reviews the findings of M. Leumann, *Homerische Woerter*,
which point to the fact that certain words found in Homer's present text origin-
ated by a process of 'mishearing' on the part of minstrels either through mis-
interpretation or through erroneous division of words which they had heard, so

that they formed fresh words on analogies supplied by these acoustic errors. Some erroneous divisions demonstrably predate the migration period, proving that we are dealing with an oral tradition which was conducted in the same language throughout.

[6] Householder in the course of his useful analysis of the comparative resources of 'pure syllabaries', 'alphabetic syllabaries' (or 'pseudo alphabets') and the alphabet, computes (p. 382) that a language 'with 20 consonant phonemes, 5 short and 5 long vowels' can be 'accurately alphabetised in 26 to 30 characters', but in a syllabary would require 210 characters 'for accuracy', a number which may be cut to 90 by allowing ambiguities. But if even a few 'syllable-final consonants' occur in the language, this inventory of 90 would be theoretically doubled or trebled. In practice, a simple consonant-vowel syllabary can be written with between 65 and 110 characters, and one which includes vowel-consonant characters 'could range between 140 and 300'. I do not entirely follow Householder when he says that for Homeric Greek the use of Linear B, containing over 80 signs, would not lead to 'any significant amount of ambiguity', but in any case the range of characters required is large enough to forbid the possibility of imposing a reading trauma on small children which alone would reduce the reading habit to an automatic reflex on a mass scale and so make 'literacy' in our sense possible (on the acrophonic principle, essential for memorising an alphabet, cf. Nilsson, 'Uebernahme', p. 1035 ff.; oral methodology still furnishes an essential key to unlock the resources of literacy). Webster, p. 273, addressing himself to the narrower problem of the minstrel's competence argues that the capacity for reading Linear B must have been restricted to scribes, and that the alphabet first made it possible for the minstrel to read a script of what he was reciting. He adduces that the alphabet was a necessary condition for composition of *Iliad* and *Odyssey* (Lord differs) and that the problematic survival of Linear B is irrelevant. Householder assumes the alphabet was not realised earlier than 700 (above, cap. 3, n. 4) and says that the Semitic system on which it depends 'may be called a vowel-less alphabet or an unvocalised syllabary'. (The latter designation seems to me more accurate; hence it is incorrect to say of the Greeks, as does Albright, p. 194, that they 'borrowed their alphabet from the Phoenicians': they borrowed the signs of a syllabary and invented an alphabet.) Householder points out that this Semitic system was a 'mad simplification' encouraged by the fact that in Semitic and Hamitic tongues many items consist wholly of consonants. It would lead to 'intolerable ambiguity' in Greek. One may add for good measure that the degree of ambiguity even in transliterating Hebrew in the Old Testament is great enough, and it could be argued that this factor discouraged new invention in the content. The older portions of the O.T. are very largely poetic; even the early prose is 'poetised', economical and thematically repetitious. These characteristics are perhaps encouraged, or rather, their converse discouraged, by ambiguity of recognition in the script.

[7] The ambivalent situation of Hesiod who, working with oral material, nevertheless attempts an organisation which depends on alphabetic resources, will be analysed in a later volume; cf. also below, cap. 15.

⁸ Cf. the very cogent observations of Sterling Dow (p. 128) on the debt owed by the oral verse technique to the lapse of Linear B.

⁹ Cf. Whitman, cap. 3: 'Athens, 1200–700 B.C.'

¹⁰ Hanfmann, pp. 4–5.

¹¹ Webster, pp. 267–8, calls attention to the evidences for 'widespread pride in the heroic past' to which he traces 'the demand for wide mythological illusion which could be found all over the Greek world but particularly among the Ionians with their very ancient and very mixed ancestry'. This is saying less than my text, but not much less.

¹² And indeed is found to be incredible by those who view Homer as the poet of a contemporary élite; thus Guthrie, p. 255, noting 'the extraordinary and to some extent artificial canonisation of the Homeric epics', adds that 'they retained their influences at least officially for centuries after the decay of the *peculiar* society which had called them into being and to which *alone* they were relevant' (italics mine).

¹³ The thesis that the epics in *their present form* constitute a Hellenic *paideia* suitable for oral preservation and transmission is consonant with the conclusion of metrists that the dactylic hexameter is itself an exceedingly formalised and indeed artificial metrical invention not easily traceable to origins in the folk meters of Indo-European or their filiates in Greek lyric. It should be realised how very odd an instrument it is for just telling tales or reciting proverbs and genealogies. Comparative studies by Meillet, Jakobson and Watkins (v. Watkins, who reviews the literature) have shown first from Sanskrit then Slavic and now Celtic that the 'epic' meters of Indo-European were (and are) much simpler and freer folk rhythms (the 'paroemiac' being selected as probable prototype by Jakobson and Watkins). This, as Watkins points out, Usener discerned in principle long ago. Watkins further remarks of Corinna, whose verse he takes to represent such a prototype, 'Length and subject and phraseology show the epic character of this fragment, while its relative simplicity contrasts with the more formal Homeric epic which has a longer and doubtless borrowed metrical line'. If as Meillet thought the dactylic hexameter was indeed borrowed from an alien Aegean culture, might the borrowing represent a decision unconsciously guided by paideutic considerations? Did some Mycenaean Greeks go to Crete to get a 'higher' education (cf. the Theseus myth) and there learn the wholly 'theoretical' convention that a long equals two shorts? and was this experience then adapted in Greek by Greek minstrels to provide an 'archetypal' line of theoretic fixed time-length, an instrument like a mediaeval chant, in which to incorporate and preserve 'archetypal' poetry? (Lorimer speculates that Greek poets had been exposed to refined executions on stringed instruments which imposed their measures on the words.) Since the iambic trimeter of tragedy adopts the same convention, may it also reflect the influence of those same paideutic motives (no doubt unconscious) which made Athenian drama into what Plato assumes to be an 'educational supplement' to epic, suitable for the formal and stable memorisation of the traditions and mores? (above, cap. 3).

¹⁴ Jaeger, *Paideia*, Vol. I, caps. 2–3.

[15] Cf. *Frogs* 1009: the poets are admired for their νουθεσία.

[16] *Od.* I.3.

[17] Mycenaean practice (despite Linear B) would reflect the same technology of oral formulation (below, n. 20), but the princes and judges of Homer are, one feels, not living behind Cyclopean walls; they are closer to their people, and have to hold their allegiance by power of speech.

[18] The relevant poems of Solon are, I assume, not retrospective justification for political acts (this tradition grew out of 'literary' conceptions of poetry) but contemporary directives, prescriptions and reports.

[19] The outline offered in the two following paragraphs of my text as to how the Homeric catalogue came to assume its present shape and content is, I think, consistent with the multitude of data bearing on the subject so impressively mustered by Page in his chapter 'The Homeric Description of Greece' (pp. 118-77), and also with some, though not all, of the inferences he draws. Thus it can be agreed that origins and transmission were oral (with the possibility however of a corresponding Linear B list or lists, enjoying for some unspecified period a separate existence), that the verbs used probably indicate an original muster-list for an expedition, that the list is not a topographical catalogue but a 'list of participants in a military campaign' (on the last two points see further below, cap. 10), that the Trojan list should not be treated separately, that the original of both is Mycenaean, that the original has been modified during transmission by later experience so that it contains 'heirlooms from the Mycenaean past' (a phrase restricted by Page to the Trojan portion), that the ships in particular are partly or wholly Ionian. I should hesitate to ascribe a Boeotian origin merely on the strength of the fact that 'about one fifth of its whole length is reserved for Boeotia and her neighbours' (p. 125). Other matters in dispute belong more strictly to the polemics waged between unitarians and separatists, on which I would observe that it is unfortunate that the controversy took shape and hardened before the full consequences of the discoveries and conclusions of Milman Parry had been mentally digested by the combatants. The separatists in particular conduct their campaign (with Page well out in front) in full reliance on standards of 'literary' consistency which are in fact literate and not oral, and on concepts of 'insertion' or 'addition' which are characteristic of documentary composition (cf. the pertinent observations of Lord, pp. 147-52, on the fallacies of the 'literary' approach to Homer). Given the conservative tenacity characteristic of preserved communication when preservation is through the personal memory, where the burden of new knowledge upon the memory must be economised and where the urgency is always to repeat rather than invent, even though invention cannot be prevented, contradictions within the living work of an oral poet become inevitable, and the more 'design' he seeks to impose upon the inherited material the more flagrant will some of the contradictions become; (cf. also the explanations of temporal inconsistency given by Lorimer, pp. 476-9, following Zielinski, and also below, cap. 10, n. 27). These principles of interpretation apply to the catalogue no less than to the rest of the *Iliad*. I would envisage within it a gradual process both of accretion and concretion compatible with the way the Greek

epic process has been reconstructed by Nilsson (cf. especially his summary, p. 211) and by Bowra, and I would extend the same law of 'oral progression' to explain the context of the catalogue in the epic as a whole. It was not preserved separately and inserted like a document at some later stage, as Page would have it. It was always around, in some form, as part of the traditional paideutic apparatus of the 'great story', part of the Greek oral encyclopedia, cf. also below, cap. 10.

[20] And in this form would have been transmitted throughout Greece by heralds or envoys as described *Il.* 11.769-81 (note especially 11.770 and 781). As Webster well remarks (*Antiquity* 113, March 1955, p. 14), 'poets as we have seen have some close connection with the tablets; heralds equally would proclaim their contents when they were operation orders and perhaps collect the information for the records. Heralds, unlike scribes and poets, appear on the tablets. I think we should consider the possibility that heralds were the scribes and poets of the Mycenaean age.' The speculative but very suggestive comparisons drawn by Webster (pp. 98-9) between the Pylos 'coastal defence' tablets and the Homeric catalogue lead him to conclude that 'the common form which underlies all the sections is: All that dwelt in Y, Z, etc., them led A, and with him followed N ships' (on this form see also below, cap. 10) and that an original of this appears in the tablets, so that 'it is difficult to deny that the catalogue of ships may go back to an actual operation order *which was absorbed into Mycenaean poetry*'. I have italicised the words which assume that the metrical version arose out of the written. This I would of course dispute, or rather, I would argue that regardless of whether the elements of an operational order happened to be itemised in syllabic script for domestic convenience or record, the order to be functionally effective and transmissible over a large area would require versification. Webster (p. 92), à propos of the metrical elements alleged to exist in Linear B, remarks that 'metrical beginnings to operation orders may prove to have been the rule'. I am proposing that this principle be extended to the oral original *in toto*.

[21] The hypothesis of a sailor's guide has been suggested or pursued by Leaf Allen Jacoby Burr (as cited by Page, pp. 166, 168, in attempted refutation), but was it 'Mycenaean' or 'Ionian'? The formula I have followed, as also much else in my text, owes a good deal to the suggestive treatment of the Ionian oral situation given by Nilsson over fifty years ago (*Rh. Mus.* 1905). Page *loc. cit.* asks in apparent incredulity 'Is it seriously suggested that the alleged mariners versified their sailing directions?' The answer is: they had no other choice; but the proviso must be added that under strictly oral conditions a wholly up-to-date poem on any subject could never get into circulation. To be mnemonically effective, all oral training remained intensely conservative. A 'brand-new' poem never had a chance.

[22] Below, cap. 10.

[23] *Clouds* 964, *Theog.* 95.

[24] Cf. Powell's *Index* s.v.

[25] *Il.* 22.490 ff.; cf. the probable mis-en-scène of Aristophanes' *Daitaleis*.

[26] Cf. Pind. *Nem.* 2.1 ff.

²⁷ Wade-Gery, pp. 14-18, and Webster, p. 270, who gives references for the Messenian choir sent to Delos festival in eighth century. Lord is sceptical of the effect of festival performance upon *length* of Homeric poems.

²⁸ Above, cap. 3, n. 14.

²⁹ Cf. Whitman, cap. 5.

CHAPTER EIGHT

The Homeric State of Mind

POETRY, with its rhythms, imagery, and idiom, has in western Europe been prized and practised as a special kind of experience. Viewed in relation to the day's work, the poetic frame of mind is esoteric, and needs artificial cultivation. Over against it there exists the secular cultural situation, which consists of the thought forms and verbal idiom employed in common transactions, in 'affairs' of all kinds. The poetic and the prosaic stand as modes of self-expression which are mutually exclusive. The one is recreation or inspiration, the other is operational. One does not burst into verse in order to admonish one's children, or dictate a letter, or tell a joke, still less to give orders or draft directives.

But in the Greek situation, during the non-literate epoch, you might do just that. At least, the gulf between poetic and prosaic could not subsist to the degree it does with us. The whole memory of a people was poetised, and this exercised a constant control over the ways in which they expressed themselves in casual speech. The consequences would go deeper than mere queerness or quaintness (from our standpoint) of verbal idiom. They reach into the problem of the character of the Greek consciousness itself, in a given historical period, the kind of thoughts a Greek could think, and the kind he would not think. The Homeric state of mind was, it will appear, something like a total state of mind.

The argument runs somewhat as follows. In any culture, one discerns two areas of communication: (a) there is the casual and ephemeral converse of daily transaction and (b) there is the area of preserved communication, which means significant communication, which in our culture means 'literature', using the word not in an esoteric sense, but to describe the range of experience preserved in books and writings of all kinds, where the ethos and the technology of the culture is preserved. Now, we tend to assume that area (a), being that of the common speech of men, is fundamental, while area (b) is derived from it. But the relationship can be stated in reverse. The idiom and content of area (b), the preserved word, set the formal limits within which the ephemeral word can be expressed. For in area (b) is found the maximum sophistication of which a given epoch is capable. In short, the books and the bookish tradition of a literate culture set the thought-forms of that culture, and either limit or extend them. Mediaeval scholasticism on the one hand, and modern scientific thought on the other, furnish examples of this law.

In an oral culture, permanent and preserved communication is represented in the saga and its affiliates and only in them. These represent the maximum degree of sophistication. Homer, so far from being 'special', embodies the ruling state of mind. The casual idiom of his epoch which we have lost should not be assumed to represent a wider and richer range of expression and thought, within which the Homeric vision of the world has formed itself on a special 'poetic' basis. On the contrary, it is only in preserved and significant speech, with a life of its own, that the maximum of meaning possible to a cultural state of mind is developed. Epic, despite its slightly esoteric vocabulary (actually, because of this vocabulary), represented significant speech, and it had no prosaic competitor. The Homeric state of mind was therefore, it could be said, the general state of mind.

The truth of this cannot of course be documented from Homer's own day, which was non-literate, but it can perhaps receive indirect illustration if we turn to those pre-Homeric cultures of the Near East which employed writing systems. These syllabaries were too clumsy and ambiguous[1] to allow fluency or encourage general literacy. Hence their idiom had no power to change the general idiom of oral communication, but on the contrary was forced to reproduce it, and in these transcriptions we get glimpses of that kind of secular converse which in a wholly non-literate situation like the Greek was not preservable so far as it did not get into the saga.

The tablets found at Knossos and Pylos represent communications of the Myceno-Cretan and Mycenaean cultures. Their decipherment seems to indicate that at the courts of Greek-speaking kings not only inventories but operational directives could be committed to writing. Some scholars have discerned in these directives a Greek that is rhythmical.[2] If they are right, it is possible to conclude that the directive shaped itself in the ear, not in the vision. It was framed orally for verbal memorisation and transmission, and then happened to get written down. The laws of its composition are acoustic, and the script, instead of being used to create the possibilities of prose, remains a servant of the dominant oral technique.

There is a less disputable example. The tablets of Assyria and of Ugarit preserve royal correspondence the idiom of which one would expect to be prosaic, since preservation and transmission are guaranteed by the existence of the visible tablet. It can, after all, be carried from one place to another. Memorisation need not come into question to make the technique of communication effective.

But we find repeatedly in these letters not only the rhythms of poetic speech but the familiar formulaic devices of oral technique—the ring form, the repetition with speakers changed, and similar devices which all at bottom utilise the principle of the echo.[3] Historians, unconsciously misled by modern mental habits, have concluded that this is a ceremonious epistolary style, the rhythms of which have affected poetry, meaning by poetry in this instance the epics, which also exist in the tablets and which exhibit corresponding metrical effects.[4] This exactly reverses the chain of cause and effect. All preserved communication in this culture was orally shaped; if it happened to get written down, the device of script was simply placed at the service of preserving visually what had already been shaped for preservation orally.

The point is of cardinal importance for understanding the progress of Greek letters after Homer. The alphabet proved so much more effective and powerful an instrument for the preservation of fluent communication than any syllabary had been. And by the fourth century its victory was nearly complete, meaning that the original functional purpose of the poetic style was becoming obsolete. You no longer needed to use it to guarantee a life for what was said. But effective as the alphabet was to prove, its functional victory was slow. Down to Euripides (to repeat what has been said earlier) it was still very largely used (aside of course from inscriptions) for the transcription of communication that had in the first place been composed not by the eye but by the ear and composed for recital rather than for reading. The writers of Greece, to repeat, remained under audience-control. That is why they are mostly poets but also poets of a very special kind. Is it worth adding that poets who composed actively till beyond the age of eighty could never in the absence of effective eye-glasses have been writers?[5] They must always have dictated to amanuenses.

Continually, as the modern mind strives to come to terms with the mind of archaic and Classic Greece, it stumbles over this obstacle to understanding and reverses the priorities of cause and effect. Thus, the navigational directives in the first book of the *Iliad*, which we have earlier proposed as a sample of rhythmically preserved *paideia*, have been understood as a metrical version of an original which was laconic and prosaic;[6] that is, we think in terms of an original which if functional must have been prosaic and which then became poetised for specifically poetic purposes. This interprets the Homeric culture in terms of our own, and stands it upside down. In the Homeric, there was no prose original. You framed directives poetically or they were no good as directives. Even a catalogue of armour would in its inception and original substance be rhythmic.

In short, all significant communication without exception was framed to obey the psychological laws of the goddess Mnemosune. This brings us to suggest that Homer and Hesiod should be accepted in the first instance not as 'poets' in the precious sense of that term but as representing a whole state of the Greek mind. In their formulaic style and their visual imagery and the like they were not behaving as a special sort of person, inspired and 'gifted'. They were speaking in the only idiom of which their whole culture was capable. The point may be illustrated from an incident which is reported to have occurred during the Gallipoli campaign in 1914-15. A series of mass charges by the Turkish soldiers upon the Allied positions had resulted only in wholesale slaughter. Moral exhaustion and sanitary necessities prompted the negotiation of a truce to bury the dead of both sides. The arrangements were concluded only under the most tense psychological conditions. Officers were alert, sentinels kept their finger on the trigger, while friend and foe met in no man's land. As the working parties carried out their grim task under a hot sun in unbelievable stench, tension among the common soldiers somewhat relaxed, and when the operation, governed by split-second timing, came to an end, the two sides before resuming hostilities exchanged greetings and farewells:

> At four o'clock the Turks near Quinn's post came to Herbert for their final orders since none of their own officers were about. He first sent back the grave diggers to their own trenches and at seven minutes past four retired the men who were carrying the white flag. He then walked over to the Turkish trenches to say goodbye. When he remarked to the enemy soldiers there that they would probably shoot him on the following day, they answered in a horrified chorus, God forbid. Seeing Herbert standing there groups of Australians came up to the Turks to shake hands and say goodbye: 'Goodbye, old chap; good luck.' The Turks answered with one of their proverbs: 'Smiling may you go and smiling may you come again.'[7]

Here briefly, in an hour of crisis, a semi-literate and a literate culture confronted each other. Each as it speaks under stress resorts to its fundamental idiom of communication. For the one this is laconic and casual prose; for the other it is the rhythm and parallelism of the shaped and preserved formula.

These were not just competing linguistic idioms, English and Turkish. Rather, the British were confronting a foreign state of mind, though one equally effective for its operational purposes. It is to be guessed that the products of modern Turkish literacy in a similar situation would not speak now as their fathers did then on that May afternoon of 1915. It is characteristic of a literate culture that if it is ever confronted with the habit patterns of a non-literature culture it tends to underestimate their efficiency. The Turkish soldiers of this same campaign were accompanied in their trenches by the Imams who chanted exhortations and the like before battle. To their British opponents, it looked at first like a non-military obstacle to efficiency, a piece of backward superstition. They learnt differently. In fact, it was a functional application of the oral technique to military discipline and morale, among a soldiery who did not read.

The ways of war bring to the surface the essential mechanisms of a culture complex. The chain of command, always there beneath the surface in civil life, holding the society together, is in warfare exposed in its most essential forms. T. E. Lawrence, describing the muster of an expeditionary force of Arab warriors, observed the improvised verses which accompanied the line-up, and the rhythms which assisted the organisation of the forward march.[8] These procedures were not the result of some special addiction to heroism on the part of the Arabs; they were not Homeric in our narrow and emasculated sense, meaning simply romantic. Rather they were truly Homeric in their functional necessity. Here was a culture, strictly non-literate, as the Balkan cultures were not. The epic style was therefore a necessity for government and not just a means of recreation. Lawrence also noticed the educational system centred on the hearth by which this epic capacity was indoctrinated.[9] Presumably, as Arabia Deserta succumbs to literacy, these mechanisms will wither away. Only a few ballad-makers will survive, a vestigial remnant divorced from functional relationship to their community, and waiting for antiquarians to collect their songs under the impression that this is truly Homeric stuff.

In such non-literate cultures the task of education could be described as putting the whole community into a formulaic state of mind. The instrument for doing this was to use the tribal epics as a paradigm. Their style is intensified to be sure. Their idiom shows a virtuosity which in common transactions might be imitated but at a simpler level of artistry. A minstrel would be a man of superior memory, and so also might be the prince and the judge. This automatically meant superior rhythmic sense, since rhythm was the preservative of speech. With superior memory and rhythmic sense would go also a greater virtuosity in the management of the formulas. The lesser memories of the populace would be content to use simpler and less elaborate language. But the whole community from minstrel and prince down to the peasant was attuned to the psychology of remembrance.

An epic might memorialise a whole area of history and manners. In a village the local head-men might be able to repeat it, the peasantry might remember only part of it. But all alike were trained to respond to formulaic directives—a military order, let us say, or a local tax assessment—in which the epic style was imitated or echoed.

This amounts to saying that the poet, and particularly the epic poet, would exercise a degree of cultural control over his community which is scarcely imaginable under modern literate conditions in which poetry is no longer part of the day's work. His epic language would constitute a kind of culture language, a frame of reference and a standard of expression to which in varying degree all members of the community were drawn. In our own culture of writers and readers the existing body of prose literature performs this same function for the common members of the language group. Their speech habits will vary in range and cultivation but in general these habits betray a relationship to the

written literature, which has been described by one authority as
follows:

> More important than the writing itself is the written tradition. In a culture
> language this exerts itself upon all levels, dictating words, formations and
> turns of phrase and constantly introducing into the spoken tongue echoes of
> the study, the church, and the technical and learned professions . . . all parts
> of a culture language may suffer this influence; phonemics through the intro-
> duction of foreign words pronounced with foreign sounds, morphology and
> syntax through the retention or revival of devices taken from literature. The
> entire question of stylistics is vitally affected by the interplay of the written
> tradition and the spoken tongue . . . the quotation, the set phrase, the technical
> expression and in general the construction modelled upon the written language
> are everyday phenomena in such a language. It is in fact not too much of an
> over-statement to say that the resources of literature constitute a blank cheque
> which the speaker in speaking can fill in to almost any amount.[10]

The term 'culture language' as used in this quotation has been
restricted to languages which have a written literature. The
theory can be supplemented by the assumption that in a society of
oral preservation it is therefore the epic, in the main, which
provides the culture language. The extent of its role in this
regard will depend on the degree of virtuosity which is used to
endow speech with survival power. The more contrived and
elaborate the devices that are used, the longer is the life possessed
by the speech thus shaped. If the written literature of a modern
culture is able to exercise over common idiom that indirect control which is described in our quotation, this is because it has a
longer life than the common speech possesses. In a sense it has
discovered the secret of making the word immortal, in so far as
the symbols on the page can be kept and copied and repeated in
unchanged form, theoretically forever. So we are continually
reminded as we read, that this, the written word, is more honorific
than our casual utterance, and we are drawn unconsciously to
accept it as a paradigm of usage, to which we expect to approximate but no more.

The Homeric epics constituted a body of invisible writing
imprinted upon the brain of the community. They represented a

monopoly exercised by the epic technique over the culture language. Such control had to be linked with functional performance to be effective. The fact that the Homeric was not the vernacular tongue only heightened its power of control. The precise times and conditions under which the Greek vernaculars separated themselves out are still obscure. But throughout archaic and Classical Greece you still said things Homerically and tended to think things Homerically. Here was not just a poetic style but an international one, a superior idiom of communication.

Control over the style of a people's speech, however indirect, means control also over their thought. The two technologies of preserved communication known to man, namely the poetised style with its acoustic apparatus and the visual prosaic style with its visual and material apparatus, each within their respective domains control also the content of what is communicable. Under one set of conditions man arranges his experience in words in some one given way; under the second set of conditions he arranges the same experience differently in different words and with different syntax and perhaps as he does so the experience itself changes. This amounts to saying that the patterns of his thought have historically run in two distinct grooves, the oral and the written. The case for this assumption has not yet been clarified. But at least Plato, if we may now return to him, seems to have been convinced that poetry and the poet had exercised a control not merely over Greek verbal idiom but over the Greek state of mind and consciousness. The control in his view had been central and he describes it as though it were monopolistic. This agrees with our own analysis of the poet's situation in the Greek Dark Age. If Plato is correct, this situation had continued virtually unchanged through Classic Greece.

NOTES

[1] Above, cap. 7, n. 6.

[2] On this cf. Webster, p. 92: the headings of three Linear B tablets (one from Knossos, two from Pylos) containing orders can be scanned, two as paroemiacs, one as pendant hemiepes; which Webster (above, cap. 7, n. 20) interprets as metrical preludes to orders (the paroemiacs *might* indicate use of Indo-European folk rhythms before the 'Aegean' hexameter had been borrowed? Above, cap. 7, n. 13). This is countered by Page, p. 211, n. 73 (who discusses only the hemiepes, from Pylos), on grounds that occurrence is accidental. He cites his own amusing collection of hexameters from Demosthenes. This argument is not quite fair, (a) Dem.'s stylistic habits as noted by Page himself encouraged accidental hexameters, (b) any large amount of Greek prose written with attention to style will expose a ratio of accidental meters (again admitted by Page), (c) the content of the tablets, so largely consisting of inventories, is *per se* hostile to metrical accident, if we assume the habits of a literate culture, so comparisons with Greek literature scarcely apply, (d) the metres discernible are anyway not apparently hexameters.

[3] Webster, pp. 71-2, citing an example each from Mari and Ugarit. At p. 77 he notes evidence that the near eastern poet dictated to a scribe but was not a scribe himself.

[4] Webster, p. 74: 'Thus the poet, like the letter writer, had a standard introduction'; p. 90: 'correspondence had its set forms which were largely adopted as the set forms of speech in poetry'. The ultimate motive for these forms W. finds in court ceremonial: p. 76: 'These compulsions all derive ultimately from the court of the king' and he finds (pp. 133, 183) origins of formulae in 'royal correspondence' and 'styles of king's court'. In short, what he traces to a political-social setting I would ascribe more fundamentally to a technological situation, although each is relevant to the other. It should be added that I am greatly in debt to Webster for his third and fourth chapters, where while noting, as have others, correspondences in the contents of near eastern and Greek mythologies, he has performed the more fundamental service of calling attention to parallels in style, manner, speech-idiom, situation, thematic repetition and the like. To his reconstruction of the Greek experience during and after the migrations I also owe much illumination.

[5] An oculist has told me that different diet patterns in antiquity would not have served to arrest impairment in vision in older people.

[6] Richardson, p. 55, tries to distinguish between those lists which he thinks were derived 'from written aide-memoires' and those 'which clearly proclaim the poet'. The distinction relies on the absence of 'pictorial adjectives' in such a passage as the 7 line ritual of sacrifice (above, cap. 4, n. 28). But the distinction breaks down if it is extended to cover the navigation passages or even the 'arming scenes', both cited by Richardson (cf. p. 68, n. 1) as reflecting compliance with written listings or written operational orders. Armstrong (pp. 341 ff.) well indicates how the latter, despite formulaic repetition. are nevertheless each

handled differently in response to four different contexts. On Homer's habit of cataloguing by 'giving the general or collective name first with the specific sub classes following in apposition in the next line' (Richardson, p. 51), cf. below, cap. 15, n. 44.

7 Alan Moorehead, *Gallipoli*, p. 188.
8 *Seven Pillars of Wisdom*, p. 153.
9 *Op. cit.* p. 206; cf. pp. 128, 160, 210, 219.
10 Quoted from Messing, p. 6.

CHAPTER NINE

The Psychology of the Poetic Performance

THE Romantics sought to revive the conception of the poet as prophet and seer possessed of a unique vision of reality and a unique insight into things temporal. These powers, however, were conceived in a sense quite alien to those wielded by the Homeric poet, for their direction was upward rather than horizontal. They aspired but they did not inform. The Homeric poet controlled the culture in which he lived for the simple reason that his poetry became and remained the only authorised version of important utterance. He did not need to argue about this. It was a fact of life accepted by his community and by himself without reflection or analysis.

So much for his content. But this could not be published or communicated except in performance, and here he was very conscious of his virtuosity. While he may not always have recognised the cultural meaning of what he was preserving, he was very vividly aware of the techniques that he wielded to make it stick. His role as the encyclopedist was shared by all members of his craft. The methods he used to hold sway over his audience were personal to himself.

Their use was an experience which had immediacy for him but was not uniquely his; it had to become equally personal to those who listened to him. To control the collective memory of society he had to establish control over the personal memories of individual human beings.[1] This in effect meant that his poetry was a mechanism of power and of personal power. He was the medium of the Muse, and the grandson of the goddess Mnemosune, whose spell he wove. What then were the psychological resources available to him to render this spell effective? They had to be available and usable in the active performance. For a relationship between the poet and the individual memory of any member of the community could be established only by audible and visual presence. The relationship must be built up and maintained during the course of oral recitation.

This surely is a clue to the reason why Plato, as he examines the ways of poets and poetry, seems so preoccupied with the conditions of the actual poetic performance before an audience; to the degree that when he seeks to analyse the content of poetry it proves difficult to separate the issue of content from the psychological effects of reciting it and listening to it. What the poet was saying was in Plato's eyes important and maybe dangerous, but how he was saying it and manipulating it might seem even more important and more dangerous.

The technology of memorisation as exploited by the minstrel will seem unfamiliar to ourselves for we have long been accustomed to dispense with it. Aside from ecclesiastical rituals where the congregation may be invited to respond to the priest and repeat after him, we normally memorise if at all something that has first been read, and read not to us but by us. This involves a complicated process by which we first use the organ of sense to see and then identify a series of printed signs. These symbols in themselves have no power over us; they are silent and lifeless. We then do one of two things or a combination of two things; we either recollect our vision of these symbols so that we can see them again in the same order if we shut our eyes, or we translate them into sounds which in practice we have to mutter or recite 'to ourselves', as we say. This act of translation combined with the solitariness of the act means that we draw exclusively upon our own psychic energies in order to get something into the memory.

Oral memorisation on the other hand could save a great deal of personal energy in a listener. For the sounds as spoken aloud by the poet were alive, and there was no need for translation from eye message to ear message. The audience simply imitated in as direct and as uncomplicated a manner as possible. The modern memoriser has to practise self-hypnotism. The Homeric audience submitted gratefully to the hypnotism of another. The situation most comparable to the Greek would in our modern culture be found in the effect upon the popular memory of verses which are wedded to popular melodies and recorded and played on machines. Particularly close is the analogy provided by Jazz and other dance rhythms so far as these are often married to words which are then remembered.

Let us seek to probe and penetrate this mechanism a little more closely. To memorise anything is like lifting a weight and carrying it; it requires physical energy. The easiest and laziest form of memorisation is sheer repetition:

Hector is dead; Hector is dead.

Even this requires a minimal output of energy, which is then increased slightly if we keep words and meaning unchanged but allow a formulaic variation of word order:

Hector is dead; dead indeed is Hector.

Then the mind, growing bolder, will venture to place a further burden on itself by keeping the same essential image— a dead man who is Hector—but looking at it from different aspects or in slightly different ways by using words and syntax which do not alter the essential situation but restate it:

> Hector is dead; fallen is Hector.
> Yea Achilles slew him
> Hector is defeated, Hector is dead.

Such devices can be pushed further and further to that extreme virtuosity found in the Homeric epic. The basic principle is however already revealed and can be stated abstractly as variation within the same. The mind's attention is continually bifocal: it preserves an identity, yet it makes room for a difference within this identity.

So far our examples have been of repeated words with repeated meanings, or recurrent mental images. But now let the speaker set up a parallel system of repetition which concerns sound alone without reference to meaning. This becomes his metrical scheme of which the units of repetition are two-fold, the foot or bar and the line.[2] Each of these in the dactylic hexameter could theoretically be an exact repetition of its predecessor, the metrical analogy of:

Hector is dead; Hector is dead.

But once more variation is sought and practised within the same, though narrowly limited. The meter would allow a foot to be followed by a variant of itself; but there is only one variant allowable. It will also allow this variation to occur irregularly. This is more daring—the rhythm of uniform repetition is broken by the licence—but not too daring. The meter is apportioned between lines of constant time length; the lines are like slow regular undulations, each of which is in turn composed of an internal pattern of ripples of two different wave lengths. The metrical effect is once more a variation within the same; the rhythmic memory constantly repeats itself.

This metrical pattern, itself innocent of meaningful statement, is then[3] wedded to the verbal formulas which express meaning. How is the marriage consummated? We are able to abstract the process and identify the two partners, but the original operation was carried out without benefit of such abstraction nor were the partners separately identified. All speech is produced by a series of bodily reflexes. Metrical speech is produced as these same reflexes are operated in special patterns and as certain other reflexes are brought into operation in parallel. 'Hector is dead' is a piece of speech articulated by a complex set of movements on the part of lungs, larynx, tongue and teeth which have to be combined unconsciously with subtle accuracy in a given pattern. Simply to repeat the statement is to set up a rhythm. But rhythms which repeat a group of words over again will not allow a fresh statement. So the main onus of sheer repetition, which the memory needs as its prop, is transferred to the meaningless metrical pattern which is retained tenaciously in the memory, and the fresh statements are then so expressed as to fit acoustically into the pattern. Thus the possible combinations of motions performed by lungs, larynx, tongue and teeth are drastically restricted, just as the possible combinations of spoken words and phrases are restricted. The requirements of memory are met in a fundamental fashion through practising a strict economy of possible combinations of reflexes. There are a million things you cannot say at all in metrical speech and it will follow that you will not think them either.

These reflexes are bodily actions; they are a form of doing, but a special form, in which doing is repetitive, but in a specially complicated way we call rhythmic. Over the whole process reigns the control of the metrical pattern. But the speaker might still forget the pattern or render it imperfectly. In the first place, it is a complicated pattern in which you have to remember several things at once or several possible variations within the same. In the second place the speaker wants to say something and not just make harmonious noises. This also might tempt him temporarily to forget the undulations and the ripples in which his vocal organs must move. And if this over-all pattern is lost, the speech becomes less repeatable and less memorisable. So a second set of physical reflexes is called into play, the purpose of which is to mark and preserve the meter only, without attention to meaning. These are performed by the fingers upon a stringed instrument; it has to be a stringed and not a wind instrument if the performance is solo, for the lungs are already required for the rhythmic verbal statement.

For the reciter this performance upon the lyre involving a motion of the hands sets up a corresponding rhythm in another part of his body which proceeds in parallel with the motion of the vocal organs. This will give him some mnemonic assistance in preserving his meter. He would not need such a prop if his attention were not preoccupied by saying something. He does need it. Therefore his strumming, arranged in some sort of melody, sets up an acoustic rhythm which in turn affects the ear drums. To the extent that the reciter as he arranges his speech-sounds and his accompaniment also simultaneously listens to this acoustic effect, or listens to himself, the melody on his strings will further add to the pattern of his bodily reflexes and so continually confirm his memory of the pattern to which he is keeping.

But the more obvious effect is directed not on himself but on his audience. Their ear drums are bombarded simultaneously by two disparate sets of sounds organised in concordant rhythm: the metrical speech and the instrumental melody. The latter must be repetitive; it cannot afford to develop as a separate technique with its own virtuosity and so become what we would call 'music'. For this would drain away attention from the main task, which is one of verbal memorisation. The Greek 'music' exists only to make the words more recollectable, or rather to make the undulations and ripples of the meter automatically recollectable, in order to free psychic energy for the recall of the words themselves.

Finally, there remain yet another part of the body and another set of physical reflexes which can also be set in motion parallel to the motion of the voice organs. These are the legs and feet and their motions as organised in dancing. Once more, as with the use of the lyre, we confront here a pattern of organised actions, the function of which is mnemonic. It moves in a rhythm which parallels that of the spoken words, and spaces and punctuates them, so that the choric recitation becomes also a bodily performance which assists in 'acting out' the recital. Yet a third set of reflexes is pressed into service to enforce the memorised sequence. Either the audience do this themselves in recitation, or they watch it being done, in which case the mnemonic assistance is mediated to them through the eyes, as they watch the dance rhythm; and perhaps as they watch their nervous systems respond sympathetically with small concealed motions of their own without necessarily agitating the legs.[4]

In the above analysis, we have been trying to explicate, however clumsily, the fundamentals of what the Greeks meant by *mousike*. We have adopted the hypothesis that, quite aside from the unconscious pleasure derived from rhythmic bodily motions, *mousike* as a recognised 'technique' was a complicated convention designed to set up motions and reflexes which would assist the record and recall of significant speech. The melody and the dance are thus the servants of preserved statement and are not in the oral stage of culture practised very much for their own sake. The dance, considered as part of the mnemonic apparatus, could be the partner of many varieties of preserved speech, particularly those we designate as ode, hymn, and dithyramb. It has been included here not only to complete the catalogue of mnemonic devices, but also because, as we shall see, it figures so prominently in Hesiod's account of the performance for which the Muses are responsible. It is not to be excluded that its mnemonic aid was invoked in epic recital.

The psychological principles governing this elaborate procedure are simple but fundamental. First, all spoken speech is obviously created by physical movements performed in the throat and mouth. Second, in an oral culture, all preserved speech has likewise to be created in this way. Third, it can be preserved only as it is remembered and repeated. Fourth, to ensure ease of repetition, and hence of remembrance, the physical motions of mouth and throat must be organised in a special way. Fifth, this organisation consists in setting up patterns of movements which are highly economical (that is, rhythmic). Sixth, these patterns then become automatic reflexes. Seventh, automatic behaviour in one part of the body (the voice organs) is then strengthened by parallel behaviour in other parts of the body (ears and limbs). The entire nervous system, in short, is geared to the task of memorisation.

So far, these elaborate mechanisms of early Greek poetry have been analysed from the standpoint of their functional purpose in the culture which they served to maintain, all of them forming a part of an unconscious design to preserve and transmit a tradition and a way of life. They served also a quite different though parallel purpose and can be looked at from a different point of view. They represented a mobilisation of the resources of the unconscious to assist the conscious. The various motor reflexes, despite the complexity of their interaction, were so organised that they operated without any need on the part of the subject to think about them. This meant that like similar reflexes of the sexual or digestive apparatus they were highly sensual and were closely linked with the physical pleasures. Moreover, they could confer upon the human subject a specific type of pleasure. The regularity of the performance had a certain effect of hypnosis which relaxed the body's physical tensions and so also relaxed mental tensions, the fears, anxieties, and uncertainties which are the normal lot of our mortal existence. Fatigue was temporarily forgotten and perhaps the erotic impulses, no longer blocked by anxiety, were stimulated.

It is therefore to be concluded that the recital of the tribal encyclopedia, because of the technology of the recital, was also a tribal recreation.[5] In more familiar terms, the Muse, the voice of instruction, was also the voice of pleasure. But the recreation was of a rather special type. The audience found enjoyment and relaxation as they were themselves partly hypnotised by their response to a series of rhythmic patterns, verbal, vocal, instrumental, and physical, all set in motion together and all consonant in their effect. These motor mechanisms were activated in as many ways concurrently as was possible. Yet these mechanisms were not all set working in a man at equal strength at all times. If he listened silently, only the ears were fully engaged; but the ears transmitted messages to the nervous system as a whole, and thus limbs, lips, and throat might perform slightly, and the nervous system in general would be sympathetically engaged with what he was hearing. When he in turn repeated what had been sung, the vocal chords and perhaps the limbs were fully activated to go through and perform in identical sequence what they had already sympathetically performed for themselves, as it were, when he had listened.[6]

This brings us back to that picture of the performance and its effect which so preoccupied Plato. For in analysing the technique used for preserving the shaped word in the living memory we have also uncovered the secret of the enormous power wielded by the minstrel over his audience. He gave them not only pleasure but a specific kind of pleasure on which they came to depend, for it meant relief from anxiety and assuagement of grief. It is this power rather than his encyclopedic role of which the poet is most conscious, and naturally so, for, although he might be consulted in his didactic role as the source of knowledge and guidance, he was far more continuously applauded as the great releaser. It is a credit to Hesiod's genius that he was able to perceive and in part to express, as we have seen, the poet's functional role in the society he served. But he was more emphatic, as is to be expected, in his description of the power that the Muses possess to charm and to assuage. First, however, let us notice what he has to say about the motor mechanisms of his art.

As he invokes the Muses at the beginning of his Hymn, what we hear first is the emphatic beat of their feet[7] till at line ten they begin to speak. Their speech is something that they 'discharge into the air'[8] as though it had an embodied existence of its own. The metaphor intended may be of arrows, the 'feathered phrases', or of a gush of liquid. The formula is used twice more at lines 43 and 67. Their speech has a shape which the poet perhaps intends to identify as formulaic when he describes the Muses as 'epos-fitters'[9] (usually translated as 'eloquent'). They are, he continues, 'in utterance concordant', and 'of consonant wit'.[10] These phrases may symbolise more than simply nine women singing in unison. Rather, if the nine separately represent different aspects of a single technique, their concordance may symbolise that intimate correlation of words, meter, music, and dance upon which the poetic effect relied. This effect, he goes on to say, is of a 'chant which flows effortlessly from their mouth'.[11] Once more the poetic utterance is identified as though it were a thing in itself which flows like a river. The metaphor urgently stresses the automatism of the performance and is used again three times over to describe the pronouncements of the prince: the Muses 'pour dew over his tongue . . . the *epe* flow from his mouth . . . the chant flows from his mouth'.[12] Part of their performance is described by the term *molpe*[13] which, on Homeric analogy, probably identifies the chanted words for which lyre and dance form the accompaniment. Then the poet reverts to the rhythmic beat of their dancing.[14] The use of the musical accompaniment is implicit in the double title Chanter and Harpist[15] which is applied to those who are sons of the Muses and Apollo.

The poet's terms for the various things the Muses do tend to be suggestive rather than precise. He can evoke aspects, but not itemise the components analytically. His phrasing suggests several operations and effects occurring simultaneously. The metaphors used have become shopworn and the translator usually takes them in his stride without looking for specific meanings. In Hesiod they are of course formulaic, part of the epic vocabulary, but this need not mean that they are simply ceremonial and conventional. Epic formulae in the period of the living epic could be specific in their reference. The poet is the first Greek to attempt to rationalise or rather to allegorise the poetic process and performance, and his vocabulary, while imprecise and non-scientific, is consistent with that analysis of Greek 'music' which we have attempted.

This is even true of the language which he uses to describe the psychological effects of poetry. He emphasises over and over again the pleasure[16] which it gives. One of the Muses, indeed, is called The Enjoyable.[17] Metaphors like 'sweet dew' and 'honeyed utterance' which 'pour' or 'gush' or 'are spread'[18] suggest the sheer sensuality of those responses which the technique could evoke from its audience. Both the dance and the chant are labelled 'desireful' (*himeroeis*) and Desire, as well as the Graces, has her dwelling near the Muses.[19] The beat of the feet and the voices speaking or singing are likewise linked by epithets with *eros*, and another of the Muses is named Erato—the 'Passionate'.[20] We have earlier suggested that as the resources of the unconscious mind were mobilised through body reflexes to assist memorisation this might result in the release of erotic emotions normally under restraint. If therefore Hesiod associates Mousike with sexual feeling this need not surprise us.

The language of the Hymn is highly emotive and suggestive. It allows us, as it were, to hear the actual performance, the effects of which are all-pervasive, for they not only penetrate the heart and mind, as when they 'rejoice the *noos* of Zeus',[21] but also at the same time seem to constitute the atmosphere in which we live, as when 'the halls of the gods laugh' and 'the surrounding earth rings aloud'.[22] At the opening of the Hymn, after setting up their 'dances of desire' on the mountain top the Muses 'fare forth through the night cloaked in mist, discharging their lovely utterance'.[23] Their voice for men is ever present in the consciousness, filling the hours of sleep as also those of waking. The poetised word acts as a kind of electricity in the atmosphere. Finally and most strikingly, in one of his most melodious lines, the poet signalises oral poetry's hypnotic and curative powers:

A forgetting of what is bad and a respite from anxieties.[24]

As the Hymn ends it is to the psychiatric aspect that he returns: the listener may have

Grief in a spirit newly wounded
And endure drought in his heart's anguish,

but once he listens to the minstrel:

Straightway he does forget his dark thoughts nor are his cares
Remembered any more.[25]

It has long been conventional to speak of the superior poet as inspired. More recently the canons of literary criticism have preferred to stress craftsmanship as the clue to success. In so doing we have returned to a point of view which is much closer to that of Hesiod and his immediate successors.[26] The early role of the Muse has often been misunderstood. She was the symbol of the bard's command of professional secrets, not of his dependence on divine guidance. When the Greek poets voice their claim to fame

or immortality they prefer to base it not as in the Hellenistic age
upon inspiration but upon their skill (*sophia*).[27] This was bound to
remain true as long as Greek poetry was responding to the conditions of an oral culture. The evocative effects described by
Hesiod and prefigured as the gift conferred by the Muse were not
a spiritual transfiguration but a set of psychosomatic mechanisms
exploited for a very definite purpose. Their effective employment required a degree of virtuosity in the manipulation of
verbal, musical and bodily rhythms which was extreme. A bard
of superior craftsmanship could increase the effect and so make
himself a more powerful poet than his fellows. But the essentials
of the craft were common to any and every poetic performance.
The contrary conception of poetic inspiration was born in Greece
precisely at that time, toward the end of the fifth century, when
the requirements of oral memorisation were no longer dominant
and when the functional purposes of poetry as a tribal education
were being transferred to prose. At this point those who thought
in prose and preferred prose—that is the philosophers, who were
intent upon constructing a new type of discourse which we can
roughly characterise as conceptual rather than poetic—were
driven to relegate the poetic experience to a category which was
non-conceptual and therefore non-rational and non-reflective.
Thus was invented the notion that poetry must be simply a
product of ecstatic possession, for which the Greek animistic term
was 'enthusiasm'.[28] Our equivalent word is 'inspiration'[29] which
is more sympathetic to the requirements of Christian monotheism
but preserves the essential point, that poetry is a possession, not an
autonomous exercise of the mental faculties.

Consonant with the new non-functional conception of Greek
poetry is that other preconception that it is an 'art' and not an
instrument of indoctrination and that therefore its content and
quality must be estimated in the first instance by criteria which
are aesthetic. This approach to poetry is of course the only one
possible in a culture where, as in our own, the poetic performance
has become divorced from the day's business. And once this

aesthetic perspective is adopted, it becomes impossible to understand the vehemence of Plato's attack upon poetry. If he impugns
the sheer pleasure of the experience, if he views with distaste the
hypnotic spell which the artist can wield, he is from our point of
view attacking not the vices but the virtues of the poetic experience—that is, if we relegate it to the sphere of a recreation
pure and simple. It is essential to understand that Plato's attack is
launched upon something which is for him not a recreation but
an indoctrination, one upon which the normal stabilities of Greek
culture had hitherto depended.

The learning process (to recapitulate) was not learning in our
sense but a continual act of memorisation, repetition and recall.
This was made effective by practising a drastic economy of
possible linguistic statements, an economy enforced by rhythmic
patterns both verbal and musical. In performance the co-operation of a whole series of motor reflexes throughout the entire body
was enlisted to make memorisation and future recall and repetition
more effective. These reflexes in turn provided an emotional
release for the unconscious layers of personality which could then
take over and supply to the conscious mind a great deal of relief
from tension and anxiety, fear and the like. This last constituted
the hypnotic pleasure of the performance, which placed the
audience under the minstrel's control, but was itself the ready
servant of the paideutic process. Pleasure in the final analysis was
exploited as the instrument of cultural continuity.

Thus in obedience to the laws of memorisation there was
established in an oral culture an intimate linkage between instruction on the one hand and sensual pleasure on the other. The
linkage moreover was normally experienced by all members of
the culture group. This fact may cast light on a baffling quality
of the Greek experience in both the archaic and high classical
periods which is best described as its automatic relish in life and
its naturalistic acceptance of life's varied and manifold moral
aspects. The Greeks, we feel, were both controlled in their
experience and yet also unfettered and free to an extent we cannot

share. They seem to enjoy themselves. They seem to take natural pleasure in fine shape and sound which we too sometimes recognise as beautiful but only after we have first pulled ourselves up by our own boot straps to an educated level of perception. Another thing noticeable about them in this period is their capacity for direct action and sincere action and for direct and sincere expression of motive and desire. They almost entirely lack those slight hypocrisies without which our civilisation does not seem to work. All this is explicable if the learning process by which the proprieties of life were mastered was itself a highly sensual experience—it had to be, in order to be effective—so that proper action and diction were inseparably associated in the Greek consciousness with pleasurable memories. You continually were encouraged to do what you remembered others had done. But this very recollection was at once linked with all the good times you had enjoyed in release from care and tension when you memorised what others had done. And hence your present acts carried out within this context were liable to be felt as pleasant acts too. There was no warfare possible between body and spirit. The pull between the pleasurable inclination to act in one way and the unpleasant duty to act in another way was relatively un-known. All this begins to change perhaps by the time the fourth century was under way. Such a change has already been noted by historians and interpreters of the Greek spirit. Is it not at least possible that the change was conditioned in part by a change in the technology of communication and hence in the technology of education? A psychological condition long encouraged by a purely oral culture was becoming no longer possible.[30]

So much may be speculative. It is at any rate clear that the learning process of Homeric man had to be pleasurable in order to be effective. We call it a 'learning process'. It is under this guise indeed that Plato attacks it, as not being a proper method of learning. But such as it was, it had been the method of indoc-trination by which the public and private law had been crystal-lised, conserved, and transmitted successively from generation to generation. Precisely how did this indoctrination work upon the mind of the recipient? What kind of learning process was this?

Surely it was one in which you learned by doing. But the doing, so far as it concerns the preservation of important language, was of a special kind. What you 'did' were the thousand acts and thoughts, battles, speeches, journeys, lives, and deaths that you were reciting in rhythmic verse, or hearing, or repeating.[31] The poetic performance if it were to mobilise all these psychic resources of memorisation had itself to be a continual re-enactment of the tribal folkways, laws and procedures, and the listener had to become engaged in this re-enactment to the point of total emotional involvement. In short, the artist identified with his story and the audience identified with the artist. This was the imperative demand made upon both of them if the process was to work.

You did not learn your ethics and politics, skills and directives, by having them presented to you as a corpus for silent study, reflection and absorption. You were not asked to grasp their principles through rational analysis. You were not invited to so much as think of them. Instead you submitted to the paideutic spell. You allowed yourself to become 'musical' in the functional sense of that Greek term.

If this reconstruction that has been attempted of the psychology of the poetic performance is near the truth, it confirms the suggestion offered earlier in Chapter Three that Plato was correctly concerned with the emotional pathology of the poetic performance, and it explains also why he chose the term *mimesis* to describe several aspects of the poetic experience which we today feel should be distinguished. The translation 'imitation', it can now be seen, does not adequately translate what he is talking about. Imitation in our language is governed by the presupposition that there is a separate existence of an original which is then copied. The essence of Plato's point, the raison d'être of his attack, is that in the poetic performance as practised hitherto in Greece there was no 'original'.[32]

The minstrel recited the tradition; and the audience listened, repeated, and recalled and so absorbed it. But the minstrel recited effectively only as he re-enacted the doings and sayings of heroes and made them his own, a process which can be described in reverse as making himself 'resemble' them in endless succession. He sank his personality in his performance. His audience in turn would remember only as they entered effectively and sympathetically into what he was saying and this in turn meant that they became his servants and submitted to his spell. As they did this, they engaged also in a re-enactment of the tradition with lips, larynx, and limbs, and with the whole apparatus of their unconscious nervous system. The pattern of behaviour in artist and audience was therefore in some important respects identical. It can be described mechanically as a continual repeating of rhythmic doings. Psychologically it is an act of personal commitment, of total engagement and of emotional identification. The term *mimesis* is chosen by Plato as the one most adequate to describe both re-enactment and also identification, and as one most applicable to the common psychology shared both by artist and by audience.[33]

NOTES

[1] Cf. the description of man in primitive society as a 'mnemotechnician' by Marcel Jousse (cited by Notopoulos, 'Mnemosyne', p. 467).

[2] Studies of either the formulae (as by Parry) or of the cola (by H. Fraenkel, and also H. Porter; cf. *Lustrum* 2.1957, pp. 30-2) within the Homeric hexameter focus attention on structure as it is determined by the words used rather than by the old-fashioned concept of a metron of six feet or bars. The very rigid conventions of quantity, however, so it seems to me, which govern the hexameter (below, n. 3) compel one to accept the musical measure of the line as a whole as constituting a separable form of control over the reciter's voice, a control non-verbal in character, and bespeaking the importance of instrumental accompaniment.

[3] My account here is intended descriptively and analytically, not historically. The formulas (or cola) of course did not emerge in independence from meter. One could reverse the equation and say that 'metre' is composed of the formulas, except that the astonishingly rigid conventions of the epic hexameter raise the

problem of whether a stock of formulas originally shaped to suit Indo-European rhythms was subsequently adapted and enlarged to suit the requirements of the Aegean metrical system (above, cap. 7, n. 13).

[4] 'Every kind of language is a specialised form of bodily gesture and in this sense it may be said that the dance is the mother of all languages': Collingwood, p. 243.

[5] Presumably I am here distinguishing, in the case of epic, what Collingwood (pp. 57-104) calls 'art as magic', versus 'art as amusement', but it is not part of our present business to decide what if any are the epic elements which correspond, in Collingwood's vocabulary, to 'art proper'.

[6] Notopoulos, 'Parataxis' (p. 15 and *passim*) places emphasis on the observed fact of the oral poet's 'intimate relation with his audience'.

[7] *Theog.* lines 3, 4, 7, 8.

[8] 10.

[9] 29, ἀρτιέπειαι, cf. the Homeric μορφὴν ἔπεσιν στέφει (above, cap. 6, n. 23) and the familiar ἔπεα πτερόεντα which, if the metaphor is of arrows, suggests the power of the formulaic phrase to attach itself to the memory.

[10] 39, 60.

[11] 39.

[12] 83, 84, 97.

[13] 69; cf. 66 and 77.

[14] 70.

[15] 95.

[16] 37, 40, 51.

[17] 77.

[18] 83, 84, 42, 97.

[19] 8, 104, 64.

[20] 65, 67, 70, 78.

[21] 37, 51.

[22] 40, 69.

[23] 7-10.

[24] 55.

[25] 98 ff. The *Helen* of Gorgias (particularly 8-10) may be said to attempt a rationalisation of this whole emotive apparatus to which Hesiod alludes. Poetry had now become *logos*, which for Gorgias is human communication, but also by definition persuasive communication, for the preserved word had always been so. It could win preservation for itself only as it cast that total spell which the sophists (mistakenly?) sought to retain for oratory.

[26] Collingwood (pp. 5-6 and 17-18) places valuable emphasis upon the classic Greek conception of 'craft' (cf. also Richardson, p. 62, who would trace celebration of 'man's mastery over tools' back to Mycenaean practice, and Dow, 'The Greeks . . .' sub. fin). Its application however he subdivides into 'old magico-religious art' versus 'new amusement art' (p. 52). He then contends that Plato, accepting the conception of poetry as a craft, wished to abolish it so far as it took the form of 'amusement poetry', but to restore it as 'magic'. Whatever

may be thought of this distinction, as applied to the history of Greek literature or the Greek visual arts, it cannot be made to work for Plato, who on the contrary specifically denies to poetry its contemporary status as a craft (cf. Rosen, pp. 142-4, and above, cap. 2, n. 28).

²⁷ *Mousike* (sc. *techne*) appears as the word for poetry at least as early as Pindar (*Ol.* 1.15) and *sophistes* appears as word for poet (*Isth.* 5.28). For the early usage of *sophos* and *sophia* to connote the skill of a *techne*, cf. Snell, 'Ausdrucke', pp. 5-8; for their early connection with poetry, the skill 'par excellence', ibid. 8-11 (cf. also Bowra, 'Problems', pp. 16-19, on the *sophia* of Xenophanes); (Snell's exx. are not exhaustive; add, e.g., Solon 13.51). Snell would place the *sophia* of the Seven Sages in a different category as being political-practical (cf. also Burnet, p. 46) but the differentiation is not necessary. It can be presumed that the label *sophoi* or *sophistai* had already in the fifth century attached itself to the presumed authors of an anthology (above, cap. 3, n. 16) of aphorisms which were ascribed to famous statesmen and perhaps introduced by the fable of the Delphic tripod (Burnet, p. 44 and n. 3), so that *sophos* here still retained its sense of 'verbally skilled' (on the origins of the notion of 'practical wisdom', cf. below, cap. 11, n. 17); cf. also Hesiod's use of ἐπισταμένως (a skill word, cf. Snell, *op. cit.*) to describe the manner of his own composition (*WD* 107) and also the power of a prince to settle litigation by the help of the Muse (*Theog.* 87; cf. above, cap. 6, n. 23). He describes the acquisition of his own gift in two ways: the Muses 'inspired' him (ἐνέπνευσαν *Theog.* 31); but they also 'instructed' him (ἐδίδαξαν *Theog.* 12 and *WD* 662); these two are reconcilable if the content of instruction had to be sympathetically memorised (cf. n. 29 below).

²⁸ Dodds (p. 82, following Delatte) points out that Democritus (B 18) seems to have introduced the doctrine. But it has not been noticed that he assigned to 'inspiration' the power to produce 'the beautiful' (B 18 καλά 112 καλόν cf. 21 ἐπέων κόσμον). Did this mean that he was prepared with an implicit distinction between artistic 'creation' and intellectual 'understanding'? Presumably the reception of ἐνθουσιασμός would be quite different from the operation of γνώμη γνησίη (B 11). Delatte, whose account of the Democritean psychological explanation of inspiration is otherwise convincing, would however apply it also to the case of the philosopher and so connect ἐνθουσιασμός with γνησίη γνώμη (pp. 52-4, where however he notes opposing views of Zeller and others), on the shaky ground provided by an enigmatic *placitum* of Aetius (FVS 68 A 116) which he translates inaccurately. The statement reads: Δ. πλείους εἶναι αἰσθήσεις περὶ τὰ ἄλογα ζῷα καὶ περὶ τοὺς σοφοὺς καὶ περὶ τοὺς θεούς. The wording with its vague περί suggests that doctrines of Dem. are being summarised in alien terms, and that the conjunction of the three terms in a single category may be a work of interpretation. Delatte also admits (p. 53, n. 1) that to include the philosopher is to involve Dem. in hopeless self-contradiction. It seems preferable to avoid this, and to relegate the theory of the poet-philosopher to its proper source in the Stoic reaction (next note). Plato (as Delatte notes) probably borrowed the Democritean account of the poetic process (with Dem. B. 18, cf. *Apology* 22c, expanded in *Ion* and *Phaedrus*) which being materialist would have

no epistemological value for him (a point Delatte ignores). So he converted the Democritean distinction between modes of knowledge into an antithesis between true and false. He modifies this position somewhat in the *Phaedrus*, but not substantially (above, cap. 2, n. 37). Both philosophers however shared a common motive (and here we return to issues created by the previous oral situation) to distinguish their own intellectual methods of gaining truth from what they felt to be the very different competence of the poets. To draw the distinction was essential, for historically the poet had claimed to be the *sophos* par excellence and his claim had been accepted (cf. also below, cap. 15, n. 22). I conclude that the words *sophos, sophia* at the end of the fifth century represented a set of prestige claims staked out in the culture. When a new variety of verbal skill began to emerge, its practitioners did not coin a new word for it. They preferred the old one, as offering a field-site already prepared, but one from which they had to eject the previous tenant. This case was not unique; it illustrates a kind of law of behaviour on the part of certain prestige words, in the cultural shift which took place between Homer and Aristotle.

29 In the Hellenistic period, Plato's classification of poetry as inspiration was revived but its pejorative colour reversed. The Stoics with success sought to rehabilitate poetry as 'philosophy' (cf. De Lacy, pp. 264, 269-71). Hence when we read in the *Ars Poetica*, 295 ff.: *ingenium misera quia fortunatius arte / credit et excludit sanos Helicone poetas / Democritus*, it is safe to infer that 'misera' and perhaps 'fortunatius' represent additions to the original sentiment. The rehabilitation was enthusiastically pursued, under Christian theological influence, in the Renaissance (Sperduti, pp. 232-3), thus preparing the conceptual groundwork of the Romantic philosophy, which assigned to poetry a power of direct access to 'higher' truth. The Greeks retained enough animism in their language to make it plausible to argue that they had 'religious belief' in the 'divine gift' of poetry (so Sperduti, *passim*, and Dodds, pp. 80-1). Yet to apply this phraseology to them is anti-historical in the sense that it reads back into the Greeks certain mental preoccupations which are post-Greek and in part post-Renaissance. Poets to be sure were sons of Zeus or Apollo or the Muses, but princes too were sons of Zeus, doctors sons of Asclepius, and so on. Moreover, as Dodds has to admit, in Homer the professions of seer and poet are distinct (to the disadvantage of the former) though in other cultures they are not, and to argue Greek beliefs about poetry from the analogy of non-Greek cultures (Sperduti, p. 212, notes 36, 37) is simply to conclude that Greek civilisation is best understood by reducing it to those terms common to barbarian Europe. A god to be sure could 'breathe songs' into Phemius (*Od.* 22.347, where P. has highly urgent personal reasons for the claim), but he could also put courage, fear, intention, and the like into any hero (and the bard Demodocus is called a 'hero', *Od.* 8.483). It is more to the point, and indicative of the essential Greek difference, that Apollo and the Muses are 'skilled' (exx. in Snell, p. 10, notes 2 and 3) and that they 'instruct' (*Od.* 8.487 ff., *Theog.* 22, *WD* 662) so that a minstrel can in the same breath speak of himself as 'instructed' and yet as 'inspired' (Phemius, lines 347 versus 348; Hesiod, lines 22 versus 31 as in note 27 above). Homer's special invocations to the Muses are connected with special feats of memory (cf. cap. 10, n. 15; Dodds, p. 100, n. 116, seeks to evade this conclusion). Pindar's claim that he was skilled φυᾷ (Ol. 2.94, cf. Nem. 3.40) reflects the natural vanity of the poet, born of that real sense of personal power which his control over his audience gave him. What Pindar does *not* say is 'Because of my native gifts, I do not need skill'.

³⁰ It might be added that as long as patterns of important behaviour had to be recorded in ceremonious language in order to be memorised, they might tend also themselves to become ceremonious. The motto of an oral culture might be phrased as ἔργον ἔπους σκιά. But in a literate culture this becomes λόγος ἔργου σκιή (Democ. B.145); that is to say, language becomes the 'description' of action instead of its 'expression' (cf. Collingwood, p. 112).

³¹ That is, the typical preserved statement, in an oral culture, is what some modern philosophers would call 'performative' as opposed to descriptive or definitive.

³² Above, cap. 3, n. 22.

³³ 'Whatever statement of emotion he (sc. the artist) utters is prefaced by the implicit rubric not "I feel" but "we feel". And it is not strictly even a labour undertaken by himself on behalf of the community. It is a labour in which he invites the community to participate; for their function as audience is not passively to accept his work, but to do it over again for themselves'—Collingwood, p. 315.

CHAPTER TEN

The Content and Quality of the Poetised Statement

WHEN Platonic *mimesis* is applied to describe the poet's act of creation, we are confronted with the question: What is the material which he creates? What is the actual content of an *epos*, or of a poem? It is only in Book Ten of his *Republic* that the philosopher trains his guns on this target. He has felt necessary first in Book Three to expose the situation of the poetic performance, and he reverts to this again in Book Ten itself, and expatiates on the psychological condition of the audience. But before he does this he turns to consider not the artist but his poetic statement, that 'phantom' of reality[1] as he calls it. We are not yet precisely aware why he thus disparages poetry as a report on the human experience. The logic of his attack will have to be defended in a later chapter. It has however now become clear that he had at least the right to consider poetry in this light, as a report and not just as an aesthetic stimulus. Poetry had indeed served as the tribal encyclopedia. We have already illustrated this fact; the body of tradition, of manners and mores and skills concealed within the narrative, has been exposed. Judged then as a kind of encyclopedia, as a body of information and direction, what kind of reporting is this? We have previously elucidated the psychological laws which govern its performance. Let us now endeavour to discover the epistemological laws which govern the arrangement of its language, the kind of syntax, so to speak, within which this type of communication is composed. Once these twin essays in understanding are completed, we may have in our hands the clues to the logic of Plato's two-pronged attack, on the performance, and on its content.

In fact, the problem of the poetic content is inseparably bound up with the condition of the performance. The two can be isolated as separate problems and considered in abstraction from each other, but Plato's instinct is sure when he insists first on analysing the relationship between performer and listener, before allowing himself to consider from an epistemological point of view the actual statements made by the performer. Preserved record (let us here recapitulate) had to be carried continually in the living consciousness: it was itself a 'live recording'. It could not be left lying around neglected until the eye by recapitulating it could restore remembrance to the consciousness. It could enlist the direct aid of only one sense, that of the ear, and the shaping of the material for presentation had therefore to be governed by mnemonic devices which obeyed acoustic laws. The other senses were then involved as much as possible by devices of sympathetic association. This required not only a selective economy of material to be preserved, but also a truly heroic effort of the psychic energies, which had to enlist the services of especially gifted men, even though the general population through habituation might have what by our standards would be an unusually good memory.

So far so good. But we must add that the mnemonic rules to which the content of preserved communication must conform had to be popular. A community can presumably throw up at any time a small number of gifted persons of unusual memories who could in theory memorise masses of material intractable to ordinary men. The jurists who in a later epoch of European history committed Justinian's Code to memory provide a case in point. In such a case, the gifted minority act as a court of appeal and a source of authority for the community. The Homeric situation was different. If tradition was to remain stable and be practised habitually, it had to be remembered in varying degrees by the whole population. Hence it must be cast in such a shape as to conform to the psychological needs of memorisation as these were present in ordinary people and not merely in the gifted.

The mechanisms set in motion among an average audience consisted, so we have argued, of activities of the nervous system common to all human beings. Here was a sort of drama of rhythmic doings in which all shared. The bodily reflexes which were required, whether of larynx or of limbs, were themselves a form of action, of *praxis*. It is easiest to excite such bodily acts through words if the words themselves evoke action and hence if they describe action. The content of the *epos* should therefore itself consist preferably of a whole series of doings. *Per contra*, it is the hallmark of a concept or an idea that it is more effectively isolated and pondered in silence and with physical immobility. Re-enactment and emotional identification have no place in the cogitative process proper. But they are essential to the rhythmic mnemonic process, and you can re-enact only a description of action. You can be stimulated by words to identify yourself with what 'they' say only when 'they' express emotions and passions in active situations.

Action presupposes the presence of an actor or agent. The preserved *epos* can therefore deal only with people, not with impersonal phenomena. In the words of Plato, *mimetike* is a *mimesis* of 'human beings acting out actions whether the action be autonomous or the result of external compulsion'; it may include 'what men think or feel about their actions, that is, how they interpret their effects in terms of weal or woe to themselves, and their corresponding joys and sorrows'.[2] Plato's context, as we have argued earlier,[3] makes it impossible that in this description he is thinking only of the drama. The epic is no less a drama of action and passion, as is all remembered poetry.

What kind of people can these be? Not anybody and everybody. If the saga is functional, if its purpose is to conserve the group mores, then the men who act in it must be the kind of men whose actions would involve the public law and the family law of the group. They must therefore be 'political' men in the most general sense of that term, men whose acts, passions, and thoughts will affect the behaviour and the fate of the society in which they live so that the things they do will send out vibrations into the farthest confines of this society, and the whole apparatus becomes alive and performs motions which are paradigmatic. The first book of the *Iliad* is a conspicuous example of this process at work: not a private quarrel but a political feud between men of power, itself exacerbated by a previous calamity which is also political—the plague in the army, which had been the penalty for a political-religious act committed by Agamemnon. In sum, the saga, in order to do its job for the community and offer an effective paradigm of social law and custom, must deal with those acts which are conspicuous and political. And the actors who alone can furnish these paradigms in this kind of society we designate as 'heroes'. The reason for the heroic paradigm is in the last resort not romantic but functional and technical.

Men and women are however in a literal sense not the only actors in the saga. It is a commonplace to say that metaphor is a staple of the poetic diet. We can take this for granted and then observe a basic principle underlying the metaphors of the saga. Phenomena other than persons can be described, but only as they are imagined to be behaving as persons would. The environment becomes a great society and the phenomena are represented as members of this society who interact upon each other as they play their assigned roles. The minstrel of the *Iliad* puts one of these metaphors before us in the first words he utters. The 'wrath' of Achilles becomes a divine demon, who destroys everything in her power, who 'saddles the Achaeans with a burden of pain', who 'hurls their ghosts to death' like an archer discharging his arrows, and who 'makes them over into a prey for dogs and birds'. The sophisticated palate of a bookish culture, savouring the vigour of these lines, will be tempted to interpret this personification as 'poetic' in the aesthetic sense, as an image which is consciously designed to replace abstract relationships of cause and effect by a substitute which is emotionally more powerful. The wrath of

Achilles did not in fact do these things in any direct sense. It had the effect of creating a situation unfavourable to the Greek army and this in turn caused the army's defeat. We say: how sure is the poetic instinct which short-cuts this train of historical reasoning, and simply presents the end result as the direct work of the anger. What we should say is: How necessary it is for the minstrel, if he is to offer any paradigm of cause and effect which our memory will retain, to present this as a series of acts performed by an agent with whom we can identify as we listen and repeat the lines. In short, a sophisticated language which analyses history in terms of causes and effects, of factors and forces, of objectives and influences and the like, is in the living oral tradition impossible because it is not amenable to the psychodynamics of the memorising process.

When we look at oral poetry from this point of view, we can see that the most common metaphor employed is a god. Which of the gods, asks the poet rhetorically, brought Achilles and Agamemnon into conflict? And he replies: 'it was Apollo, who became wroth with Agamemnon, and raised up an evil plague against them, and the people were destroyed'. This way of telling it again provides an agent in place of historical cause. His vivid behaviour, easily re-enacted, takes the place of a causal connection between a series of events which are fairly complex and which had the unforeseen result of embroiling the two leaders in a quarrel. Thus, the plague in the army was a natural phenomenon, and the poet is aware that it was, when he describes how it was ended by sanitary measures.[4] But the only way to describe its onset is to attribute it once more to an agent, or rather, to the successive acts of several agents, and this type of explanation is provided when Calchas tells how Agamemnon has committed sacrilege against Apollo by appropriating Chryseis the daughter of his priest. The plague is an expression of the god's anger. But the remedy—the cancellation of this impiety—is to be achieved at the expense of Achilles who is to lose his prize to Agamemnon, and so the two collide in a conflict, the ultimate cause of which was either the plague, or the previous act of impiety which in turn caused the plague. Thus presented, the story has a historical logic of its own. The chain of causation can be presented as a system. But no living memory could deal with the relationships and categories necessary for such a system. They have to become 'alive' and 'perform' as living beings, greedy, resentful and the like. So they become Apollo, a powerful agent who takes two men and throws them into collision, an agent who is hostile to one of them and indirectly hostile to everybody concerned because he is protecting a protégé.

This example furnishes a law by which the use of the gods in oral saga can be widely explained. They constantly provide an apparatus by which causal relations can be rendered in a verbal form with which the listener can identify. They become imitable and so memorisable. The complexity of the causative chain is simplified; the abstract factors are all crystallised as the interposition of powerful persons.

Once viewed in this light, as a kind of recurrent metaphor for constant conjunction of causes and effects, polytheism can be seen to have a great descriptive advantage over monotheism. It can more vividly report the variety of the phenomenal experience, of seasons and weather, of war and catastrophe, of human psychology, of historical situation, by referring a given phenomenon to the act or decision of some god whose activity can be limited to the given phenomena, without extending it to cover all other phenomena. The temptation to over-simplify the behaviour of the external world, as also the inner workings of man's own impulses, is thus avoided.

The minstrel's mentality however could not remain satisfied with a purely arbitrary and random use of a large variety of divine beings to suit given occasions and crises. The law of economy basic to the diction of the preserved record must be practised here too. So the gods do indeed become a kind of apparatus organised in families on the analogy of men, and they have personal attributes that remain fairly constant. For a given phenomenon, a given god becomes appropriate (though Homer

shows some flexibility in his choices) and these divinities in order
to be remembered with constancy themselves become incorporated in their own saga, so to speak. They love and quarrel,
rule and obey, in situations and stories which imitate the human
political drama. Their stories thus in turn become paradigms of
the operation of the public and private law which it is the business
of the saga to preserve. They constitute a second society super-
imposed upon the society of the heroes.

It can be objected that this line of reasoning, which explains the
gods in terms of the psychology of oral memorisation, fails to take
account of them as objects of cult and of worship. To which it
can be replied that the Homeric saga is itself largely indifferent to
the gods as objects of cult, and Hesiod as we shall see in a later
chapter is equally so. Cult is not absent; indeed, the plot of the
Iliad is set in motion by an offence committed against an official
who presides over a local rite. Nevertheless, cult subsists only on
the margins of the story, not at its centre. If we had to depend on
Homer for our knowledge of Greek cults we would not know
very much about them. The gods in the saga seem to function
largely as we have sought to describe them.

Let us recapitulate. The psychology of oral memorisation and
oral record required the content of what is memorised to be a set
of doings. This in turn presupposes actors or agents. Again, since
the content to be preserved must place great emphasis on public
and private law, the agents must be conspicuous and political
people. Hence they become heroes. All non-human phenomena
must by metaphor be translated into sets of doings, and the
commonest device for achieving this is to represent them as acts
and decisions of especially conspicuous agents, namely gods.

Now, to return to the hero himself, it is to be noticed that a
conspicuous human being who wielded power was remembered
within the context of a very fundamental human sequence. He
had been born, then became powerful, and then died, and his acts
and words intervene between the twin events which marked the
boundaries of his life. His birth had followed a previous be-

getting; his doings had been involved automatically in the doings of previous human beings. Behind him lay his parents' marriage. Before him, after he was born, lay his own marriage which would lead to the birth of his descendants. They being born survived when he died. The hero of the *Iliad* is no sooner brought on stage in his magnificent wrath than he is transported to the seashore in confrontation with his mother who celebrates his birth and his death. His most poignant utterances, as the story moves to its conclusion, recall his father and his own possible failure to maintain the succession.[5]

The hero's life and acts were the receptacle in which the tribal mores were contained and illustrated. He tended therefore to become a moral phenomenon which arose and passed away. But the image of passing away and of perishing threatened the continuity of the tradition. This must at all cost survive in the record as something permanent; it could not survive abstractly but only as a paradigm of doings. So the lives and the deaths of heroes are linked in endless series by formal and ceremonious marriages and equally ceremonious funerals in which the obsequies to the dead repeat and re-enforce the tribal imperatives which the survivors must preserve. It is remarkable in this connection to notice to what extent the arts of sculpture and painting, from the geometric to the high classical periods, are preoccupied with the representation of weddings, births, deaths, and funerals which as they threatened the sense of group permanence and group survival were therefore arranged deliberately to suggest their unbroken sequence and their causal relationship.

The verbs which identify birth and death suffered a very early metaphorical shift, by which they were linked with a predicate to represent an action or the result of an action. A new situation is so to speak 'born' or created by a previous action; a new phenomenon is born out of a previous one.[6] The Homeric formula 'they gathered and were "born" together'[7] illustrates the metaphor at its crudest. 'Born together' is added as a variant of the previous expression, 'they gathered'. Modern translation automatically substitutes the verbs 'became' or 'came to be', ignoring the fact that the Homeric Greek is innocent of any connection with the verb to be. This metaphor and the correlative metaphors of be-getting, putting forth (like a plant), dying, withering, perishing and the like are then extended to what we would call phenomena. A feud or battle, a plague or a storm, can do things to other people. They can also themselves 'be born' or 'arise' or 'wither' or 'perish' or 'give up'. The only phenomena to which the death metaphor cannot be applied are the gods. They can however be born and beget and give birth, and full advantage is taken of the fact. Their deathlessness on the other hand stands in the saga as an eternal contradiction to the endless succession of perishings in which the human drama has to be described.

The content of the poetic record can thus be viewed on the one hand as an endless series of actions, on the other as an equally endless series of births and deaths which when applied meta-phorically to phenomena become 'things happening' or 'events'. The verb 'happen' is indeed another favourite translation of the Greek verb 'to be born' just as 'pass away' is a favourite method of rendering the Greek for 'be destroyed'. This quality of the tribal report as an event-series—that is as a series of births and deaths—does not become fully evident until Hesiod attempts to rationalise the record into a system of births in generations or families. We are not ready for him yet. The saga in its purest oral form spoke far oftener of doings than of happenings. But it can fairly be generalised that the saga considered from the standpoint of a later and more sophisticated critique is essentially the record of an event-series, of things-happening,[8] never of a system of relations or of causes or of categories and topics. Only a language of act and of event is amenable to the rhythmic-mnemonic process, and the *nomoi* and *ethe* are memorialised only as they are things done or as things occurring. There are exceptions to be found in the Homeric aphorisms, pointing in the direction of a syntax which is designed to escape from the event. But these can be temporarily ignored. The fundamental units of the tribal encyclopedia are sets of doings and of happenings. Information or prescription, which in a later stage of literate culture would be arranged typically and topically, is in the oral tradition[9] preserved only as it is transmuted into an event.

The examples already cited in an earlier chapter of the encyclopedic content of the saga all conform to these syntactical rules. The character and function of the staff of authority which Achilles dashes to the ground are recalled only as they are cast into the form of active and specific performances:

> Verily by this staff—it never will leaves and shoots
> Put forth again when once it has left its stump in the mountains
> Nor will it ever bloom again. Round about it the bronze has peeled off
> The leaves and the bark. And now the sons of the Archaeans
> Bear it in their handgrip, even the arbitrators of rights who the precedents
> Do guard under the eye of Zeus.[10]

Achilles' words evoke several sudden image situations: there is the staff being cut in the woods and peeled, and there is the committee of judges in the speaking piace holding up the staff in their hands. This is not a still-life tableau; they are doing things; gestures and speech are implicit in the description. Past and future tenses, and a present tense which is limited to the here and now as a vividly present event, replace our sophisticated syntax of a timeless present used to connect a subject with a universal predicate: 'the staff is a symbol of authority and of law'.

The navigation procedures, as we earlier extracted them from the narrative, are in fact not reported as universal procedures but recited as specific commands for action or as specific acts. 'As for now, a black ship let us draw down . . .' is followed by four more imperatives. Then the operation is carried out in the past tense: 'the son of Atreus a swift ship to the salt sea drew down, and therein oarsmen he selected', etc. As these vignettes are narrated, the audience can identify psychologically with them, for they are doings, and so they become memorisable.

A doing or a happening can occur quite obviously only in the context of what we might call an episode, a little story or situation.

The rhythmic memory does not wish to be interrupted in its performance and have to start again. It wants to glide from a doing to a doing so that item B is remembered only as it flows out of A, and C only as it flows out of B. This chain of narrative association groups itself most naturally around the acts of an agent whose image has been evoked in an episode and whose words and acts then become the vehicles which are made to carry items of the tribal encyclopedia. Thus is established the law of narrative relevance[11] as essential to the successful preservation of a tribal record, and the superior bard is he who most successfully commands this art of relevance so that he masks as it were the content of the encyclopedia which the group memory has somehow to retain. The statement of the function of the staff of authority, itself an image, is placed in an episode which makes it relevant—the anger of Achilles, the solemnity of his oath. The navigation procedures arise in the narrative as a logical response to a given situation: the king has become convinced he has to make amends; how do you do this except by giving orders to transport the girl back to the shrine from which she had been ravished? Hence embarkation, loading, the voyage, the docking, the unloading are not described for their own sake as general operations but as particular directives carried out in the course of an active situation.

Finally, while the rhythmic memory can in theory accommodate a great range of short episodic stories, a sophisticated oral culture demands a *paideia* which shall be coherent, a corpus of semi-consistent mores transmissible as a corpus from generation to generation. The tighter is the group structure, or the sense of common ethos shared by communities who speak a common tongue, the more urgent is the need for the creation of a great story which shall compendiously gather up all the little stories into a coherent succession, grouped round several prominent agents who shall act and speak with some over-all consistency. For the patterns of public and private behaviour, as recalled in a thousand specific episodes, are multiform and various, not reducible to a catechism, but nevertheless to be recollected and repeated at need. What shall be the frame of reference, the chapter headings, the library catalogue, within which the memory can find markers which shall point up relevant saws and wise instances? Only the over-all plot of a great story can serve, a plot memorised in thousands of lines but reducible to specific episodes which shall yield specific examples.

'You ask me how should one confront death? Well you remember Achilles after the death of Patroclus; how his mother came to him—she was a goddess, you know—and what he said to her about his duty and what she said to him and how he replied again to her.'[12] Only the frame of the *Iliad* can supply the initial recall of this paradigm in its place in the story. The paradigm itself, considered as an episode, is recalled in its specific dynamism; its message may be general but only in sophisticated retrospect. The contexts of the *Iliad* are the page references for the oral memory.

These laws governing the syntax of the tribal encyclopedia, the verbal texture of act and event, the need for episodic location in a narrative situation, the need to place that narrative situation in the context of a great and compendious story—are all illustrated in the case of that most conspicuous of all didactic items contained in the *Iliad*; namely the so-called Catalogue which forms the second half of the second book. We are not here concerned with the possible historical sources of this 'document'. Was it a Mycenaean muster-list? Did it once exist in Linear B? Was it a rescript issued to summon a fleet to Aulis? Is it not rather a 'heroolgy', a celebration of certain great families? Or is it not a navigational guide to the islands and coasts of the Aegean reflecting the needs and circumstances of the ninth and eighth centuries? All these questions have been asked of it.[13] But our business here is with the simple fact that this as we have it in Homer is not a document at all but a piece of oral record. We are concerned here solely with its syntax and its context. It is to be a list of names and numbers: 'Tell me now, ye Muses that dwell in the mansions of Olympus... who were the captains of the Danaans and their lords?'[14] So does the minstrel announce the purport of the episode to come. But a list is a scheme or a system divorced from act and event. How can it possibly be retained in memory either of minstrel or of audience? As though aware of this problem, the bard utters a special and rather tense invocation to all the Muses; their powers must conspire to help him in a very difficult task. By contrast, the opening of his great story, which plunged at once into the vocabulary of action, needed only a casual invocation of the goddess. The present context shows how true it is that the Muses symbolise the minstrel's need of memory and his power to preserve memory, not a spiritual inspiration which would certainly be inappropriate to a muster-list.[15] However, it is not going to be a straight list after all; the syntax of the sheer catalogue is impossible for a non-literate composer. It is not going to be a set of data but of doings. The leading item, the most ambitious in length of them all, is typical:

'Over the Boeotians Peneleos and Leitos were ruling (three more personal names added). . . . These were they that were pasturing Hyria and rocky Aulis and Schoinos (twenty-six more place-names added with some repetition of "pasturing" and "holding"). . . . Of these fifty ships were coming, and in each young men of the Boeotians 120 were embarking.'[16]

A geographic area—Boeotia—is identified not as such but by the name of its men. These are then linked to certain powerful agents whose leadership is not however stated in the abstract but given as an act of power. Then the geographic entity, namely Boeotia, is broken down into localities but these are presented only as objects of personal action on the part of those who were pasturing or holding them. Then, as if the long list of names had exhausted the mnemonic powers of the bard, he closes by evoking two simple but active images, of ships on their way, of men coming on board. The Boeotian 'entry', we might say, is converted into an active episode.[17]

Variations of this syntactical pattern are followed in all the items of the list, all of them dominated by images of powerful

persons in the lead or ruling or dominating. In the case of some
heroes, the bard as he names them is drawn into a little episode
which enlarges the narrative context of the name—the mere
datum—and renders it more alive and available for sympathetic
identification.

Sometimes the facts surrounding a hero's parentage are
recorded, but if so it is never simply that he was the son of
Ares or Heracles or the like, but rather a picture of the putative
father seducing the mother under given circumstances. In short,
these are not footnotes, but rather reversions to that syntax of
event or act without which the preserved record flags and fails.
Such narrative inserts are added to the names of twelve heroes
and also to three place-names. Nor can these narrative additions
be viewed as borrowed from honorific genealogies of families.
For in the conspicuous cases of Agamemnon, Menelaus, Achilles,
Protesilaus and Philoctetes,[18] the narrative addition is used to
place the hero in the context of the bard's great story, as though
he repeatedly felt an overriding need to get back into his narrative
even while offering what purports to be a list. Naming Achilles
twice, he also twice in variant versions reminds us how he lay
idle by the ships in anger and so forth.[19]

So much for the verbal texture of the list itself. It is next to be
noted that the list as a whole is preserved and therefore recalled
as it occurs and is prompted by a specific episode. It must have
narrative relevance. The Greek army before Troy has been
thrown into panic and is ready to abandon the war, but a strong
speech from Odysseus rallies them and Nestor then clinches the
argument for continuing the siege. He urges Agamemnon to
hold a muster of the army in order to raise morale to fighting
pitch. The muster is then described, with the captains exhorting
their respective contingents as they pour forth on to the Sca-
mander plain: 'Tell me now, ye Muses, who were the leaders of
the Danaans and their lords.' Thus it is that the minstrel employs
narrative relevance as the key which unlocks a hoard of traditional
data. The catalogue information can be recorded and carried in

the living memory only as it forms part of a great episode which suggests it and leads us into it.

Finally this episode in turn itself constitutes a memorable crisis in the great story, the Tale of the Trojan War, as that war in turn is remembered in connection with the theme of Achilles' great quarrel. This over-all plot, the structure of the epic as it has coalesced during the non-literate centuries between 1000 and 700 B.C., forms the general library which is to comprise and carry its contained materials, and in this case the material is didactic to a special degree. The Catalogue is at once a kind of history of the Greek folk and a kind of geography of their world, an appropriate part of the general education of the Greek ethnic group as it had come to live on the coasts of the Aegean by the eighth century B.C. If Homer were being rewritten to conform to the logic of a literate expository style of discourse, we would start the account of the war with this catalogue of information required as a background for the particular story we propose to tell. But the oral memory reverses this procedure. Dynamic narrative must have priority to establish its spell over the rhythmic memory before it attempts to carry such a burden. The information cannot exist independently; it rises up in recollection only as it is suggested by the great story of which it forms a part. The catalogues of epic, sometimes described as the 'Hesiodic' element, are often discussed as though they formed the most ancient layer of tradition in the poems.[20] This can mislead us, for in oral tradition they never could have existed as sheer catalogues. Always they had to be recalled in a narrative context and themselves be rendered in terms of events, of things happening, or of actions performed by living persons.[21] The catalogue in its purest and most laconic form may have existed in Linear B documents during Mycenaean times, though this is doubtful. It could never in this pure form have formed part of the oral tradition. The activity of Hesiod, the first extant cataloguer, therefore heralds the first beginnings of a later style of composition which craft literacy had rendered possible. Only with the growing help of the written word would

catalogue material begin to be separated out from narrative contexts and appear in a more harsh, informative, and less memorisable dress.

If preserved 'knowledge' (we place the term deliberately in
quotation marks) is compelled to be obedient in these ways to the
psychological requirements imposed by the memorised saga, it
becomes possible to define its general character and content under
three separate aspects, none of which agree with the character of
'knowledge' as it is assumed to exist in a literate culture. First of
all, the data or the items without exception have to be stated as
events in time. They are all time-conditioned. None of them can
be cast into a syntax which shall be simply true for all situations
and so timeless; each and all have to be worded in the language
of the specific doing or the specific happening. Second they are
remembered and frozen into the record as separate disjunct
episodes each complete and satisfying in itself, in a series which is
joined together paratactically. Action succeeds action in a kind
of endless chain. The basic grammatical expression which would
symbolise the link of event to event would be simply the phrase
'and next . . .'.[22] Thirdly, these independent items are so worded
as to retain a high content of visual suggestion; they are brought
alive as persons or as personified things acting out vividly before
the mind's eye. In their separate and episodic independence from
each other they are visualised sharply, passing along in an endless
panorama. In short, this kind of knowledge which is built up in
the tribal memory by the oral poetic process is subject precisely
to the three limitations described by Plato as characteristic of
'opinion' (*doxa*). It is a knowledge of 'happenings' (*gignomena*)
which are sharply experienced in separate units and so are
pluralised (*polla*) rather than being integrated into systems of
cause and effect. And these units of experience are visually
concrete; they are 'visibles' (*horata*).

Let us consider a little further the first and perhaps the most
fundamental of these three characteristics. A story has to be time-
conditioned and we can take that for granted. But what we are

looking at here is the fact that this time-conditioning extends also to the encyclopedic materials contained in the story, that is, it extends to the 'knowledge' retained in the tribal memory. The story itself is committed to a syntax of past, present, and future, all available in classical Greek, or to 'aspects' of time available in other languages. The contained material, involving information, precept and custom and the like, is equally likely to occur in the future or the historic past as event or as command, since the given instance has to occur in a narrative connection and be itself presented as a 'doing'. The navigational procedures are an instance of this. It may however occur in the present tense, as often in aphorism. Achilles described how the elders 'do now hold' the staff of office. But this kind of present is not a timeless present (if the paradox may be allowed). It is used to describe an act occurring temporally and vividly before the mind's eye, of minstrel and of audience: 'There they are, holding it.'[23] Hence neither technical information nor moral judgment can be presented reflectively in the saga as true generalisation couched in the language of universals.

There is a notable passage near the opening of the *Odyssey* which might seem to provide an exception, but the exception is only apparent. Zeus in council exclaims before the rest of the gods:

Lo, how vainly mortals accuse the gods.
From us, they say, are their evils. But it is they themselves
Who by their own wilfulness and wildness have pains beyond their
    portion.[24]

This is not the syntax of true universal definition. We still are presented evocatively with a doing, as mortal men accumulate disasters, and the whole utterance is conditioned in the narrative by the instance of Aegisthus whom Zeus remembers and for whose fall he wishes to disclaim personal responsibility. This is as near as the oral record can get to philosophical reflection. What it cannot do is to use the verb to be as a timeless copula in such a sentence as: 'human beings are responsible for the consequences of their own acts'. Still less can it say 'the angles of a triangle are equivalent to two right angles'. Kantian imperatives and mathematical relationships and analytic statements of any kind are inexpressible and also unthinkable. Equally an epistemology which can choose between the logically (and therefore eternally) true and the logically (and eternally) false is also impossible. This temporal conditioning is an aspect of that concreteness which attaches itself to all preserved Homeric discourse.

We have argued that this kind of discourse, just because it is the only speech which in an oral culture enjoys a life of its own, represents the limits within which the mind of the members of that culture can express itself, the degree of sophistication to which they can attain. Hence all 'knowledge' in an oral culture is temporally conditioned, which is another way of saying that in such a culture 'knowledge' in our sense cannot exist.

To this fundamental trait of the Homeric mind Plato and also the pre-Platonic philosophers address themselves, demanding that a discourse of 'becoming', that is of endless doings and of events, be replaced by a discourse of 'being', that is of statements which are in modern jargon 'analytic', are free from time-conditioning. The opposition between becoming and being in Greek Philosophy was not motivated in the first instance by those kinds of logical problems proper to a sophisticated speculation, still less was it prompted in the first instance by metaphysics or by mysticism. It was simply a crystallisation of the demand that the Greek language and the Greek mind break with the poetic inheritance, the rhythmically memorised flow of imagery, and substitute the syntax of scientific discourse, whether the science be moral or physical.

If the saga has to be composed of doings and happenings, it is equally true that these can occur only in a series in which the separate doings are so to speak self-contained, each of them in turn registering an impact upon the audience, who identify with them successively without attempting to organise them reflectively in groups within which subordinate acts are attached to principal acts. The word-order will in general be that of time; the connection, implicit or explicit, between each doing will be 'and then'. Thus the memorised record consists of a vast plurality of acts and events, not integrated into chained groups of cause and effect, but rather linked associatively in endless series. In short, the rhythmic record in its very nature constitutes a 'many': it cannot submit to that abstract organisation which groups 'manys' into 'one'. Stylistically, this truth can be stated as an opposition between that type of composition which is paratactic,[25] as in the epic, and that which is periodic, or beginning to be so, as for example in the speeches of Thucydides. But the issue cuts far deeper than mere style. To illustrate its truth let us analyse the opening lines of the *Iliad* from the standpoint of this opposition:

Chant Oh goddess the wrath of Achilles
(that) destroying (wrath); it (or which) placed ten thousand tribulations
  upon the Achaeans
And hurled forth many mighty ghosts to Hades
(ghosts) of heroes, and made the men into a prey for dogs
and for all birds, and the council of Zeus was fulfilled.
From whence at the first the two having fallen to feuding stood asunder
even Agamemnon son of Atreus and divine Achilles.

This version translates the verbs and participles in their Greek order. A more categorical organisation of the same material might run as follows:

My song is of a military catastrophe involving heavy casualties
Which befell the Achaeans as the result of the wrath of Achilles
A wrath prompted by his great quarrel with Agamemnon
And rendered effective by the co-operation of Zeus.

In the Homeric version the image of the powerful wrath of Achilles leads at once into an image of activity which by habit men are prone to associate with such wrath—that of killing people; the killing in turn is then filled out by adding the image of the ghosts despatched to Hades and the bodies lying on the

battle-field. And then without apology the locus shifts abruptly
to the mind of Zeus planning and plotting. There is an associative
linkage even here; Achilles is the most powerful of men, Zeus the
most powerful of gods; the two are paired in common action.
Then the minstrel attempts a temporal retrospect (which may be
partly causal) of the starting of the feud between the two leaders.
The feud is suggested by the wrath; the addition of the second
leader is prepared for by the presence of the first. The images
evoked in the verbs and in the nouns succeed each other paratactically; each unit of meaning is self-subsistent; the linkage is
essentially that which is rendered possible by adding fresh words
which exploit or vary associations already present in previous
words. In fact this kind of speech is constructed on that principle
of variation within the same which we characterised in a previous
chapter as typical of rhythmic memorised speech.

By contrast our second version begins by searching out and
stating the over-all situation of the epic (that is as far as Book
Seventeen), namely a military defeat; to this fact, the anger of
Achilles is then reflectively subordinated as the cause, and the feud
with Agamemnon is in turn subordinated causally to the wrath;
and finally the council of Zeus, now reserved for the last place in
the cause-effect series, is likewise subordinated to the wrath as the
last essential condition of its effectiveness. This process constitutes
an act of integration in which, out of a series of multiple paratactic doings, one doing is selected as principal and the other
doings are then arranged in subordinate relationship to the central
doing, so that in thought a single composite reflection takes the
place of the many successive impressions.

Homer is not entirely innocent of periodic composition.
Indeed the introduction to the *Iliad* if pursued further will be
found to yield examples of attempted subordination. For the
introduction is unusually sophisticated. Thus we are told that
'Apollo in anger had sent a plague because the son of Atreus had
dishonoured Chryses the priest'.[26] The temporal-paratactic order
would have been: the son of Atreus had dishonoured the priest

and Apollo was angry. This simple instance illustrates however why what we have called integration of experience into chains of cause and effect was difficult for the oral medium. The causative type of thinking presupposes that the effect is more important than the cause and in thought is therefore to be selected first before you seek for its explanation. This reverses what we may call the temporal-dynamic order, or the natural order, in which the doings are linked in that series in which they occur in sensual experience, and are each in turn appreciated or savoured before the next one occurs.[27]

But though Homer can manage such rearrangements of experience and so construct little unities out of the pluralities, they are not characteristic. It is the essential genius of the rhythmic record that its units of meaning are like vividly experienced moments of doing or happening.[28] These are linked associatively to form an episode, but the parts of the episode are greater than the whole. The many predominate over the one.

This law is likewise applicable to all that 'knowledge' which the tribal encyclopedia may contain. It too must survive in isolated units each sharply presented as doings with which the audience can momentarily identify. If one reviews those contained materials, that is those typical statements, which in Chapter Four we disentangled from the text of the first book of the *Iliad*, it can easily be seen how true this is. In short, the *nomoi* and *ethe* are presented and are put on record not as a system of law, public and private, but as a plurality of typical instances which have the coherence proper to an organic but instinctive pattern of life. To organise them in a system, in their genera and species and categories, would be to create a one out of the Homeric many. This was to be a task reserved for the Greek mind of the fifth and fourth centuries before Christ. As to technical information, the example of the navigation procedures is characteristic. These are not gathered together and grouped and topicalised as navigation procedures. On the contrary they occur in four disjunct passages each of them prompted by its specific narrative context and it is

only the reflective mind of the sophisticated reader, who rereads
and reviews the text, that can group them together and unify
them under a single heading.

The necessity to preserve the moral tradition in this disjunct
series of memorised units explains why, taken in detail, the
tradition is not only repetitive but subject to variant versions and
is also to a degree contradictory, if judged by the standards of a
logically consistent ethic. Since a given piece of exhortation or
prescription was presented episodically, it was coloured by its
narrative context, the particular situation in the story, and hence
it was framed as what was appropriate in that context. The result
was that the epic could furnish examples of suitable behaviour or
of suitable speech for many different types of occasion, examples
which at times would cancel each other out if gathered into a
single credo, but which made sense, in given contexts, of the
multiplicity of heroic experience.

As an example of this, the great speeches in the ninth book of
the *Iliad* will serve. Odysseus leads a deputation, the business of
which is by aphorism and example to exhort Achilles to rejoin the
army. Achilles replying quotes aphorism and example to support
his refusal. Their speeches—as also those of Phoenix and Ajax—
are full of quotations eminently applicable to given moral
situations. The audience who memorised such passages might
instinctively recall and apply portions of any of these speeches to
their own experience as it arose. There are for example times
when it is appropriate to back out of a situation (Achilles) and
there are times when it is proper to confront it (Odysseus); times
when co-operation with one's fellows seems a duty (Odysseus)
and times when self-assertion of one's own dignity seems essential
(Achilles). The tendency of the saga to typify such reflections
as unconscious paradigmata of proper behaviour explains the
secret of the Homeric grand manner. But this very virtue of the
poet later became a vice in the eyes of the rationalists who in the
fifth century began to seek a consistent rationale of morality.[29]
The search is pursued to its conclusion in the pages of Plato. It was

such flexible poetic moralities that Plato sought to define when he spoke of the poetic content as: 'human action whether this action be autonomous or the result of external compulsion and also including what men think or feel about their actions; that is how they interpret their effect in terms of weal or woe to themselves and their corresponding joys and sorrows'.[30]

Mnemonic necessity also required the content of the epic to wear a third aspect. Not only had it to consist of acts and events, not only had these to be presented pluralistically and independently, but they had to be presented visually, or as visually as possible. The psychological effort of recall was assisted in the first instance by the rhythm, by acoustic echo, by one word or phrase evoking a variant word or phrase; that is by similarity of sound. It was assisted in the second instance by the fact that the doings as they followed each other tended to suggest each other because they bore some correspondence to that kind of sequence we are used to in everyday life. Destruction suggests death; anger suggests feud. But a third method of suggestive leading-on of the memory could be supplied by visual resemblance between the items of the record; that is if one agent looked something like another or one performance looked something like another. The picture of an angry man leads to the picture of that man drawing his sword; but the drawing of the sword may link to the picture of someone else holding on to it from behind. Achilles the mighty hero looks, as a hero, about like Agamemnon the mighty hero. Zeus of the thunderbolt may draw us on to contemplate Apollo of the arrows. The wrath placed many woes on the Achaeans and then hurled many ghosts precipitately to Hades. Here the use of the plural—not woe but a heap of woes—helps to make the burden visually appreciable, and the crowding woes are half visually balanced against the crowding ghosts. The Homeric epithet can be seen to have a double function. It fills in a portion of the rhythm by automatic reflex, and this saves the bard effort. But equally it visualises the object more keenly. If the ships are fleet, we see them as ships briefly sailing. The priest does not come to promise a ransom; he carries it in his hands, and in his hand also is a golden staff with the badge of office on it. The attributes, unessential to the main story, evoke a visualisation of the scene and the actors.

Earlier, in discussing the way in which the minstrel created and repeated his tribal encyclopedia, we used the simile of a house crowded with furniture among which he threads his way touching this object and that. If you are looking at a table, the original temptation is to let the glance shift to another table or to a chair, not to ceiling or stairs. To be effectively retained in the memory, the epic had to utilise this psychological aid as far as it could. So its units of meaning are highly visualised in order that vision may lead on to vision.

We are here determining the basic sense of that much-used word the 'image'. It starts as a piece of language so worded as to encourage the illusion that we are actually looking at an act being performed or at a person performing it.

Actions and their agents are in fact always easy to visualise. What you cannot visualise is a cause, a principle, a category, a relationship or the like. The abstract can be defined in many ways and at varying degrees of linguistic sophistication. Is the goddess Memory an abstraction? Is the wrath of Achilles an abstraction? In the terms in which we have defined the characteristics of preserved communication they are not. To be effectively part of the record, they have to be represented as agents or as doings particular to their context and sharply visualised. As long as oral discourse retains the need of visualisation it could not properly be said to indulge in abstraction. As long as its content remained a series of doings or of events none of these could properly be regarded as universals, which emerge only through the effort of rearranging the panorama of events under topics, and of reinterpreting it as chains of relation and cause. The era of the abstract and the conceptual is yet to come.

We can be misled by some of Homer's vocabulary into thinking that he can manage an abstraction. We draw this conclusion however only if we ignore syntactical context and concentrate on the word itself, which is an improper method of evaluating its effect on the consciousness of the audience. The arrival of the abstract is near at hand in Hesiod, as topical groupings and categories are imposed upon the image-flux, and as causal relations are sought between phenomena. But it is not really achieved until these headings and categories are themselves identified and named by the use of the impersonal neuter singular.[31] To be sure, Homer in aphorism can himself exploit this usage. But it is exceptional, a sign-post pointing forward to a diction and a syntax which would destroy poetry altogether.

The visualisation thus exploited by minstrels was indirect. Words were so grouped as to stress the visual aspects of things, and so encourage the listener to see with his mind's eye. The direct techniques of memorisation were all acoustic, and appealed for rhythmic acceptance in the hearing. With the arrival of the written word, the sense of sight was added to the sense of hearing as a means of preserving and repeating communication. The words were recallable now by the use of the eye and this saved a great deal of psychological energy. The record did not have to be carried round in the living memory. It could lie around unused till you had need to recognise it. This drastically reduced the need of framing discourse so as to be visualised, and the degree of this visualisation consequently drops. It may indeed be suggested that it was increasing alphabetisation which opened the way to experiments in abstraction. Once rid of the need to preserve experience vividly, the composer was freer to reorganise it reflectively.

We have, to repeat, been distinguishing three aspects of orally-preserved communication, which correspond to Plato's definition of 'opinion' as a state of mind that deals with becoming rather than being, and with the many rather than the one, and with the visible rather than with the invisible and thinkable. One can add for good measure another aspect which also corresponds to something he has to say about this state of mind. The hurrying pano-

rama is so constructed and sung that we are seduced into identifying with its doings, its joys and griefs, its nobilities and cruelties,
its courage and its cowardice. As we pass from experience to
experience, submitting our memories to the spell of the incanta-
tion, the whole experience becomes a kind of dream in which
image succeeds image automatically without conscious control
on our part, without a pause to reflect, to rearrange or to general-
ise, and without a chance to ask a question or raise a doubt, for
this would at once interrupt and endanger the chain of association.
When we summarised Hesiod's account of the pleasurable spell
cast by the honeyed Muse upon her audience, the effect he seems
to be trying to describe we spoke of as a kind of hypnosis. If
the characteristics of the preserved communication were such as
we have described, then indeed, in contrast to reflective and
cogitative speech, it was truly a form of hypnosis in which
emotional automatism played a large part, as doing leads to doing
and image precipitates image. This surely is the reason why Plato
so often describes the non-philosophical state of mind as a kind of
sleep-walking, nor was he alone in passing this judgment.[32]

The effect would be more pronounced in antiquity. We after
all do not expect to memorise the *Iliad*, nor to identify with it nor
to live by it. In sum, these aspects conferred on the Greek epic
powers of evocation, of grandeur, of psychological fulfilment,
unique after their kind. They could not supply the descriptive and
analytic discipline, but they could supply a complete emotional
life. It was a life without self-examination, but as a manipulation
of the resources of the unconscious in harmony with the conscious
it was unsurpassed.

NOTES

[1] *Rep.* 601b9, cf. 600e5.
[2] *Rep.* 603c4 ff.
[3] Above, cap. I.
[4] *Iliad* I.314.
[5] *Iliad* I.352, 414 ff. (cf. 18.54 ff., 95-6); 24.534 ff. (cf. 19.326 ff.).

[6] *Iliad* I.49, 57, 188, 251, 493; only 5 instances in 611 lines: (add 280 γείνατο). The entry in LS(J) under γίγνομαι furnishes an instructive example of how an analytic presentation can stand the actual history of the Greek abstractive process on its head. The generic or fundamental sense is given as 'come into a new state of being'; from this universal is deduced the genus 'come into being', as opposed to εἶναι; and from this in turn are then deduced the various species 'be born', 'be produced', 'take place', and 'become'. No wonder that the editors, in order to illustrate the genus, have to resort to the philosophers Empedocles and Plato, while the Homeric instances begin to appear only in the species.

[7] *Iliad* I.57; cf. 9.29, 430, 693.

[8] Holt, p. 79, notes of the noun γένεσις, found only thrice in Homer and always in *Iliad* 14 (201, 246, 302), that Chantraine described its meaning as signifying a latent power' (puissance cachée) and translated it by 'principe vital' (cf. also the accompanying discussion of φύσις, found in Homer only at *Od.* 10.303). Holt argues for a close connection with γενετή or 'birth', and suggests γένεσις is a Greek 'invention' designed to express the sense of birth 'so far as it is beyond the reach of human experience, and thus different from γενετή which signifies a specific birth'. Here, one may say, is an instructive example of the beginning of 'proto-abstraction' in Homer. *Genesis* is still a 'birth' of some sort, i.e. still a process-word to which the actual memory of being born is attached. Yet it is this process thought of in typical fashion. So it hovers between 'birth' and 'origin'; the latter English term is 'Aristotelian' in its fixed conceptual colour, and 'vital principle' still more so.

[9] It is perhaps a pity that the issue of abstraction, or its absence, in Homer has become entangled with the controversy over the relative dating of the *Odyssey*. Webster (pp. 280-2) reviews the statistics on abstract words gathered by Cauer in *Grundfragen*, as they are used by Page in *Homeric Odyssey*, and feels compelled to correct Page's conclusions. The transition from the Homeric to the post-Homeric vocabulary and state of mind is far more significant than shading of difference, if any exists, between *Iliad* and *Odyssey*.

[10] *Iliad* 1.234 ff.

[11] Above, cap. 5.

[12] Cf. *Apology* 28b9 ff.

[13] Above, cap. 7, notes 19, 21.

[14] *Iliad* 2.484, 487.

[15] At 493 the minstrel in his own person makes regular announcement of the list to follow: (a) I will proceed to declare the captains of the ships and (the sum of) all the ships. (This line presumably belongs to the 'Ionian' stage of composition; cf. above, cap. 7, n. 19). He prefaces this announcement by a paragraph of nine lines in which (b) he invites the Muses to make declaration:

(c) for you are goddesses and are present and know all
(d) what we hear is only glory nor do we know at all
(e) who were the princes of the Greeks . . .
(f) I could not tell the tale of the number nor name them over
(g) even if I had ten tongues and mouths and voice unbreakable and brazen gut

(h) if you did not memorialise the numbers that came up under Troy.

This statement is not such as to divide human knowledge from divine or inspired knowledge (as argued by Dodds) for item (a) assumes the list to follow is the poet's, while (b) assumes it is the Muses' list, and (f) and (h) assume it is the joint list of both. (c) and (d) distinguish songs of great deeds from songs of information, assigning the former to the poet and the latter to the Muse, but we know from numerous Homeric contexts and from Hesiod (*Theog.* 100) that the former are just as much the Muse's gift as the latter; the difference between them is that the information is of a general sort, the fruit of a universal experience or 'presence', whereas the lay of great deeds is (by implication) more specific or limited. (h) stresses fact that this information is an act of recollection and record, and (g) stresses that for such a list the Muses' help has to be physical and psychological; reciting the list (and remembering it) takes enormous energy.

[16] *Iliad* 2.494 ff.

[17] Cf. cap. 7, n. 19.

[18] *Iliad* 2.577 ff., 587 ff., 686 ff., 699 ff., 721 ff.

[19] 685, 769 ff.

[20] Chadwick, vol. I, chapters 10, on 'Antiquarian Learning' in the epics, and 12, on 'Gnomic Poetry', avoids this assumption (p. 276: '. . . the encroachment of antiquarian interest upon the heroic story . . .' and p. 399: 'in Greece cultivation (of gnomic poetry) would seem to be later than that of heroic poetry').

[21] A striking parallel to this rule, as it is exhibited in the syntax and context of the Homeric Catalogue, is furnished by the presence of a catalogue of the tribes of Israel in the Song of Deborah (Judges 5). This very ancient epic song celebrates a memorable victory over the Canaanites by a combination of Hebrew tribes. But some of them stayed aloof. The minstrel's encomia, blended with reproaches at the expense of the 'neutrals', furnish occasion for the preservation in his song of the first available register of the Hebrew tribes and their location.

[22] This does not mean however that primitive epic is a chronicle, for the notion of proper sequence in time, which resists subjectivity on the part of the poet, is sophisticated (cf. Thucydides). Chronology depends in part on the mastery of time as an abstraction (cf. below, n. 27). Hence I remain doubtful of the thesis of Kakridis, *Homeric Researches*, p. 91 ff. (cited by Webster, p. 273), that the existence of earlier chronicle epics is a necessary presupposition for the 'dramatic' epic exemplified in the *Iliad*.

[23] *vid.* cap. 4, n. 12.

[24] *Od.* I.32-4; cf. 22.412-16; the passage is discussed by Nestlé, p. 24.

[25] Notopoulos, 'Parataxis' (p. 13): '. . . parataxis and the type of mind which expresses it are the regular forms of thought and expression before the classical period'; (p. 14): 'The foundation of the new criticism (sc. of oral poetry) must rest on the fact observed by students of the primitive mind that the interest is on the particular first and foremost instead of the whole.'

[26] *Iliad* I.11 ff.

[27] Zielinski points out that epic 'time' cannot admit of unfilled intervals where nothing happens and which the narrator can therefore leap over. Conversely,

any one event series once narrated completely fills up the available time space: heroic epic has no way of saying 'meanwhile'. Contemporary events have to be presented paratactically. The epic action is a stream, and you cannot stand on the bank and survey it to and fro. Lorimer (pp. 476-9) makes perceptive and very effective use of this thesis to support a unitarian conception of Homer (cf. also above, cap. 7, n. 19). Fraenkel's analysis (pp. 1-22) of the concept of time in early Greek literature offers a valuable supplement to Zielinski: the Homeric epos is innocent of any concept of time in the abstract; concretely, the idioms in which *chronos* appears denote periods of waiting or delay or doing nothing, as though it was through waiting that the idea of time was discovered (pp. 1-2); the epic depicts course of events in terms of a single stream; the 'day' (a concrete experience) is Homer's preferred symbol; it can be filled with any action (p. 5) in the *Iliad*, and with experience in the *Odyssey* (p. 7).

28 'The general distinction between imagination and intellect is that imagination presents to itself an object which it experiences as one and indivisible: whereas intellect goes beyond that single object and presents to itself a world of many such with relations of determinate kinds between them'—Collingwood, p. 252.

29 The new standards of fifth-century rationalism thus exposed inconsistencies within the poets which the teaching sophist might seek to reconcile, as in that paradigm of method presented (and parodied?) by Plato in the 'Simonides Interlude' in the *Protagoras*.

30 *Rep.* 10.603c4 ff.; above, notes 2, 3.

31 This is an oversimplification of a complex process, one fundamental aspect of which has been well denominated by Diels (quoted in Holt, p. 109): 'The verb signifies incidence of process generally, the substantive determines the typical situation; the former is viewed concretely, the latter abstractly. Here is a pattern of linguistic behaviour indicating that language proceeds from the perceptual to the conceptual. . . . In the course of this gradual advance of the substantival usage, as it supplants the verbal, prose emerges from poetry.' I would add for good measure that even the noun as it 'emerges' is still often more of a gerund, a doing or happening, than a phenomenon or thing. Abstraction is a mental process not available to examination except as we infer it from changing linguistic behaviour. Its linguistic tools include the coinage of new nouns (e.g. the 'action' nouns in —σις assigned by Holt to Ionian literature), the 'stretching' of old ones (e.g. *arete, cosmos, soma*), and finally the attempt to 'destroy' the noun altogether via the neuter singular (Snell, *Discovery*, cap. 10). These procedures as they occurred between Homer and Plato I hope to illustrate in a later volume.

32 *Rep.* 5.476c5 ff., Heraclitus B 1, 21.

II

THE NECESSITY OF PLATONISM

CHAPTER ELEVEN

Psyche or the Separation of the Knower
from the Known

AT some time towards the end of the fifth century before
Christ, it became possible for a few Greeks to talk about
their 'souls' as though they had selves or personalities
which were autonomous and not fragments of the atmosphere
nor of a cosmic life force, but what we might call entities or real
substances. At first this conception was within reach only of the
more sophisticated. There is evidence to show that as late as the
last quarter of the fifth century, in the minds of the majority of
men, the notion was not understood, and that in their ears the terms
in which it was expressed sounded bizarre.[1] Before the end of the
fourth century the conception was becoming part of the Greek
language and one of the common assumptions of Greek culture.

Scholarship has tended to connect this discovery with the life
and teaching of Socrates and to identify it with a radical change
which he introduced into the meaning of the Greek word *psyche*.[2]
In brief, instead of signifying a man's ghost or wraith, or a man's
breath or his life blood, a thing devoid of sense and self-consciousness, it came to mean 'the ghost that thinks', that is capable both
of moral decision and of scientific cognition, and is the seat of
moral responsibility, something infinitely precious, an essence
unique in the whole realm of nature.

In fact it is probably more accurate to say that while the discovery was affirmed and exploited by Socrates, it was the slow
creation of many minds among his predecessors and contem-

poraries. One thinks particularly of Heraclitus and Democritus.[3] Moreover, the discovery involved more than just the semantics of the word *psyche*. The Greek pronouns, both personal and reflexive, also began to find themselves in new syntactical contexts, used for example as objects of verbs of cognition, or placed in antithesis to the 'body' or 'corpse' in which the 'ego' was thought of as residing.[4] We confront here a change in the Greek language and in the syntax of linguistic usage and in the overtones of certain key words which is part of a larger intellectual revolution, which affected the whole range of the Greek cultural experience.[5] There is no need in this place to attempt a full documentation of it.[6] The main fact, that such a discovery occurred, has been accepted by historians. Our present business is to connect this discovery with that crisis in Greek culture which saw the replacement of an orally memorised tradition by a quite different system of instruction and education, and which therefore saw the Homeric state of mind give way to the Platonic. For this connection the essential documentation lies once more in Plato himself and most specifically in his *Republic*.

Let us recapitulate the educational experience of the Homeric and post-Homeric Greek. He is required as a civilised being to become acquainted with the history, the social organisation, the technical competence and the moral imperatives of his group. This group will in post-Homeric times be his city, but his city in turn is able to function only as a fragment of the total Hellenic world. It shares a consciousness in which he is keenly aware that he, as a Hellene, partakes. This over-all body of experience (we shall avoid the word 'knowledge') is incorporated in a rhythmic narrative or set of narratives which he memorises and which is subject to recall in his memory. Such is poetic tradition, essentially something he accepts uncritically, or else it fails to survive in his living memory. Its acceptance and retention are made psychologically possible by a mechanism of self-surrender to the poetic performance, and of self-identification with the situations and the stories related in the performance. Only when the spell is fully effective can his mnemonic powers be fully mobilised. His receptivity to the tradition has thus, from the standpoint of inner psychology, a degree of automatism which however is counterbalanced by a direct and unfettered capacity for action, in accordance with the paradigms he has absorbed. 'His not to reason why.'

This picture of his absorption in the tradition is over-simplified. There are clear signs in Homer himself[7] that the Greek mind would one day reach out in search of a different kind of experience. And any estimate of the mental condition of Homeric man will depend upon the point of view from which the estimate is made. From the standpoint of a developed self-conscious critical intelligence he was a part of all he had seen and heard and remembered. His job was not to form individual and unique convictions but to retain tenaciously a precious hoard of exemplars. These were constantly present with him in his acoustic reflexes and also visually imagined before his mind's eye. In short, he went along with the tradition. His mental condition, though not his character, was one of passivity, of surrender, and a surrender accomplished through the lavish employment of the emotions and of the motor reflexes.

When confronted with an Achilles, we can say, here is a man of strong character, definite personality, great energy and forceful decision, but it would be equally true to say, here is a man to whom it has not occurred, and to whom it cannot occur, that he has a personality apart from the pattern of his acts. His acts are responses to his situation, and are governed by remembered examples of previous acts by previous strong men. The Greek tongue therefore, as long as it is the speech of men who have remained in the Greek sense 'musical' and have surrendered themselves to the spell of the tradition, cannot frame words to express the conviction that 'I' am one thing and the tradition is another; that 'I' can stand apart from the tradition and examine it; that 'I' can and should break the spell of its hypnotic force; and that 'I' should divert some at least of my mental powers away from memorisation and direct them instead into channels of critical inquiry and analysis. The Greek ego in order to achieve that kind of cultural experience which after Plato became possible and then normal must stop identifying itself successively with a whole series of polymorphic vivid narrative situations; must stop re-enacting the whole scale of the emotions, of challenge, and of love, and hate and fear and despair and joy, in which the characters of epic become involved. It must stop splitting itself up into an endless series of moods. It must separate itself out and by an effort of sheer will must rally itself to the point where it can say 'I am I, an autonomous little universe of my own, able to speak, think and act in independence of what I happen to remember'. This amounts to accepting the premise that there is a 'me', a 'self', a 'soul', a consciousness which is self-governing and which discovers the reason for action in itself rather than in imitation of the poetic experience. The doctrine of the autonomous psyche is the counterpart of the rejection of the oral culture.

Such a discovery of self could be only of the thinking self. The 'personality', as first invented by the Greeks and then presented to posterity for contemplation, could not be that nexus of motor responses, unconscious reflexes, and passions and emotions which had been mobilised for countless time in the service of the mnemonic process. On the contrary, it was precisely these which proved an obstacle to the realisation of a self-consciousness emancipated from the condition of an oral culture. The *psyche* which slowly asserts itself in independence of the poetic performance and the poetised tradition had to be the reflective, thoughtful, critical psyche, or it could be nothing. Along with the discovery of the soul, Greece in Plato's day and just before Plato had to discover something else—the activity of sheer thinking. Scholarship has already called attention in this crucial period to changes that were occurring in the significance of the words denoting various kinds of mental activity. Their complete documentation need not be treated here. It may suffice to point to one symptom among many; namely that the same sources which testify to a sort of virtuosity in the use of the words for 'soul' and 'self' testify also to the same kind of virtuosity in the words for 'thinking' and 'thought'.[8] Something novel is in the air, not later than the last quarter of the fifth century before Christ, and this novelty might be described as a discovery of intellection.

One way of expressing this novelty would be to say that a psychic mechanism which exploited memorisation through association was being replaced, at least among a sophisticated minority, by a mechanism of reasoned calculation. We cannot correctly say that the imaginative powers were yielding to the critical, though this, in the Alexandrian Age, seemed to be the practical result for Hellenism. The term imagination as it is used today seeks to combine the Homeric and the Platonic states of mind in a single synthesis. Another and more correct way of stating the effect of the revolution, if we are to employ modern terms, as we must, would be to say that it now became possible to identify the 'subject' in relation to that 'object' which the 'subject' knows. The problem of the 'object', the datum, the knowledge that is known, we shall explore in the next chapter. Here we concentrate on the new possibility of realising that in all situations there is a 'subject', a 'me', whose separate identity is the first premise to be accepted before we pass on to any further statements or conclusions about what the situation is.

We are now in a position more clearly to understand one reason for Plato's opposition to the poetic experience. It was his self-imposed task, building to be sure on the work of predecessors, to establish two main postulates: that of the personality which thinks and knows, and that of a body of knowledge which is thought about and known. To do this he had to destroy the immemorial habit of self-identification with the oral tradition. For this had merged the personality with the tradition, and made a self-conscious separation from it impossible. This means that his polemics against the poets are not a side issue, nor an eccentric piece of Puritanism, nor a response to some temporary fashion in Greek educational practice. They are central to the establishment of his own system. Within the confines of this chapter let us take up the pertinent documentation of his *Republic*, as it reveals and illuminates the direct connection in his own mind between the rejection of the poets on one hand and the affirmation of the psychology of the autonomous individual on the other.

Soon after the beginning of Book Three, his programme for censoring the stories told by the poets is concluded. He has so far been dealing, as we recall, with content (*logoi*) and now he proposes to take up *lexis*,[9] the 'medium' by which the content is communicated. At this point he introduces the conception of *mimesis* and at first sight he seems content to use the term, as we have earlier pointed out, in a purely stylistic sense to distinguish dramatic impersonation from straight description. But when he asserts that the artist who employs the former in effect 'likens himself' and not simply his words to another, and is in this sense a mimer, we realise that he is assuming a condition in the artist which must involve psychological identification with his subject matter. It is no longer merely a question of styling. In fact, as we have seen, his argument as it develops the theme of identification seems to draw little distinction between the artist, the performer, and finally the pupil who learns the poetry from either the artist or the performer. For it is surely the pupil who is to become the future guardian, and as Plato's argument develops, it focuses more and more on the psychological protection of the guardian during the course of his education. He stresses the profound effect which "imitations starting in early youth" can have upon "characters" and warns against the habit of "likening oneself to the inferior" (model). The precise effects which are registered upon the pupil's personality are not analysed in detail, but in general their impact is stated to be one of dispersal and distraction, of loss of focus and moral direction. This suggestion is first supported by appealing to the previous doctrine in Book Two of natural specialisation. The poetic mimer cannot select his one proper speciality for imitation; he is continually involved with a series of identifications, all of them inconsistent. When the medium used is expository rather than mimetic, the shifts and changes are small. That Plato's words apply to the content, with its variety of character and situation, and to the response of the pupil, is indicated a few sentences later: 'we do not want our guardian to be a "two-aspect man" nor a "many-aspect man" nor do we want an artist who can become "any kind of person".' Then he leaves these matters and passes on to problems of mode and melody.

Later he resumes and summarises what for the young guardian should be the general objective of his education. He has to be 'an effective guardian of himself and of the music he has been learning, presenting himself rhythmically well-organised and harmonised'.[10] This comes near to a conception of an inner stability of the personality, self-organised and autonomous, a stability not possible under the existing practice of poetic education. But it is noteworthy that in this, the first programme of educational reform offered in Books Two and Three, the conception of the autonomous personality is not put forward and defended as such. True, the *Republic*, even in the earlier books, can use the term *psyche* in the Socratic sense. We should hardly expect otherwise in a thinker whose thinking begins within the Socratic orbit. But a systematic explication of the term and the doctrine behind it is reserved for Book Four, at a point where the cardinal virtues, already defined in a social context as attributes of the political community, are now to be defined as attributes of the individual personality. Here, in a context divorced from the problem of imitation, Plato first makes formal use of the assumption that the individual man has a *psyche* comprising three 'forms' which are correspondingly found in the three classes in the state.[11] He warns however against committing ourselves to the notion that this means that the *psyche* is divisible into real parts. Its three divisions have a convenience which is apparently descriptive only.[12] It does however have powers or capacities corresponding to our power of 'learning', to our 'spirit' (or 'will' ?) and to our 'appetition' or 'desire'.[13] The fundamental distinction to be drawn lies between the calculative or rational, and the appetitive capacities, with spirit or will lying between, potentially the ally of either.[14] He then, using this descriptive mechanism, states the psychological doctrine which is to support his moral doctrine. Spirit or will is properly the ally of the calculative reason. With its help the task of reason is to control the appetitive instincts and bring the whole *psyche* into a harmonised and unified condition, in which the virtue of each faculty, demonstrated in the performance of its proper role within its proper confines, is united with its fellows into a condition of over-all 'justice'. This is the true inner morality of the soul and as Plato sums up, he recalls and now explicates his previous description[15] of the guardian who has won self-mastery:

> Righteousness pertains to the inner action not the outer, to oneself and to the elements of the self, restricting the specific elements in one's self to their respective roles, forbidding the types in the *psyche* to get mixed up in one another's business; requiring a man to make a proper disposition of his several properties and to assume command of himself and to organise himself and become a friend of himself . . . becoming in all respects a single person instead of many. . . .[16]

We are justified in calling this a doctrine of the autonomous personality, one which self-consciously rallies its own powers in order to impose upon them an inner organisation, the inspiration for which is self-generated and self-discovered.

When we read Plato, we can sometimes be convinced that there was no salvation outside of society, while at other times it is the kingdom within man which is all-sufficient. The *Republic* is bifocal in its emphasis. In the present passage at least the philosopher speaks as though, if justice were founded within one's own soul, it would be occupying the only entity which exists beyond time and place and circumstance. This, when he wrote, was a very new conception for Greece. It is put forward in this place with only indirect reference to the problems raised by poetic 'imitation', or, as we have interpreted it, psychological identification. The connection is there, for Plato's description of this subject who has become 'one person' instead of many recalls his previous description of that condition proper to the young guardian who has had the proper kind of education, and has escaped the dangers of *mimesis*.

The next stage in the unfolding of Plato's psychology comes only in Book Seven. He has in the meantime confronted us with society's need to be governed not simply by guardians but by intellectuals, the philosopher-kings. What is the difference? It lies in the crucial distinction between the average experience of average men and a knowledge of the Forms; between the kind of mind which accepts and absorbs the passing show uncritically, and the intelligence which has been trained to grasp formulas and categories which lie behind the panorama of experience. The parables of the Sun, the Line and the Cave have been offered as paradigms which shall illuminate the relationship between ideal knowledge on the one hand and empirical experience on the other, and shall suggest to us the ascent of man through education from the life of the senses towards the life of the reasoned intelligence.

And what then, asks Plato, is the process, properly understood, that we name education? Not the implanting of new knowledge in the *psyche*. Rather there is a faculty (*dynamis*) in the *psyche*, an organ which every man uses in the learning process, and it is this innate faculty which, like a physical eye, must be converted towards new objects. Higher education is simply the technique of conversion of this organ. 'Thinking' is a 'function' (*arete*) of the *psyche* supreme above all others; it is indestructible, but it has to be converted and refocused in order to become serviceable.[17]

In Book Four Plato had sought a descriptive outline of the competing impulses and drives or 'faculties' (*dynameis*) in the *psyche*, which would at the same time not compromise its essential unity and absolute autonomy. Here the conception of that autonomy is now elevated to a plane where the soul attains its full self-realisation in the power to think and to know. This is its supreme faculty; in the last resort its only one. Man is 'a thinking reed'.

And what is to be the *mathema* or object of study which shall produce this effect of conversion?[18] As he seeks the answer to this question and proposes 'number and calculation', as the first item in his curriculum, Plato drops into a linguistic usage which re-affirms, over and over again, the conception of the *psyche* as the seat of free autonomous reflection and cogitation. It is the learning process associated with arithmetic which 'leads to thought pro-cesses'. Sense experience *per se* 'fails to challenge the thought process to undertake inquiry' and 'the *psyche* of most men is not compelled to put a question to the thought process'.[19] Plato does not here mean that *psyche* and thought process are distinct, for a little later he speaks of 'the *psyche*, caught in a dilemma', asking questions of the senses, and again 'the *psyche* challenges calculation and thought process to undertake examination'. There are situations where sense impressions are contradictory. It is these which 'offer challenge to the intellect and stimulate thought pro-cess' so that 'the *psyche* in its dilemma sets moving the thought process in itself'.[20]

In this way, that autonomous self-governing personality defined in Book Four becomes symbolised as the power to think, to calculate, to cogitate, and to know, in total distinction from the capacity to see, to hear, and to feel. In Book Ten, as Plato at last returns to the problem of poetic *mimesis*, we discover how in-timate in his own mind is the connection between this problem and the doctrine of the autonomous *psyche* which is able to think.

In Book Three the mimetic process had not been totally rejected; a degree of identification was possibly useful to the pupil in primary education if it helped him to imitate models which were morally sound and useful. Even so, Plato could not help suggesting that there was something psychologically un-sound about the mimetic process as such.

But now, before reaching Book Ten, he has expressed in full the doctrine of the autonomous personality and identified the essence of the personality with the processes of reflection and cogitation. He is now therefore in a position[21] totally to reject the whole mimetic process as such. He has to propose that the Greek mind find an entirely new basis for its education. Hence the

SEPARATION OF KNOWER FROM KNOWN 207

extreme position in the matter of the arts put forward in Book
Ten, so far from being a piece of eccentricity or a reply to some
fleeting fashion in education, becomes the logical and inevitable
climax to the systematic doctrine of the *Republic*.

Roughly the first two-thirds[22] of the attack is levelled at the character of the content of the poetised statement. The problem here
is epistemological, and we shall come to it in our next chapter. It
is met by using presuppositions about the character of knowledge
and of truth which had been laid down in Books Six and Seven,
and which are comprised within the so-called Theory of Forms.

Plato's argument, thus armed, and having disposed of the
problem of poetry's content, turns upon[23] the character of the
poetic performance as an educational institution and renews that
attack which he had launched in Book Three. But now the
victory has to be total. Since he is now equipped, and has now
equipped his reader, with the doctrine of the autonomous
personality and identified it as the seat of rational thought, he is in
a position to re-examine *mimesis* from the basis of this doctrine,
and he finds the two wholly incompatible. For the imitative
process already described in Book Three as 'making yourself like
somebody else' is now disclosed with compelling force to be a
'surrender' of one's self, a 'following-along' while we 'identify'
with the emotions of others; it is a 'manipulation' of our *ethe*.[24]
He even includes a reference to the fact that these experiences are
'recollections';[25] that is, the task of the poetic education is to
memorise and recall. To this pathology of identification Plato
now opposes the 'polity in oneself',[26] the city of man's own soul,
and affirms as he had in Book Three the absolute necessity of
building an inner self-consistency. This becomes possible only if
we reject the whole process of poetic identification. And this
identification is pleasurable; it appeals to the unconscious
instinct. It means the surrender to a spell.[27] Plato's description
cannot but recall the terms in which Hesiod had first described the
psychology of the reflexes which assist memorisation. Plato
himself is well aware that he is entering the lists against a whole

cultural tradition. That is why his peroration ends with a challenge to man to resist the temptations not only of power, wealth, and pleasure, but of poetry herself.[28] The appeal translated into terms of modern cultural conditions sounds absurd. Plato was not given to absurdity.

Did this conception of the autonomous rational personality derive from a previous rejection of the spell of oral memorisation, or did it precipitate this rejection? Which was cause and which was effect? The question is not answerable. The two phenomena in the history of the Greek mind are different ways of looking at the results of a single revolution; they are formulas which complement each other. One is entitled to ask however, given the immemorial grip of the oral method of preserving group tradition, how a self-consciousness could ever have been created. If the educational system which transmitted the Hellenic mores had indeed relied on the perpetual stimulation of the young in a kind of hypnotic trance, to use Plato's language, how did the Greeks ever wake up?

The fundamental answer must lie in the changing technology of communication. Refreshment of memory through written signs enabled a reader to dispense with most of that emotional identification by which alone the acoustic record was sure of recall. This could release psychic energy, for a review and re-arrangement of what had now been written down, and of what could be seen as an object and not just heard and felt. You could as it were take a second look at it. And this separation of yourself from the remembered word may in turn lie behind the growing use in the fifth century of a device often accepted as peculiar to Socrates but which may well have been a general device for challenging the habit of poetic identification and getting people to break with it. This was the method of dialectic, not necessarily that developed form of logical chain-reasoning found in Plato's dialogues, but the original device in its simplest form, which consisted in asking a speaker to repeat himself and explain what he had meant. In Greek, the words for explain, say, and mean could coincide. That is, the original function of the dialectical question was simply to force the speaker to repeat a statement already made, with the underlying assumption that there was something unsatisfactory about the statement, and it had better be re-phrased.[29] Now, the statement in question, if it concerned important matters of cultural tradition and morals, would be a poetised one, using the imagery and often the rhythms of poetry. It was one which invited you to identify with some emotively effective example, and to repeat it over again. But to say, 'What do you mean? Say that again', abruptly disturbed the pleasurable complacency felt in the poetic formula or the image. It meant using different words and these equivalent words would fail to be poetic; they would be prosaic. As the question was asked, and the alternative prosaic formula was attempted, the imaginations of speaker and teacher were offended, and the dream so to speak was disrupted, and some unpleasant effort of calculative reflection was substituted. In short, the dialectic, a weapon we suspect to have been employed in this form by a whole group of intellectuals in the last half of the fifth century, was a weapon for arousing the consciousness from its dream language and stimulating it to think abstractly. As it did this, the conception of 'me thinking about Achilles' rather than 'me identifying with Achilles' was born.

Thus the method was one means of separating the personality of the artist from the content of the poem. Hence it was that in his *Apology*, which whatever its historicity certainly attempts a summation of the Socratic life and of Socrates' historical signifi-cance as Plato saw them, the disciple represents his master's famous mission as in the second instance a resort to the poets to ask them what their poems said.[30] The poets are his victims because in their keeping reposes the Greek cultural tradition, the fundamental 'thinking' (we can use this word in only a non-Platonic sense) of the Greeks in moral, social and historical matters. Here was the tribal encyclopedia, and to ask what it was saying amounted to a demand that it be said differently, non-poetically, non-rhythmically, and non-imagistically.

It is of some interest in this connection to note that when Plato in his own elaborate development of Socraticism proceeds to construct the outline of the actual curriculum of his Academy, he too faces the same problem of awakening the prisoners in the cave from their long illusion. The first subject on the curriculum proposed for this purpose is arithmetic. This takes the place of the Socratic interrupting question. Why arithmetic, if not because it is a primary example of a mental act which is not one of recollection and repetition, but of problem-solving? To establish a numerical relationship is to achieve a small leap of the mind. Plato by number and calculation did not mean just 'counting' but 'counting up'. He is not asking for a repetition of the same series of symbols in fixed order, but rather the establishment of simple ratios and equations. This cannot be a mimetic process; it involves not identification with a series or list of phenomena, but the very reverse. One has to achieve personal separation from the series in order to look at it objectively and measure it.

That Plato thought of this discipline as some kind of equivalent for the elementary dialectic of Socrates is shown by the fact that he links arithmetical thinking with the uncovering of 'mental dilemma' (*aporia*),[31] and this in turn is created by the occurrence of contradiction in the sense data. In Book Ten he finds the same kind of contradiction in the poetised description of phenomena. The soul is puzzled, disturbed, and in malaise.[32] 'Arithmetic', the prototype of all calculation, is then challenged to solve the dilemma. This means a challenge to the autonomous *psyche* to take over the sense experience and the language of sense experience in order to remodel them.

So it is that the long sleep of man is interrupted and his self-consciousness, separating itself from the lazy play of the endless saga-series of events, begins to think and to be thought of, 'itself of itself', and as it thinks and is thought, man in his new inner isolation confronts the phenomenon of his own autonomous personality and accepts it.

NOTES

[1] *Clouds* 94, 319, 415, 420, 714, 719; *Birds* 1555 ff.

[2] J. Burnet, 'Socratic Conception of the Soul'; A. E. Taylor, *Socrates*, pp. 35-88; F. M. Cornford, *Before and After Socrates*. The summary of the Socratic mission at *Apology* 29d8 reads: χρημάτων μὲν οὐκ αἰσχύνῃ ἐπιμελούμενος ὅπως σοι ἔσται ὡς πλεῖστα, καὶ δόξης καὶ τιμῆς, φρονήσεως δὲ καὶ ἀληθείας καὶ τῆς ψυχῆς ὅπως ὡς βελτίστη ἔσται οὐκ ἐπιμελῇ οὐδὲ φροντίζεις;

[3] For Heraclitus, psyche remains the Homeric 'breath', whether fiery or smoky, but at least three of his sayings imply that this breath in the individual is the seat or source of his intelligence: B107 (ghosts that are 'barbarian'); 117 ('a drunk man has a wet ghost'); 118 ('the dry ghost is the most intelligent'—reading αὔη ψυχὴ σοφωτάτη). By Democritus psyche is distinguished as the seat of intelligence (Diodor. 1.8.7 = *FVS* B5, 1: ἀγχίνοια ψυχῆς, and B 31: *sophia* is the *iatrike* of *psyche*); and as seat of happiness (170, 171); of moral choice (72 and 264); of cheerfulness or its opposite (191); of grief (290). It is likewise opposed to the body as superior to inferior or as controller to controlled (37, 159, 187).

[4] *Clouds* 242, 385, 478, 695, 737, 765, 842, 886, 1454-5; cf. *Phaedo* 115c6: οὐ πείθω, ὦ ἄνδρες, Κρίτωνα, ὡς ἐγώ εἰμι οὗτος Σωκράτης, ὁ νυνὶ διαλεγόμενος καὶ διατάττων ἕκαστον τῶν λεγομένων, ἀλλ᾽ οἴεται με ἐκεῖνον εἶναι ὃν ὄψεται ὀλίγον ὕστερον νεκρόν, καὶ ἐρωτᾷ δὴ πῶς με θάπτῃ.

[5] The assumptions expressed in the *Phaedo* passage (previous n.) are the exact reverse of those that lie behind the language of the *Iliad*, I.3-4: πολλὰς δ᾽ ἰφθίμους ψυχὰς Ἄϊδι προΐαψεν ἡρώων, αὐτοὺς δὲ ἑλώρια τεῦχε κύνεσσιν. Cf. *Iliad* 23.103-4: ὢ πόποι, ἦ ῥά τίς ἐστι καὶ εἰν Ἀΐδαο δόμοισι ψυχὴ καὶ εἴδωλον, ἀτὰρ φρένες οὐκ ἔνι πάμπαν. This does not mean that Homeric man was a shadowy creature, unsure of himself or his existence. On the contrary, since the emotions which accompany the senses are the foundation of all consciousness, and since, as these are intensified and enriched by their own expression, consciousness is intensified also (cf. Collingwood, cap. 10), an Achilles can 'live fully' as a human being without benefit of any Socratic belief that he must 'tend his soul'. The gulf between the two men is bridged by a transition from the imaginative consciousness to the intellectual self-consciousness.

[6] The discovery of self which is ascribed to the lyric poets by Snell (*Discovery*, cap. 3: 'The Rise of the Individual in Early Greek Lyric') is undocumented so far as vocabulary is concerned.

[7] Perhaps particularly in the *Odyssey*.

[8] *Clouds* 94, 137, 155, 225, 229, 233, 740, 762, 950; 695, 700 and below, n. 17 .

[9] *Rep.* 392c ff. What follows in our text is a brief recapitulation of the argument of cap. 2, pp. 20 ff.

[10] 413e3-4.

[11] 435b.

[12] 435c4-d8.

[13] 436a9-10 μανθάνομεν μὲν ἑτέρῳ, θυμούμεθα δὲ ἄλλῳ τῶν ἐν ἡμῖν, ἐπιθυμοῦμεν δ᾽ αὖ τρίτῳ τινὶ κτλ.

14 440e–441a.
15 Above, n. 10.
16 443c9 ff.
17 518e2 ἡ δὲ τοῦ φρονῆσαι παντὸς μᾶλλον θειοτέρου τινὸς τυγχάνει, ὡς ἔοικεν, οὖσα, ὃ τὴν μὲν δύναμιν οὐδέποτε ἀπόλλυσιν, κτλ. Since φρονεῖν, like other terms describing psychic process (cf. Snell, *Discovery*, cap. 1, where however the phren- phron- words are not treated), had hitherto enjoyed a wide and from our standpoint ambiguous range of signification (pride, purpose, decision, intention, awareness, state of mind; cf. also Aristotle, *de An.* 3.3, and Fraenkel's *Agamemnon* 11.105, as cited by Holt, p. 60; the formula γιγνώσκω, φρονέω, τά γε δὴ νοέοντι κελεύεις occurs at *Od.* 16.136, 17.193, 281, on which Merry notes that 'there is not much shade of difference between the three verbs'), it may be inferred that here Plato deliberately narrows the verb (or extends it, depending on the point of view) to the signification of sheer thinking or intellection, a sense not substantiated with certainty in any previous author except Heraclitus B.113 (cf. Kirk's discussion, pp. 60–1; B.112 and B.116, as emended by Diels, would indeed anticipate Plato, but Kirk, p. 56, regards both as 'weak paraphrases' of B.113; as for Parmenides B.16.3 and Emped. B.108.2, the richer Homeric sense, a complex of thought feeling and perception, is probably still intended by both, though Kirk argues otherwise for Parm). Adam's note *ad loc.* says 'The meaning of φρόνησις has changed since 4.433b in conformity with the intellectualism of Books 6 and 7'. This infers that the history of φρονεῖν is linked with that of φρόνησις, and raises the question of whether, even at *Rep.* 6.505b6, the *phronesis* which is named by οἱ κομψότεροι as the *summum bonum* may not be 'intellection' (the process) rather than 'wisdom' or 'knowledge' (the objectified product). In that case, at 505c2, φρόνησιν γὰρ αὐτό φασιν εἶναι ἀγαθοῦ means 'thinking about the good', and Plato's objection, that prior 'comprehension' (σύνεσις 505c3) of the good is required in order to be able to 'think' about it becomes more plausible. Moreover, the fifth-century history of *phronesis* and other phron-words suggests that the present passage provides a better index to the character of the original Socratic quest than is furnished in earlier books of the *Republic*. *Phronesis* (cf. also on *mimesis*, above, cap. 3, n. 22, and on *genesis* above, cap. 10, n. 8) is an action noun originating in Ionic prose, before its entry into Attic (Holt, pp. 117–20, who cites Her. B.2 and Democritus B.119, 193, and then Sophocles, twice, and Euripides, once). Holt translates it as 'intelligence' and, in Her., as 'faculté de penser'. It thus represents (a) an attempt at abstraction but (b) an abstraction of a process or faculty. Holt explains this type of noun in—σις as an invention designed to denominate general traits shared by a class of actions regardless of whether they are 'actual' or not (réel versus irréel). This is a philosopher's or thinker's motive. Previous vocabulary had limited itself to denominating specific action. The evidence of Old Comedy (cf. Denniston, p. 120, for instances of phron-words, to which add the chorus of *phrontistae* in the *Connos* of Ameipsias, and 'miscarriage of a *phrontis*' in the *Clouds* line 137) points to the dawning awareness of intellection as a mental phenomenon in the sophistic-Socratic period, and to the attempt to express the notion by exploiting these

terms. Hence *Apol.* 29e1-2 (above, n. 2) should be translated 'You do not give any concentration (*ἐπιμελῇ*) nor thought (*φροντίζεις*) to thinking (*φρονήσεως*) and truth and the psyche, to put it in perfect condition (*ὅπως ὡς βελτίστη ἔσται*)' where the improvement of the psyche (cf. also 30b2) is not primarily ethical but intellectual. Its powers of intellection must be maximised (from which would follow ethical improvement). The passage in *Rep.* 7 (considered in our text) is thus to be understood simply as an expansion of the Socratic enterprise as stated in the *Apology*. To 'put the psyche in best condition' is to realise its *arete*, which equals *τὸ φρονεῖν* or *φρόνησις*. Per contra, as Adam notes, phronesis, as already used at *Rep.* 4.433b, has connoted intelligence as applied to practical politics— *εὐβουλία*. The above throws doubt on Jaeger's statement (p. 81, à propos of the usage of *phronesis* in the *Protrepticus*) that 'for a long time it had been split into two systems, one predominantly practical and economic, the other moral and religious . . . it was then taken over by Plato . . . and became pure theoretic reason, the opposite of *what it had been* in Socrates' practical sphere' (italics mine). Jaeger is undoubtedly correct in emphasising the contribution made by *E.N.* 6.5 ff. to the establishment of the concept of *phronesis* as 'practical wisdom' or 'prudence', but it would seem that the previous career of the word had been more complicated. Originally taken up by Socraticism in the sophistic-Ionic sense of 'intellection', it was (a) retained by Socratics in this sense as they explored the laws, linguistic, epistemological and psychological, of intellection and also (b) extended (by Plato, or earlier? Xenophon is an unreliable witness) specifically to *applied* political and ethical thinking, as expressing the most important or at least pressing use of the faculty, and identified with the kind of intellectualist virtue proper to a guardian, as at *Rep.* 4.433b (c) this split in application, which may have remained implicit in Plato, was then rationalised by Xenocrates (cf. Burnet, *Ethics*, p. 261 note). (d) The practical application was then selected by Aristotle and its definition amplified, and the term was thereafter confined within these limits. That the sense of 'political sagacity' or 'prudence' may not be pre-Platonic is perhaps indicated by the parallel case of *phronimos*, which in the sense of 'politically sagacious', 'prudent' (as opposed to 'in one's senses', Soph. *Aj.* 259, or 'intelligent', *OT* 692, *El.* 1058), does not seem to be earlier than the fourth century (Eurip. *frag.* 52.9 cited in this sense by *LSJ* is of dubious meaning, and its authenticity rightly doubted by Nauck). Hence when Aristotle says, *E.N.* 6.5.5 (justifying his own definition of *phronesis*), 'we think of Pericles and his like as *phronimoi*, in virtue of their capacity to objectify their own good and that of men generally, and we assume that the *oikonomikoi* and the *politikoi* belong in this category', he is appealing to a verbal usage which would not readily have been understood in the Periclean age itself, but one which developed as the philosophers discussed in retrospect and analysed the statecraft of that period. The editors of *LSJ* s.v. *φρονεῖν,*, by equating 'understanding' with 'prudence' as the basic sense of the verb, indicate the influence of the *Ethics*.

[18] 521c10.

[19] *νόησις* 523a1, b1, d4.

[20] 524a7 *ἀναγκαῖον . . . τὴν ψυχὴν ἀπορεῖν.* 524b4 *πειρᾶται λογισμόν τε καὶ*

νόησιν ψυχὴ παρακαλοῦσα ἐπισκοπεῖν ... 524d3 ... παρακλητικὰ τῆς διανοίας
... ἐγερτικὰ τῆς νοήσεως ... 524e4 ἀναγκάζοιτ᾽ἂν ἐν αὐτῷ ψυχὴ ἀπορεῖν καὶ
ζητεῖν, κινοῦσα ἐν ἑαυτῇ τὴν ἔννοιαν.
   21 Cf. 10.595a7 ἐναργέστερον ... φαίνεται, ἐπειδὴ χωρὶς ἕκαστα διῄρηται τὰ
τῆς ψυχῆς εἴδη.
   22 595a–603d.
   23 605c–608b.
   24 605d3 ἐνδόντες ἡμᾶς αὐτοὺς ἑπόμεθα συμπάσχοντες.
   25 604d8 τὰς ἀναμνήσεις ... τοῦ πάθους.
   26 Above, cap. 1, n. 4.
   27 607c6 σύνισμεν γε ἡμῖν αὐτοῖς κηλουμένοις ὑπ᾽αὐτῆς; cf. c8.
   28 608b4 ff.
   29 This rephrasing will substitute for a poetised image of act or event (above,
cap. 10) a paraphrase thereof, which will yield a descriptive statement or proposition of some kind, which then becomes the basis of what Robinson (p. 51)
calls 'Socrates' primary questions', namely, 'Is X Y?' or 'What is X?'.
   30 Apol. 22b4.
   31 524a7, e5; cf. n. 20.
   32 602c12 πᾶσά τις ταραχὴ δήλη ὑμῖν ἐνοῦσα αὕτη ἐν τῇ ψυχῇ; d6 τὸ μετρεῖν
καὶ ἀριθμεῖν καὶ ἱστάναι βοήθειαι χαριέστεραι πρὸς αὐτὰ ἐφάνησαν.

CHAPTER TWELVE

The Recognition of the Known as Object

T HE concept of the autonomous personality was not one that could be achieved in the abstract as though it were a scientific solution to a problem in external nature. True, it was a discovery which once made could be generalised as pertaining to all human kind, but in the making of it the thinker could proceed only by personal introspection of himself. For any Greek of this period, from the time of Heraclitus to that of Plato, it was a personal and intimate discovery. The exhortation to know thyself became a motto approved not only by the Delphic aphorism but by the dialectic of Socrates.

It would have been theoretically possible, one can suppose, for Greek thinkers, once they were armed with this postulate and the language in which to express it, to have developed a philosophy of total subjectivism in which 'I' in my fully realised condition of self-consciousness and inner freedom become the universe, a sort of existentialist centre of reality supplying the source of all moral imperatives and all criteria of true and false. There were two obstacles to this occurring, or perhaps a single obstacle under two guises. It was inherent in the temperament of the Greek people that they should take nature and the external environment seriously. Their plastic arts demonstrate this conclusively, for while the geometric beginnings are the product of an inner vision which could stress the mental design at the expense of the external phenomena, the succeeding development through the archaic, classical and Hellenistic periods shows with equal force the profound respect with which the artist confronted the 'facts', so to speak, outside himself and sought to imitate these facts even as he retained inner control over them. Correspondingly in philosophy, as the existence of the self was progressively clarified, there occurred a parallel and simultaneous effort to bring the self into relation with what is not self. The existence of the subject in short, for the Greek, came to presume the existence of the object.

The *Republic* remains faithful to this bifocal objective when, after asserting and describing the organisation of the autonomous *psyche* in Book Four, it proceeds in Book Seven to identify the proper faculty of this *psyche* as the activity of 'thinking'. For if you think, you have to think about something.[1] If you reflect and calculate, there must be data outside your thinking for you to master and to organise. Correspondingly while in Book Four[2] Plato can perhaps incautiously suggest that justice within the soul, the justice of inner conviction, is enough, he later abandons any contentment with this intellectual position. Only a just society can ever make possible the existence of the fully just man; and for the just society the patterns exist beyond man himself in the structure of the cosmos.

Yet admitting the proper virtue of the soul is to think and to know, and that thinking must have an object, why could not this object still be the self? As we have said, the great respect for the social and natural environment prevented this solipsist solution. But it was equally forbidden by the character of the mental and cultural revolution which had brought the soul so to speak to birth. What was Greece, or rather the Greek intellectual leadership, revolting from? Plato has supplied the answer; it was the immemorial habit of self-identification with the poem. This psychological identification had been the necessary instrument of memorisation. And why was memorisation essential if not to preserve the private and public law of the group, its history and traditions, its social and family imperatives? If therefore the habit was to be given up, if the knowing self was to be isolated as subject, it would follow that the object known by the subject became the content of the tribal encyclopedia.

'I' am therefore to be separated from the poem. If this is done, does not the poem then become the object of my knowledge?

No, for the poem's structure, rhythm, syntax, and plot, its very substance, have all been designed for a situation in which 'I' do not exist. They provide the machinery of self-identification, the magic of the spell, the drug that hypnotises. Once I end my absorption in the poem, I have ended the poem too. Its structure must change and become a re-arrangement of language suitable to express not a performance or a re-enactment but something that coolly and calmly and reflectively is 'known'.

What kind of change must come over the poem which shall conform to the change that has come over me? What will make it an object of my knowledge? Its function has been to record and preserve in the living memory the public and private law of the group, and much else. Where was this to be found in the poem? As such, it did not exist. The contents of the encyclopedia can be identified by retrospective analysis, as they were in Chapter Four, but in the epic story they are implicit, not explicit. They appear only as acts and events performed by important persons or happening to important persons. This was inevitable as long as the law was to live in memory. For memory could identify effectively only with acts and events. But now that it becomes possible to know the law, the act and event become irrelevant. They should be discarded; they are the accidents and incidentals of place, time and circumstance. What we require to think about and to know is 'the law itself'.

So it must be somehow isolated from its setting in the great story and set 'itself by itself' and identified 'per se'. It must be 'abstracted' in the literal sense of that word. The Greek for this object, thus achieved by an effort of isolation, is 'the (thing) in itself',[3] precisely the equivalent of the Latin *per se*. And so the Platonic pages are filled with the demand that we concentrate not on the things of the city but on the city itself, not on a just or unjust act but on justice itself by itself, not on noble actions but on nobility, not on the beds and tables of the heroes but on the idea of bed *per se*.

This simple idiom in short is designed to crystallise in the first instance that initial and essential act of isolation which separates a law or topic or principle or concept from its instances, or abstracts it from its context. But how is this done? You can take a word, justice, city, courage, bed, ship, and treat it as a common name and demand a general definition of it which will cover all the possible poetised instances. But this procedure is sophisticated. It becomes possible only when the spell of the poetic tradition has been already broken. It imposes itself upon the poetic process as an alternative and wholly alien procedure. But how, while still working within the tradition, can one start to extrapolate such topics and principles out of the narrative flux?

The answer is that you can take similar instances and situations which are severed and scattered through different narrative contexts but which use many of the same words and you can proceed to correlate them and group them and seek for common factors shared by all of them. Navigation and its rules do not constitute a topic of the first book of the *Iliad*. But the four different narrative contexts in which embarkation and landing are in question do in effect provide a paradigm of the rules. This can be seen if the pluralised instances are unified, if the 'many' can become a 'one'. So another way of putting the mental act of isolation and abstraction is to say it is an act of integration. The saga will contain a thousand aphorisms and instances which describe what a proper and moral person is doing. But they have to be torn out of context, correlated, systematised, unified and harmonised to provide a formula for righteousness. The many acts and events must somehow give way and dissolve into a single identity. In short 'the thing *per se*' is also a 'one'.

Once it becomes this, the original syntax of the poem has been destroyed. For the poem was in its very nature a story, an event-series. Otherwise it was not memorisable. And an event-series is conducted in verbs of past, present and future, or, if these tenses are not distinctively developed, in verbs of action and happening in time phases. Putting it another way, the only data which can live in the memory are experienced data with which we identify in act and in situation, and acts and events are 'happenings'; they 'become' or 'are done'. *Per contra*, once the abstracted integration, the law or principle, has come into being, nothing can happen to it. It just is. It can be expressed in language the syntax of which is analytic; that is, terms and propositions are organised in relationships which are timeless. The angles of a triangle are two right angles; they do not gain possession of two right angles; they were not once three right angles and now have become two. They never did anything; they just are. Such a statement is totally divorced from the idiom and syntax of the saga. In short, the absolute isolated identity is not only a 'one', it is also a 'being', in the sense that its linguistic expression is innocent of tense and time. It is not an act or event but a formula; *per contra*, the whole syntax of the poem from which it has emerged is now seen to be one of 'becoming'.

And finally this abstracted object, divorced from concrete situation, no longer needs to be visualised; in fact it cannot be. For visual experience is of colour and shape which occur only as they are pluralised and made specific and so concretely visible in their sharp differentiations from their neighbours. We see the ship, and the men and cargo, and the sea over which they sail, the sail bellying in the wind, the wave breaking foamy and white, even as we hear the wind whistling and the wave hissing. These effects are all there in the saga language—they have to be in order to enlist the indirect aid of mental vision and so reinforce the acoustic resources of the ear. But as the specific sensual nuances of this situation dissolve into a treatise on navigation the visible becomes invisible, the sensual becomes dissolved into an idea. So the abstracted object of knowledge has to lose not only plurality of action in time but also colour and visibility. It becomes 'the unseen'.

Thus the autonomous subject who no longer recalls and feels, but knows, can now be confronted with a thousand abstracted laws, principles, topics, and formulas which become the objects of his knowledge. These are the essences, the *auta ta*, the things *per se.* Are they a heterogeneous and random collection? Or do they in their turn exhibit a new kind of mutual organisation, some sort of counterpart to the old narrative organisation of the great poem? Platonism assumes from the beginning that they do; that the new objects of sheer thought constitute an over-all area of the known which has its own inner logic and constitutes a system. In short, the knower confronting the known is coming to terms with a new complete world of knowledge.

Theoretically this world can be regarded as systematic and exhaustive. All the abstracted essences somehow gear in with each other in a relationship which is no longer that of narrative but of logic. They all fall into a total ground plan of the universe. It is theoretically possible to exhaust the area of the known; at least the mind of a Supreme Knower might manage this. For the known, in order to be known, must be definite; it cannot go on forever as the story could. It must be a system and a system to be such must be closed. Hence in its over-all aspect the world of knowledge itself furnishes the supreme example of a total integration, within which a thousand minor integrations disclose themselves in ascending and descending hierarchies. The abstracted object *per se* is a one, but so also is the world of the known taken as a whole.

To confirm the picture we have drawn of the Greek or rather Platonic discovery of the known, and of the new properties[4] which were a condition of its being knowable, we can turn back again to the *Republic*.

That work, if we accept Plato's own description of the first book as a 'proem',[5] proceeds in the second book to confront the protagonist Socrates and hence also the reader with a fundamental challenge. The cause of righteousness has already been defended against Thrasymachus, but this effort leaves both Glaucon and Adimantus unconvinced. Prove if you can, says Glaucon, that righteousness is acceptable 'on account of itself as well as for its effects'. He then uses the more abstract formula: 'What is the power possessed by vice and virtue respectively itself *per se*, as it inheres in the *psyche*? Please ignore the rewards and effects'; and again 'I want to hear it praised itself *per se*'.[6] Then to give point to this challenge he describes a sophisticated doctrine which traces the rise of justice to a reluctant social compact, formed in defiance of our instinctive preference for injustice (provided, that is, that we manage to be the aggressors rather than the victims).

Following him, Adimantus sharpens the challenge still more by pointing out[7] that, theories aside, the traditional moral education to which the young are submitted never meets the condition laid down by Glaucon. Parents approve not righteousness 'as a thing itself'[8] but only the prestige it gains among men and the rewards it wins from heaven. Or else, virtue is approved reluctantly as a doubtful and painful achievement, while vice it is suggested is not only pleasant but is rewarded so that the wicked can flourish and the virtuous are afflicted. As for heaven, it can turn a blind eye if we use the right form of prayer and appeasement. The youth can only conclude that 'virtue *per se*' is irrelevant; a specious decorum[9] of behaviour becomes the goal, while below the surface we pursue our selfish ends in order to succeed in life. For these traditional views Homer and Hesiod are both cited and quoted, as also are Musaeus and Orpheus and the poets and poetry.[10]

And then Adimantus returns to the language used by Glaucon and repeats and enlarges the fundamental challenge. All statements so far made on this subject, all encomia of righteousness, have concentrated purely on the factors of reputation and social prestige and reward. But virtue and vice respectively, 'each a thing itself by its own power inhering in the *psyche*, have never been adequately followed through in discourse to the conclusion that the one is the maximum of evils and the other the maximum good'.[11] And he concludes his peroration by repeating this language thrice: 'Prove what each itself by itself does to its possessor; take away the social effects. . . . Praise only this (property) of righteousness, namely, that which itself becomes of itself through itself beneficial to the possessor. . . . Explain what

each of them itself through itself does to its possessor and leave the
rewards and the social effects to others to describe.'[12] The demand
for a mental act of isolation could not well be more emphatic. It
also amounts to a demand that the right thing to do in given circumstances be translated and transmuted into a concept of
'righteousness'. The demand is primarily intellectual and it is
fairly novel.[13] That is why it is reiterated, for it is to set the stage
for the massive argument of the remaining books. The formula
kath' auto, per se, is thrust into the argument by the intellectual
Glaucon. Adimantus adverting to the tradition distinguishes
between a righteousness which can be defined intrinsically for its
own sake and one which is always involved in extrinsic situations.
His language is in Platonic terms a little less stringent than
Glaucon's.[14] But the joint impact of both demands is clear: we
are going to be required to think of righteousness as an object
isolated from its effects and treated as a neuter, as a formula, or as
a principle, not as an example geared to a specific situation or act.

Does the challenge also disclose that this object could be integrated only at the expense of the poetic idiom and syntax? No,
not here; exposition of the intellectual insight required must
wait until popular virtue has been defined and disposed of. But
the implication is there; it is the poets who are saddled with the
responsibility of describing only the rewards and effects of
righteousness.

Now if the mnemonic tradition could preserve only situations
and acts which illustrated the public and private law, it was in fact
limited to describing the effects of the law. Your example of
virtue in action had to be that of a superior man acting successfully. This meant the saga was confined to describing the honour
and the prestige of virtue, for only these were concrete. It
memorialised what happened to a hero as he acted, how others
responded to him, and his own affirmation of his own honour and
pride. The plot of the *Iliad* provides a conspicuous example.
When Glaucon says: leave the effects of virtue to others, he denotes the events which in the saga continually clothe the principle

in concrete situations, and which constitute an illustration of its 'effects' in terms of rewards or punishments.[15] We learn the importance of piety, or its reverse sacrilege, from what happens to Agamemnon and to the army in the opening of the *Iliad*. We are not treated to the notion, still less to the definition, of 'piety *per se*'. This would require a new language and a novel mental effort. As Adimantus says, 'no one has followed this through adequately in discourse'.

Here then is the concept of an 'object', fiercely isolated from time, place and circumstance, and translated linguistically into an abstraction and then put forward as the goal of a prolonged intellectual investigation. We have to contemplate it with our mind, for it is invisible. But this is not said yet, nor for a long time. The ultimate intellectual purport of this challenge, the implications of the expression 'itself *per se*', are actually postponed till Book Five. In the meantime, as the state and the soul are respectively expounded and defined according to a tripartite pattern of classes and of faculties, a working definition of justice is attempted. Can it be anything but an example of that specialisation, of division of labour, which had guided the development of society from its primitive beginnings?[16] Applied to the state as a whole, this means that each class does its own business or keeps to its own. Is this not in fact a rule sanctioned by popular tradition? asks Plato. Is it not the principle which guides any judge in a lawsuit, to assign to each his own?[17] Applied to the individual, this must mean a strict observance by his three psychic faculties of their several roles, without trespassing on each other's territory.[18] But Plato offers this suggestion cursorily, as though even he were not satisfied with it, and proceeds to a peroration in which the righteous man is presented in completely traditional and also conventional terms. He is a reliable trustee, he does not rob temples, nor commit adultery, nor steal, nor neglect his parents or the gods.[19]

Now his Greek audience did not need to have the *Republic* written for them in order to arrive at these elementary and time-honoured truths. So far from breaking with the poets and with current practice he has arrived at a simple summary of current morality. Plato in fact, as has often been pointed out, offers here a formulation of virtue suitable for popular consumption and guidance, to produce a docile and well-behaved population, before he proceeds to the much more controversial task of proposing a curriculum for his philosopher-kings. The doctrine of Book Four therefore postpones the answer to the essential challenge of Book Two.[20] 'Justice *per se*', as an intellectual object, has been set before us but then left suspended in mid-air. We have described this interruption only to stress the fact that while the intellectual premise that justice must be objectified and treated as an abstraction had to be offered in Book Two as a stark contrast to the whole idiom and thought world of the previous poetic tradition, this premise is not met and fulfilled[21] until Book Five, when the procedures of the intellect itself are taken up and examined.

This becomes possible only in the aftermath of a political challenge: 'The intellectuals must be given political power.'[22] But what is this intellect, this subject who thinks and knows? Or rather; what are the objects of its intellection, for only as these are defined can the true character of the subject also emerge.[23] And Plato then returns to the linguistic formula 'the thing *per se*' and expands it.

'The beautiful and the ugly are opposed and therefore distinct from each other, so that each is a one. The same formula applies to just unjust, good bad and so forth; each itself is a one' . . . and in the same context he proceeds to stress over and over again the existence of the 'beautiful *per se*' or of 'beauty *per se*' and so forth. This is the object which the mind (*dianoia*) should embrace, and, searching for a word to describe this mental faculty, he pitches on *gnome*—it is the 'knowing faculty' which addresses itself solely to these abstracted objects in their self-sufficient isolation.[24]

Amplifying this relationship (for he is conscious that it is unfamiliar) and seeking to overcome the objections of an imaginary opponent, he then asks: 'does the knower know *something*?' That is, does knowledge have to have an object?[25] In answering his own question he defines some attributes of this object, which we for a moment postpone. But after defining them he challenges his reader to recognise the existence of the 'beautiful *per se*' and the 'just *per se*', and even adds by implication 'the double', 'the half', 'the great', 'the small', 'the light', 'the heavy *per se*' to his list of examples of objects which have to be abstracted and isolated from their application. These are the specific objects of knowledge (*gnosis*).[26]

From here on, the *Republic* when necessary will always assume the absolute necessity of the isolation of the 'per se'. It represents after all a method with which the procedure of earlier dialogues has made us familiar. But it is in the *Republic* that the original genius of the method as constituting a break with previous concrete experience is most clearly exposed. For even as he introduces these objects in the first context quoted from Book Five they are described primarily as integrations, that is as 'ones' concealed behind or among the pluralised appearances where they lurk. 'Each is itself one but appears as many images presented wherever you turn because of its involvement with action and bodies, and also with other objects like itself.' The import of this last phrase can here be neglected. It refines upon but does not alter the basic theory, which is that the all-various actions and the multiple physical objects (which we infer to be the stuff of the narrative experience) break up sets of abstract unities and disperse them into pluralities of images and image situations. Plato does not here suggest how you reverse the process. We have cited as a possible example the integration of four different instances of sailing methods, in order to discover the topic or form of navigation. But in any case it is this integrative aspect of the abstract object which first monopolises Plato's emphasis as he proposes it for us to think about. It is a 'one'.[27] Later, he is to suggest it is like a grouping of all possible instances under a common name;[28] the single name, the sheer noun, then itself becomes the unifying factor in the mind. Here he simply emphasises over and over again the contrast between 'the beautiful sounds and colours and shapes and all that is created out of them' on the one hand, and 'the beautiful *per se*' on the other: the contrast between 'beautiful acts-and-events (*pragmata*)' and 'beauty *per se*'.[29] The 'many', it is clear, are equivalent to the pluralised instances, the various scattered situations and not merely to the physical things in which the many beautifuls may occur.

Now, since he has already cited more than one example of this kind of object—that is, has applied the abstractive method to several words and will apply it to many more—it is obvious that these objects of knowledge themselves constitute a 'many' but a new sort of 'many'.[30] What is the difference between a group of such objects and a group of events or situations? He replies: these objects severally just 'are' or (in the participle) each of them is simply 'being'.[31] What precisely is being? To ask the question in this form is to prepare the wrong answer. Being we might say is not a noun but a syntactical situation (though later Plato will use a noun—*ousia*—to describe this situation).[32]

The abstracted objects of knowledge, as known and as stated, are always identical with themselves—unchanging—and always when statements are made about them or when they are used in statements these statements have to be timeless.[33] Their syntax excludes tenses of the verb 'to be'. Principles and properties and categories and topics just 'are'. When placed in relationship with each other they provide the terms of analytic statements or of equations, which cannot share in the syntax of process and time, for they are not statements of specific situations and instances, not statements of action.

We need not ask here whether Plato does not sometimes seem to confuse timelessness with immortality. That his prime preoccupation is with linguistic syntax is indicated in the fact that he raises this issue by first posing the problem: 'What is the character of the known? What is it the knower can know?' And he answers: 'He can only know what is'.[34] This cannot mean a metaphysical entity. He has already told us that the knower knows the abstracted identities. These then are what 'is'; in the plural they continually 'are', as the angles of a triangle 'are' always two right angles. If you integrate the rules of navigation till you have exhausted them, then, *qua* 'rules *per se*' in contrast to the story which uses them, they just 'are'. Hence he says 'the object of science is that which is'.[35] Because his argument in this context insists, for reasons to be examined in the next chapter, on the contrast between 'what is' and 'what is not', we can become distracted and imagine we are being asked to look at entities rather than at syntactical relations. That it is timelessness on which he has his gaze focused is indicated by the fact that he thrice describes the object *per se* as 'always holding itself self-identical within the same'; 'always being self-identical within the same'; 'always itself identical within the same'.[36] In short he tries to focus on the permanence of the abstract whether as formula or as concept, as opposed to the fluctuating, here-today-gone-tomorrow character of the concrete situation.

This fluctuation is one way of describing that change and variety of situation which alone can inform a story which is time conditioned. Plato's expression for it in this context is 'rolling' or 'wandering'.[37] He uses these terms to describe an endless alternation between the condition of being and that of not being. That is, Agamemnon is noble in one context and base in another; therefore he is both noble and not noble, base and not base. Achilles is now angry and now remorseful; that is, he is and is not angry; he is and is not remorseful. For that matter, Achilles is alive and then dead; he wanders between is and is not. This is a way of dramatising the fact that concrete narrative deals with concrete objects and situations which are all different, or else there would be no narrative, rather than with categories, principles or formulas which persist unchanged.

In the next book Plato continues the argument by focusing upon the character of the subject, namely the intellectual (*philosophos*)[38] and his knowing mind. How can the subject's mind however be described? Plato had already indicated the answer. It is describable in terms of the kind of objects it thinks about and these have now been defined. So we are now told the philosopher is the man who 'lays hold on the always itself self-identical within the same', and again 'knowledge is of each being (thing)'.[39] These expressions indicate that whole group of isolated abstractions which have been already described. Then comes the question: Is there any overarching discipline (*mathema*) which can train the subject to think about this kind of timeless object?[40] The final answer is to wait till Book Seven. But Plato replies in general terms that it will be a '*mathema* of that beingness (*ousia*) which always is and is not put into wandering by becoming and perishing'.[41] The phraseology once more may tempt the reader to think he is being asked to look at a metaphysical super-reality rather than at a syntactical situation. But it is the latter that Plato intends. The term *ousia*[42] or 'beingness' is used to suggest that the several abstracted objects, the principles, formulas, categories and the like, compose an area of final knowledge outside ourselves. The contrasting syntax of narrative is here properly rendered as the realm of becoming (more strictly of 'birth')[43]; the realm of the endless event-series. It is the realm of those multitudinous situations which happen.

Plato now begins to talk about 'all', or 'the whole', of that area potentially to be known by the subject. It is 'all truth' and then he adds that the subject 'contemplates all (or every) time and all (or every) beingness', which is the nearest his language can get to that notion of 'timeless statement' which we have adopted in our exposition of his meaning.[44]

This then affirms by implication that the known constitutes, in theory at least, a total area of knowledge, a 'world', an order, a system, populated by abstractions which, being themselves achieved by an act of integrating previous experience, also interconnect in a series of over-all relationships which constitute a 'super-integration'. Plato constructs his parable of the Line to identify this total area as the *noetos topos*—the area of the intel-

ligible, or as the *noeton genos*, the genus of the intelligible.[45] It is
the over-all sum of objects known by the subject, encyclopedic in
its scope, but its content is invisible and abstract as the content of
the poetic encyclopedia was not. Below it lies the area of the
visible, which is really not a physical location as we are tempted to
think from the vividness of Plato's language, but a level of human
experience where the sensual consciousness absorbs the concrete
panorama of things 'as they seem', performing their endless
narrative of birth and death, action and passion. We have to
ascend from the lower to the upper portion of the Line; that is,
both portions represent psychic activities but of different kinds.
Plato here is less concerned to suggest how the objects of intellect
are integrated and abstracted out of the sensual than to stress the
totally different type of experience which the intelligible represents. He dramatises this antithesis as one between the visible
and the intelligible worlds. So it is here, as he advances the notion
of the known as a sum-total of knowledge, that he is drawn also
to stress that non-visual[46] and non-imagist condition, which
dissolves the vividness of the story into a language which is
wholly abstract. This non-visualness, when added to integrity
and to timelessness, completes the trilogy in which are comprised
the non-epic properties of the sheer idea.

Plato's quest has been for a simple but decisive terminology
which shall define both the various abstract objects known by the
knowing subject and also that super-object, the realm of final
knowledge, in which they are comprised. That quest is now
achieved, and as he pursues in Book Seven the problem of the
specific disciplines to which our personalities must be submitted
in order to wake them up and make them think, he is able to
assume that the knowing psyche has to be converted 'from that
which becomes towards that which is'; or 'dragged from that
which becomes toward that which is'.[47] This language describes
the rupture of age-long mental habits of recollection and of discourse which had dealt with concrete events that 'become'. It
proclaims the learning of a new mental habit,[48] that of conceptual

thought directed towards abstractions which are outside time. Hence arithmetic 'drags us toward beingness'. The intellectual 'must try and grasp beingness after emerging from becomingness'.[49] The mind must be taught to enter a new syntactical condition, that of the mathematical equation, in preference to the syntax of the story. The content of this beingness he says is not a set of metaphysical entities but 'the great, the small', and similar categories and relationships, or 'the nature of number viewed by sheer intellect'.[50] In short, the content consists of those same isolated abstractions, existing *per se* because divorced from all immediate context and all specific situation, which were first proposed in Book Five in the guise of 'the just *per se*' and 'the beautiful *per se*'.

NOTES

[1] Cf. n. 25 below. This proposition, so fundamental to Plato's system (for it carries the corollary that the Forms cannot themselves be thoughts; cf. *Parmenides* 132b3–c12, and also below, cap. 14), was probably anticipated by Parmenides, or at least latent in the language he used (B 2.7 and 8.35–6). The *Charmides*, to be sure, explores the possibility that knowledge is to be found in self-converse, but the result of the inquiry is an *aporia*.

[2] 443c9 ff.

[3] Undoubtedly a Socratic formula: *Clouds* 194 is decisive. In the *Apology* it occurs only at 36c8. In 'early' Plato its implications are spelled out at *Euthyphro* 5di ff. ἦ οὐ ταὐτόν ἐστιν ἐν πάσῃ πράξει τὸ ὅσιον αὐτὸ αὑτῷ καὶ τὸ ἀνόσιον αὖ τοῦ μὲν ὁσίου παντὸς ἐναντίον, αὐτὸ δὲ αὑτῷ ὅμοιον καὶ ἔχον μίαν τινὰ ἰδέαν κατὰ τὴν ἀνοσιότητα πᾶν ὅτιπερ ἂν μέλλῃ ἀνόσιον εἶναι; where the ἰδέα may represent the Platonic addition unless the well-known views of Burnet and Taylor carry conviction (cf. Havelock, 'Evidence').

[4] These could be described as belonging to the mental situation which 'knows that' as against the one which 'knows how' (cf. Gould, cap. 1). But historically, the one evolved from the other: *techne* was the mother of *philosophia*, and *episteme* the consort of both. The complexities of this semantic relationship need not however preoccupy us here; cf. below, cap. 15, n. 22.

[5] 357a2 and above, cap. 1, n. 37.

[6] 357b6 αὐτὸ αὑτοῦ ἕνεκα 358b5 αὐτὸ καθ'αὑτὸ ἐνὸν ἐν τῇ ψυχῇ 358d2 αὐτὸ καθ'αὑτὸ ἐγκωμιαζόμενον.

[7] 362e1 ff.

⁸ 363a1 οὐκ αὐτὸ δικαιοσύνην ἐπαινοῦντες.

⁹ 365c4 σκιαγραφίαν ἀρετῆς.

¹⁰ 363a7-d2; 364c5-365a3; 365e3-366b2.

¹¹ 366e5 ff. αὐτὸ δ'ἑκάτερον τῇ αὐτοῦ δυνάμει τί δρᾷ, τῇ τοῦ ἔχοντος ψυχῇ ἐνόν κτλ.

¹² 367b4 τί ποιοῦσα ἑκατέρα τὸν ἔχοντα αὐτὴ δι'αὐτὴν ἡ μὲν κακόν, ἡ δὲ ἀγαθόν ἐστιν. 367d3 ὃ αὐτὴ δι'αὐτὴν τὸν ἔχοντα ὀνίνησιν κτλ. 367e3 τί ποιοῦσα ἑκατέρα τὸν ἔχοντα αὐτὴ δι'αὐτήν κτλ.

¹³ It is usually interpreted less stringently, as, e.g. by Gould, p. 142: 'Glaucon and Adeimantus together appeal to Socrates to convince them in effect of the *primacy of moral demands*' (my italics). This would be true if Plato's language was written as though it assumed moral concepts familiar to us. In that case, the repetition of the demand would be a rhetorical device. But in fact the concept of 'the moral' or 'morality' which gives meaning to the phrase 'primacy of moral demands' is itself only being born, as an object of cognition, before our eyes as we read the *Republic*. Hence Plato's repetition of the demand is a measure of the mental effort and of the achievement implicit in the step of isolating 'the right' as an abstract object, or of converting 'the right thing' into 'rightness'.

¹⁴ Contrast the δι'αὐτὴν of Adeimantus (n. 12) with the καθ'αὑτό of Glaucon (n. 6).

¹⁵ These *doxai* and *timai* (*Rep.* 366e4) are the sole object of heroic endeavour, typified in *Iliad* 1.353 τιμήν πέρ μοι ὄφελλεν 'Ολύμπιος ἐγγυαλίξαι. Saga by definition was a celebration of *kleos*.

¹⁶ 433a1 ff.

¹⁷ 433e3 ff.

¹⁸ 441d12.

¹⁹ 442e6-443a11.

²⁰ Cf. Gould, p. 154: 'It seems that the definitions of ἀρεταί (*sc.* in Book 4) are too feeble and circumscribed to be the adequate end of any quest . . . The discovery of the real nature of justice is referred, in spite of the definition only recently concluded, to the future once again . . .'

²¹ Cf. Book 6, 484a5-7 ἐμοὶ γοῦν ἔτι δοκεῖ ἂν βελτιόνως φανῆναι εἰ περὶ τούτου μόνου ἔδει ῥηθῆναι, καὶ μὴ πολλὰ τὰ λοιπὰ διελθεῖν κτλ, which could be interpreted to mean that in the grand design of the *Republic* all else is subordinate to the definition of the philosophic intellect.

²² 473c11; cf. below, cap. 15.

²³ 475e3-4.

²⁴ 475e9-476d7.

²⁵ 476e7.

²⁶ 478e7-480a1; cf. also 484c7 τοῦ ὄντος ἑκάστου . . . τῆς γνώσεως.

²⁷ 476a5 αὐτὸ μὲν ἓν ἕκαστον εἶναι κτλ. Cf. 479a4 ἄν τις ἓν τὸ καλὸν φῇ εἶναι κτλ. At *Philebus* 15a4 ff. Plato supplies the terms ἑνάς and μονάς to describe these integrations, as he probes the problem of their relation to phenomena.

²⁸ Cf. below, cap. 14, p. 270.

²⁹ 476b5 ff., 476c2 ff.

³⁰ 479e7 τοὺς αὐτὰ ἕκαστα θεωμένους 484c6 τοῦ ὄντος ἑκάστου d6 ἕκαστον τὸ ὄν.

³¹ 479e7 ἀεὶ κατὰ ταὐτὰ ὡσαύτως ὄντα 480a4 ὥς τι ὄν 484c6 τοῦ ὄντος ἑκάστου 484d6 ἕκαστον τὸ ὄν.

³² That the syntactical situation has priority in Plato's mind over the metaphysical is indicated at *Parmenides* 135b: however difficult it may be to define the relationship of the Forms to each other or to particulars, they have to exist, or else 'descriptive discourse' (διαλέγεσθαι) will be impossible. The nature of this situation is explored in the *Sophist*, especially 257d ff. On *ousia* vid. below, n. 42.

³³ Vid. n. 31, and 479a2 ἰδέαν . . . ἀεὶ μὲν κατὰ ταὐτὰ ὡσαύτως ἔχουσαν 484b3 τοῦ ἀεὶ κατὰ ταὐτὰ ὡσαύτως ἔχοντος.

³⁴ 476e7 ff.

³⁵ 477b10 ἐπιστήμη μὲν ἐπὶ τῷ ὄντι πέφυκε, γνῶναι ὡς ἔστι τὸ ὄν.

³⁶ *Vid.* n. 33.

³⁷ 479d3 μεταξύ που κυλινδεῖται 484b5 οἱ δὲ . . . ἐν πολλοῖς καὶ παντοίως ἴσχουσιν πλανώμενοι οὐ φιλόσοφοι 485b1 (cf. n. 41 below). (Cf. *Od.* 1.1-3; *Parmenides* B 6.6; and Havelock HSCP, 1958, pp. 133-43.)

³⁸ Below, cap. 15, pp. 280 ff.

³⁹ 484b4 (above, n. 33); 484c6 (above, nn. 30, 31).

⁴⁰ 485a1 cf. 521c1.

⁴¹ 485b1 μαθήματός γε ἀεὶ ἐρῶσιν ὃ ἂν αὐτοῖς δηλοῖ ἐκείνης τῆς οὐσίας τῆς ἀεὶ οὔσης καὶ μὴ πλανωμένης ὑπὸ γενέσεως καὶ φθορᾶς.

⁴² Its use in the *Republic* has been postponed by Plato to this point, but it appears in its philosophical sense as early as *Euthyphro* 11a7. Its habitual translation 'essence' (cf. Robinson, p. 52, where οὐσία and εἶδος are treated as equivalents) tends to veil the fact that in the Socratic quest for 'what each thing is' (Robinson, p. 74, commenting on *Rep.* 533b and 334b) the 'what' in the Greek is, if I may so put it, less important than the 'is'; for usage of *ousia* cf. Berger.

⁴³ 485b2 μὴ πλανωμένης ὑπὸ γενέσεως καὶ φθορᾶς cf. cap. 10, n. 6.

⁴⁴ 485b5 πάσης αὐτῆς (i.e. τῆς οὐσίας) d3 πάσης ἀληθείας . . . ὀρέγεσθαι 486a5 τοῦ ὅλου καὶ παντὸς ἀεὶ ἐπορέξεσθαι a8 θεωρία παντὸς μὲν χρόνου, πάσης δὲ οὐσίας.

⁴⁵ 509d2. 'Knowledge', though it expresses a conception which seems obvious to us, is not easily translatable into pre-Platonic Greek, and the 'known object' still less so. Heraclitus B 32 ἓν τὸ σοφὸν μοῦνον and 108 ὁκόσων λόγους ἤκουσα, οὐδεὶς ἀφικνεῖται ἐς τοῦτο, ὥστε γιγνώσκειν ὅτι σοφόν ἐστι πάντων κεχωρισμένον may adumbrate this conception; the upper portion of Plato's Line constitutes a declaration that it has now crossed the threshold of the European consciousness.

⁴⁶ Cf. especially 511a1 ἃ οὐκ ἂν ἄλλως ἴδοι τις ἢ τῇ διανοίᾳ.

⁴⁷ 518c8 σὺν ὅλῃ τῇ ψυχῇ ἐκ τοῦ γιγνομένου περιακτέον εἶναι. 521d3 μάθημα ψυχῆς ὁλκὸν ἀπὸ τοῦ γιγνομένου ἐπὶ τὸ ὄν.

⁴⁸ The 'mental situation', which in Greece preceded the 'separation of the knower from the known' and the 'recognition of the known as object', may be thought of as analogous to that situation defined by Collingwood as the 'aesthetic experience'. Thus, p. 292: 'It is a knowing of oneself and one's world, these two

knowns and knowings being not yet distinguished'; and again, p. 290: 'In the case of art, the distinction between theory and practice or thought and action has not been left behind, as it has in the case of any morality that deserves the name. . . . Such a distinction only presents itself to us when, by the abstractive work of the intellect, we learn to dissect a given experience into two parts, one belonging to "the subject" and the other to "the object". The individual of which art is the knowledge is an individual situation, in which we find ourselves. We are only conscious of the situation as our situation, and we are only conscious of ourselves as involved in the situation.' If this be accepted as a definition of the conditions under which the aesthetic sensibility operates, does it follow that it was difficult for a pre-Platonic Greek to create something genuinely ugly? Cf. Collingwood, p. 112; 'The reason why description, so far from helping expression, actually damages it, is that description generalises. To describe a thing is to call it a thing of such and such a kind: to bring it under a conception, to classify it.'

⁴⁹ 523a2 ἑλκτικῷ ὄντι παντάπασι πρὸς οὐσίαν 524e1 ὁλκὸν . . . ἐπὶ τὴν οὐσίαν 525b5 διὰ τὸ τῆς οὐσίας ἁπτεὸν εἶναι γενέσεως ἐξαναδύντι.

⁵⁰ 524c6 μέγα αὖ καὶ σμικρὸν ἡ νόησις ἠναγκάσθη ἰδεῖν 525c2 ἕως ἂν ἐπὶ θέαν τῆς τῶν ἀριθμῶν φύσεως ἀφίκωνται τῇ νοήσει αὐτῇ.

CHAPTER THIRTEEN

Poetry as Opinion

LET us look back for a moment over the road that has been travelled. The original departure-point lies in those Homeric days when the Greek culture had been one of oral communication. This fact created a set of conditions for the preservation and transmission of the Greek ethos which were only starting to change radically in the generation just preceding Plato's. By ethos is meant, concretely speaking, a linguistic statement of the public and private law (including history and technology) common to the group and expressive of its coherence as a culture. This statement had been orally memorised and repeated by successive generations of Greeks. The function of the poet was primarily to repeat and in part to enlarge the tradition. The Greek educational system, if the term may be used, was placed wholly at the service of this task of oral preservation. It would effectively preserve and transmit the mores only if the pupil was trained to a habit of psychological identification with the poetry he heard. The content of the poetic statement had to be phrased in such a way as to allow this identification. This meant it could deal only with action and event involving persons.

Plato himself in his *Republic* sufficiently documents the functional character of poetry and the mechanisms of psychological identification by which it was memorised. We have gone on to argue that the same work is systematically organised behind two doctrinal goals which constitute the core of early Platonism: the affirmation of a 'subject', that is, of the autonomous thinking personality, and the affirmation of an 'object', that is, of an area of knowledge which shall be wholly abstract. We have also argued that these twin goals of Platonism are both directly conditioned by his perception of the need to break with the poetic experience. That experience had been central; it had constituted an over-all state of mind; let us call it the Homeric. And he proposes to substitute a different state of mind, the Platonic. The Homeric had been expressed in a given kind of language with a given kind of syntax. He proposes a different kind of language and a different syntax.

It is not perhaps difficult to accept the conclusion that the autonomous psyche was indeed a doctrine which can be directly related to its opposite, the submergence of the self-consciousness in previous poetic education. But is it not going rather far to assume that the whole doctrine of an area of knowledge populated by abstract objects, the area of the 'ones', of 'beingness', of the 'invisibles', is also in effect designed as a total correction of the poetic account of experience; that these objects are conceived as a direct replacement of the acts and events which constituted the content of the epic narrative?

What are the labels which Plato himself applies to the non-abstract and non-philosophic experience? It recognises, he says, only the many and the visibles. It is an area of becoming, of distraction, and of ambiguous movement. We have quoted this kind of terminology from his text. Over-all, is he as early as Book Five prepared to give a name to this kind of experience? Yes, he firmly labels it as *doxa*, or opinion.[1]

What proof then is there that by *doxa* he means to identify the Homeric state of mind?[2] Is it not usual to assume that opinion denominates the opinion of the average common-sense man, the unthinking materialist, or 'realist', who does not philosophise, who uses language superficially and illogically, whose vision is fixed purely on physical externals? All this Plato says of him, and the modern Platonist is therefore inclined to identify this person with the modern average man so far as he does not think, reflect, or penetrate behind obvious appearances.

We have on the contrary assumed frequently in the preceding argument that when Plato defines this mental condition he is attacking a problem specific to his own culture, and one which is indeed created by the previous poetised experience of Greece. It was a mental condition which to be sure has something in common with common sense even today, but not much. We have assumed that it had certain specific characteristics, that it spoke in a specific idiom, which were the direct result of the mnemonic procedures we have described; and these had to pass away. If we are correct, what Plato is pleading for could be shortly put as the invention of an abstract language of descriptive science to replace a concrete language of oral memory.

At any rate it is time to ask: does Plato's own text give any support to the thesis that the experience of the many visibles which become and perish, one which is labelled, not merely in the *Republic*, as 'opinion', is really intended to denominate the content and idiom of the poetised tradition?

If it is, then the many fluctuating visibles correspond to the acts and events which, so we have argued, could alone be retained in the oral memory. They are an interpretation in effect of the narrative syntax in which a specific something is always being done or is happening but in which topics, categories, formulas, and principles never appear. Is Plato ever prepared to identify poetry as essentially a system of narrative syntax? Not very explicitly, it must be admitted, although the implication is there in his assumption, maintained fairly consistently, that the content of poetry is *mythos* as opposed to dialectical *logos*. He can call it *logos* too, but then he is using *logos* as a general term for 'content'.

Everything said by a *mythologos* or poet, he says, is a 'going through of what has happened or is or will be'.[3] The phraseology points to his awareness of the time-conditioning which, as we have argued, is inseparable from the syntax of the memorised material. He says this in Book Three as he first introduces the problem of the medium (*lexis*) in which poets speak. By Book Seven he is prepared to establish a complete philosophic alternative to the entire poetic curriculum. Can it be music? he asks.

No: 'music educates in habit patterns and it transmits a sort of harmonised and rhythmic condition by using harmony and rhythm. It does not transmit science. As for its content, this has a second set of characteristics which correspond, whether the content be mythic or of a more reliable kind. It contains no discipline of any use for what we want . . .'.[4] What those characteristics of content are, which correspond to the rhythm and harmony of meter and accompaniment, he does not say.

At Book Ten, having put forward *mimesis* as the label now not only of personal identification but of the artistic representation, he asks, What does the poet represent? and he replies 'He represents human beings involved in action, whether this action be autonomous or the result of external compulsion and including what men think or feel about their actions; that is how they interpret their effect in terms of weal or woe to themselves and their corresponding joys and sorrows'.[5] Here certainly the content of poetic representation is limited to action and to situation, to doings and to events, and to the thoughts and feelings only as they emerge as reflexes to acts and events, not as isolated and objectified reflections.

To this extent, Plato's formulas for poetic content do tend to place the accent on a purely narrative series. This does not mean narrative at the expense of drama. On the contrary, dramatised representation merely has the effect of transferring the action to the speaker's own person but without altering one whit the narrative syntax. Indeed dramatic impersonation is if anything less capable of an alternative syntax than is impersonal statement, which is one reason why Plato had given some preference in Book Three to the latter.

This poetised panorama of the act and event in which we become involved is in Book Ten explicitly labelled as the enemy of science and as wholly alien to being. As these terms are used, they carry with them those previous contexts in Books Five and Seven in which their significance had been explained. The argument of Book Ten, when compared with those doctrines of the two earlier books which it uses, can conveniently be broken down and itemised as follows:

(1) Poetry is first introduced as the corruption of the intellect. This *may* be a reminiscence of the parable of the Line where the mathematical intellect presides over the third section of the Line.[6]

(2) This reminiscence of the Line is reinforced when the objects of mimetic are compared to those physical appearances reflected at random in a revolving mirror—of all kinds, shapes, and sizes without discrimination. That is, *mimesis* corresponds to the bottom-most division of the Line, where even the objects of sense are only reflected in water and the like.[7]

(3) The quality of this mimetic content is then exposed, so far as the painter is concerned, as consisting of phantom appearance. This is because *mimesis* can portray only one aspect, frontal or sidewise and so forth, of an object, never the whole object at once. This portrayal is in contrast to what is.[8]

(4) On this ground, mimetic is then placed in stark antithesis to science (*episteme*).[9]

(5) Then after a long polemic against Homer and the poets as educators Plato sums up the poet's function as 'mimetic of a phantom of virtue' . . . 'he uses words and expressions to put what we might call coloured surfaces upon all the techniques . . . and these devices possess an inherent spell.'[10]

(6) The next stage[11] in Plato's analysis of what is represented by *mimesis* is to try to define it in terms of those psychic habits within ourselves to which it makes appeal.

(7) And what, asks Plato, are these habits? or what is their area of experience? His answer is: optical deception which communicates contradictory reports concerning identical

objects, as these are distorted by the 'wandering' of the coloured surfaces and by distance.[12]

(8) By contrast the calculative element in the soul corrects such distortion by measurement and number and so avoids contradiction within the same.

(9) It should be impossible to entertain contradictory opinions which defy the science of measurement.[13]

(10) The appeal of *mimesis* is therefore alien to 'thinking' (*phronesis*).[14]

(11) And if we turn specifically to poetry we find that its content consists of continual action and passion fluctuating and inconsistent.

(12) It can therefore appeal directly to that faculty which is the enemy of calculation—the pathological part of us which the calculative power and law try to control and restrain. A mimetic poet for emotional reasons cannot have a relationship with the calculative faculty.[15]

(13) Besides, he cannot distinguish great and small but holds the same to be now one and now the other.[16]

Plato may have written this polemic at white heat. It is filled with terminology with which readers of the *Republic* should be familiar, but the terminology is not explicated and the philosopher employs shortcuts in his argument to drive home his final thesis— that thesis which first showed over the horizon at the beginning of the treatise when in Book Two he confronted the 'enemy' in the guise of current morality as it is found in the accounts of the poets. Here this poetised account, so it is hinted, like a mirror reflects a content consisting of a plurality of unorganised visibles of which it cannot be said that they are. The poetic experience is the function of a faculty which is the antithesis of science; it is a condition of opinion which accepts a constant wandering and contradiction in physical reporting; one which is alien to number and to calculation. We conclude that if we cannot apply the term 'is' to reports of this kind, this is because the report shifts and contradicts itself. The same physical thing now appears to be of a given size or dimension and yet again of a different dimension; it both is and is not.

The pattern of this terminology and the doctrine behind it have been developed earlier in the *Republic*, first in one passage we have already examined in Book Five where the doctrine of the isolated abstracted objects is first introduced, and secondly in Book Seven where the doctrine of the conversion of the soul towards thinking about what is (another passage already noticed) culminates in the introduction of arithmetic as the first discipline which shall begin the conversion. Let us here turn back first to Book Five, and consider the entire context in which the theory of the object *per se* is first proposed as a theory of philosophic knowledge.

Plato had proposed the *philosophos* as the only proper source of political authority in the state. What kind of person is this type? Obviously he is a man who 'likes what is intellectual' (*sophia*) and therefore 'likes to study' (*philomathes*) anything and everything. To which objection is at once made that this description exactly fits those who 'like sights and sounds', the sight-seers who are certainly not philosophers.[17] It is to clarify the distinction between these two types of men that Plato then offers a definition of what it is the philosopher thinks about and knows: namely the abstracted objects *per se* which are ones and are not many. *Per contra*, those who like sights and sounds embrace beautiful sounds and coloured surfaces and shapes. They are 'familiar with beautiful actions-and-events' but not with 'beauty *per se*'.[18] They live in a dream, and this mental condition is one of opinion, a condition intermediate between scientific knowledge on the one hand and of blank unconsciousness on the other. This opinion is a faculty which has its own specific object, and this object is also intermediate.[19]

Furthermore this condition is one of continual mental confusion. He who likes sights and sounds is continually passing contradictory judgments about the same thing, and their moral content seems to shift (so that just becomes unjust), even as their proportions and properties shift (so that light becomes heavy). He is continually saying of the same thing 'it is and it is not'.[20] We conclude that the 'many familiar conventions (*nomima*) of the many'[21] dealing with moral and other judgments are always wandering. This is a condition of opinion not of knowledge, a condition in which noble sounds and coloured surfaces are the objects embraced. We have therefore distinguished two main classes of human beings: those who like opinion (*philodoxoi*) and those who like what is intellectual (*philosophoi*).[22]

So much for the analysis of opinion in Book Five. A cross-comparison with the analysis of poetry in Book Ten reveals the continuity of the two. There is a distinction drawn in each case between a concrete state of mind (which is confused) and one which is abstract and exact. The former is called the 'opinion of the many' in Book Five, and in Book Ten is identified once as 'opinion'[23] and otherwise as the mental condition of the poet and of his report on reality. In both cases, this concrete state of mind reports a version of reality which is pluralised, visual, and various. This pluralisation in both cases is then translated into terms of contradiction. The judgments made about colours, shapes, and sizes are contradictory. The statements made about actions and events and their moral properties are contradictory also. The same thing is now good and bad, now great and small. Consistent moral judgment and consistent physical measurement are alike impossible. If they could be achieved, it is implied, they would in each case be effected by the same faculty. *Per contra*, the condition of opinion is like a dream-state (Book Five) or like being under a spell (Book Ten).

The comparison clarifies one problem. In Book Ten, Plato uses the painter and his pictures of physical objects as an analogy for the poet and his stories of action and passion. Does he however mean that the poet like the painter gives a report of physical reality in the same erroneous language in which he reports the acts and the moralities of human beings? The language of Book

Ten can be regarded as ambiguous on this point. The coloured surfaces employed by the poet could be a mere metaphor for his rhythm and his poetic skills. But when it is realised that the fascination of the vision with isolated colours and surfaces and shapes is also the basic flaw in the 'many' who are prisoners of 'opinion' in Book Five, and that it is this general opinion which gives distorted and contradictory reports of physical reality because of its obsession with these colours, it becomes impossible to avoid the conclusion that Plato intends to judge poetry as a report on the physical environment as well as on the moralities of men, and that he finds it as unsatisfactory in the one case as in the other. And essentially for the same reason. It cannot employ the measuring, calculating and reasoning faculty either in representation of physical objects or in representation of human manners. In the latter case, since the poetic representation becomes effective only as audiences identify with it personally in order to memorise, their reasoning faculty is likewise inhibited from controlling or measuring their personal reactions.

What then is the relation of the poetry of Book Ten to the opinion of Book Five? Obviously they are described in terms of similar states of mind. Since, however, for us poetry represents a much more esoteric experience than does opinion, we would at first conclude that the poet and his poetry happen to be a particular example of the general error inherent in opinion, an example which Plato pillories for some special purpose of his own.

But a different answer is possible. Suppose the poetry of Book Ten is coextensive with the opinion of Five? It is certainly described as though it were. Suppose in fact that it is in Book Ten that Plato fully reveals what he has been getting at in Book Five, when he called his target opinion?

This would certainly be in line with the thesis we have been defending throughout, namely, that the Homeric state of mind was a general state of mind. For in that case, the poets represented the public medium and the only one by which the general state of mind could express itself. They and they alone furnished the 'culture-language', as we called it, and hence also the cultural norms, within which was formed the 'opinion of the many'. And the intensity of Plato's epistemological attack on poetry, as an erroneous report on physical fact and moral value, would be explained, because he is thereby attacking error as it exists in society generally.

If that were so, we would expect that the attack on the many in Book Five should betray some evidence that the ultimate target does lie in poetry; even if that target is fully unfolded only in Book Ten. And it does. Taken as a whole, the passage is devoted to a formalisation of the relationship between knowledge on the one hand and opinion on the other and the definition of the gulf between them. But the antithesis is prepared for us initially by introducing us to two human types, the 'philosopher' versus the 'sight-seer', who represent respectively these two levels of human experience, and the passage concludes by reaffirming these as two fundamental and opposed types of humanity. The sight-seer is precisely defined before the analysis ends as a man who rejects the abstracted object *per se* and whose type of comprehension is enmeshed in contradictions so that he cannot report the physical or the moral world with consistency. He is specifically equated with the 'opinion-lover'.[24]

Now who is the sight-seer? As introduced, he is portrayed as a kind of theatre-goer who perpetually makes the rounds of the Dionysiac choruses both metropolitan and provincial.[25] But why, we should ask, does Plato in seeking to define the new intellectual standards of the Academy imply that the obstacle to their achievement is simply a habit of attending the theatre? This seems more frivolous than the deep seriousness of his purpose required. Theatre-goers in our culture are a sophisticated minority of the better educated. The whole passage makes it clear on the other hand that Plato's target is the average man of average mind. In what sense was the average Greek mind a theatrical mind? The answer can be found only by supposing that Plato's real target here is the poetic performance, by which the cultural tradition was stored, kept alive, and memorized, and with which the living memories of the audience had to identify. In short, though here as sometimes in Book Ten he focuses on dramatic performance because it is the most contemporary form of the tradition, his target (as in Book Three also) is 'the poets and Homer', the epic performance no less than the tragic. It is not poetry as it might be read from a book that he is attacking. It is the act of memorisation through identification in the poetic performance which to him is inseparable from the poem itself, and which constitutes a total act and condition of *mimesis*.

His phraseology in Book Five supplies more than one hint that this is indeed his target. The 'devoted sight-seers' are equated with the 'devoted hearers of sounds', and the equation stresses the acoustic relationship which is fundamental to the performance. The fond object of their devotion is 'fair sounds and coloured surfaces and shapes and all that is fashioned therefrom'.[26] This accent on sound and colour and shape as the field of experience of opinion is repeated in the conclusion of the argument[27] when he seeks to clinch the contrast between this field and the field of vision of the philosopher. The phrasing is suggestively ambiguous and deliberately so; it describes on the one hand the acoustic-visual content of the poetised tradition and the degree to which it concretely visualises situations and things, no less than its use of rhythm, meter, and music to do this. Yet it also describes the physical things and artifacts[28] with which the external world is so variously and indiscriminately populated. The same double reference covering the content of the poetic record and the outward appearance of the physical world is exploited in Book Ten.

Again, this contrast is also described as issuing from a 'familiar acquaintance with acts-and-events (*pragmata*)' and as a plurality of familiar conventions held by the many about the just and so forth'.[29] Such language can refer only to the moral and social content of what we have called the tribal encyclopedia, the fountain head of all social convention for the Greeks.

At one point in Book Five Plato uses the triple classification of 'sight-seers, devotees of technique and practical men'.[30] No excuse is furnished in the immediate context for this surprising combination as an over-all definition of the average man and his opinion, but it is a recollection of the famous tripartite classification in the *Apology* where Socrates describes his mission undertaken to the politicians, the poets and the craftsmen.[31]

Finally, as already noticed, the over-all experience of these theatre-goers is likened to a dream. This is the equivalent of that rhythmic and emotional spell so necessary to the act of identification, which is described in Book Ten as the accompaniment of poetry.

It now appears, if we are right, that the over-all plan of the *Republic* calls for a progressive definition of a new education in Platonic science which, at every stage of its development through the secondary to the advanced levels, finds itself in collision with the general mind of Greece. This mind in turn is defined always in terms of the mental habits and conventions acquired through long practice in the oral poetry of Greece considered as a vehicle of moral guidance and also of physical description. Whenever the epistemology of Plato's own system is in question he feels compelled to define it in contrast to the psychology and the language employed in the poetic performance. We have added, what he does not explicitly reveal, that this habit and this language had been required by the conditions of oral memorisation and preservation of the group experience.

Books Two, Three, Five, and Ten therefore progressively reveal the enemy of Platonism to be this poetised state of mind, and the attack on poetry becomes progressively more drastic as the theories of Platonism have been progressively expanded and deepened. What then of Book Seven, where Plato, as we have seen, identifying the autonomous *psyche* of the thinker and of the knower, calls for it to be awakened and converted away from becoming toward the abstracted object which constitutes timeless and intelligible knowledge? Does he here, in Book Seven, repeat his rejection of poetry as a candidate for this task? Yes he does, for as we have seen he summarily dismisses all music as now irrelevant to his purpose[32] and proposes arithmetic as the discipline which shall accomplish this awakening. He says no more of poetry in this place, yet the analysis he proceeds to offer of that mental condition which arithmetic can correct is one that he is going to use again when he comes back to the poet in Book Ten. It is an analysis which selects contradiction as the root error of the concrete state of mind. This is a dialectical weapon. Let us look for a moment at the over-all use to which Plato puts it.

Poetry, he says in Book Ten, is not a viable method of discourse, because it reports reality only in terms which are self-cancelling. In fact it embraces contradiction almost as a principle. Like the painter, the poet reports of the same thing that it is now great, now small. The poet is therefore essentially irrational and the same contradiction pervades all his moral statements about action and passion. A hero, that is to say, behaves now well and now badly, thus failing to furnish any one pattern of goodness in the abstract. This epistemological contradiction in the content of the poem sets up a corresponding psychological contradiction in the *psyche* of the listener, who identifies with the tale and so becomes now good, now bad, now angry and now calm.[33]

What we observe here is that, viewing the pluralisation and the concreteness and the confusion of the poetised statement, Plato has reduced all these objectionable aspects to one: they violate the principle of consistency. This must mean that in poetry anti-thetical statements are made of the same person and antithetical predicates are attached to the same subject. He or it is now good and now bad, now big and now small depending apparently on the point of view.

It was in Book Five that he had first used this weapon. He had proposed opinion as the label of that experience which is aware only of the many. But suppose, he continues, our objector asks for proof that opinion (that is, this experienced and vivid impression of the multi-changing panorama of appearances) is not knowledge: we reply: knowledge must be of something that is;

ignorance, its opposite, is of what is not. Since the object of opinion can be neither, then, since opinion is a faculty distinct from both knowledge and ignorance, its object can be neither. The only possibility left is that its object, its area of discourse, lies in between. It is the area of the 'is plus the is-not'.[34]

Now, continues Plato, warming to his theme, to illustrate what I mean, the vision of your ardent sight-seer is filled with many beautifuls, uglies, justs, and unjusts, doubles and halves. But every one of this many can at another time appear ugly instead of beautiful, half instead of double. It is therefore no more beautiful than it is not beautiful and this is true of all the many familiar conventions entertained by the many. And so this condition we call opinion is one which continually apprehends is and is not.[35]

What Plato is getting at, if the contexts of Books Five and Ten are compared, is a contrast between two syntactical situations. In any account of experience which describes it in terms of events happening, these have to be different from each other in order to be separate events. They can only be different if the situations of 'characters' in the story, or of phenomena, are allowed to alter, so that Agamemnon is noble at one point and base at another, or the Greeks at one point are twice as strong as the Trojans and at another point are half as strong. Hence the subjects of these predicates 'are and are not'. He does not mean that they cease to exist, but that in this kind of discourse it is impossible to make a statement which will connect a subject and a predicate in a relationship which just 'is', and which is therefore permanent and unchanging.

What kind of statements then does he want and what kind of syntax will they require? Now we can turn to Book Seven to find out. There as he introduces number and calculation as the key discipline which shall train the mind to abstract the intelligible out of the visible he proposes a dichotomy not between knowledge and opinion but between 'intelligence' and 'sensibility'.[36] The latter reports the fact of three visible fingers as such;

but it goes on to report that one of them is both great and small, both hard and soft, meaning both greater than one and smaller than the other, harder than one and softer than the other.[37] Hence in the language of Book Five it both 'is and is not'. The sensations reported are contradictory; so 'intelligence and calculation' are summoned to solve the mental dilemma and they do so by asking the question: 'What do I mean by the hard or by hardness, by the big or by bigness, etc.?' And they proceed to distinguish and to recognise the mental objects hardness versus softness, bigness versus smallness. These, and not the fingers, are what are counted up and calculated, so that they emerge as separate abstract objects of the intelligence even though our sensible experience keeps confusing them.[38] It is as the intelligence is trained to apprehend them that 'it cleaves to beingness' instead of to 'becomingness'.[39]

Thus when Plato in Book Ten argues that the artist is a man of opinion who confuses his dimensions and cannot reason or calculate and who deals with physical appearances which both are and are not he is continuing the doctrines of Book Five and of Book Seven and reducing the root disease of poetry to this kind of contradiction. But contradiction is a disease only if we assume that it is not the immediate events and situations that are real but the isolated abstractions such as greatness and smallness or right and wrong. It is only of these that statements can be made which are never contradictory. Agamemnon in varying aspects of his behaviour is and is not noble. But nobility always 'is' a virtue. In short, the appeal to banish contradiction is another form of the appeal to name and to use and to think about abstracted identities or principles or classes or categories and the like, rather than concrete events and acts of living passionate people.

Doxa or 'opinion' (or 'belief') is the word which in the *Republic* is preferred as the label of the non-abstract state of mind. There were historical reasons for its choice, later to be explored.[40] Book Ten equates *doxa* with *mimesis*, the latter representing both the content of poetry and that psychological condition which experiences poetically. But in Book Seven, in the passage about the fingers, where the problem about the plural and the concrete and the visible is reduced to one of physical contradiction, the term *doxa* is replaced by *aisthesis*, in both the singular and plural.[41] This word is usually rendered as 'perception' or 'sensation'; we have preferred the translation 'sensibility' to indicate the connection of the word in its original usage with emotional reflex as well as with percipient organ. The use of the term here is of obvious importance for the development of Platonic epistemology. It begins to remove the problem of cognition from the area of the poetised experience of narrative events and to place it in the context of sense experience of physical objects. It is more technical and professional in its overtones. Of the sight-seers in Book Five it is not said that they used 'sensibility', but only that they had been 'familiar with' or had 'embraced' or had 'looked at' the visible panorama.[42] But here it is said of the subject that he is 'sensible' of a finger. The use of *aisthesis* gives promise of greater precision in a debate which will turn on the merits of different theories of cognition and differing criteria of truth.

The structure of the argument in the *Republic*, however, shows how 'opinion' and 'sensibility' and 'mimetic experience' are all bound up together, at least in Plato's mind at this stage of his thinking. In Book Five, it is opinion that passes contrary judgments on great and small, light heavy, and the like. In Book Seven it is sensibility that reports conflicting judgments on size and smallness, hard soft, heavy and light. In Book Ten, it is in *mimesis* that size does not appear equal when it should; and the case is not otherwise with crooked and straight, great or less.[43] And as with sensibility in Book Seven, so also with *mimesis* in Book Ten, it is numbering and measurement that is needed as the weapon wielded by the calculative faculty. Whether Plato speaks of opinion or of sensibility or of poetry, they are all three alike judged and found wanting by the light of the same standard; they cannot become aware of those sheer abstracted identities represented by such terms as size or greatness or smallness. Of opinion

in Book Five as of *mimesis* in Book Ten it is also said that they fail
to apprehend moral abstractions.

Thus it is possible to argue that the problem of physical perception and its confusions and contradictions, a thesis developed and
examined in later Platonism, was originally developed within the
larger context of the poetised experience and its inherent confusions. In both alike, according to Platonism, there is a failure to
separate out clearly the abstracted objects, which are categories,
relations, moral principles, and the like, from the concrete. But
the narrowing down of the problem of experience to one of
physical perception had the effect also of narrowing the object of
experience from the total event-series down to the physical things
in the series. Philosophy gradually forgot its original objective[44]
which had been to throw off the mnemonic spell of the narrative.
It substituted the attempt to throw off the spell of material things.
In either case, the rival candidate for our philosophic allegiance is
an abstract reasoning power which knows identities which are
unchanging. But these identities when opposed to physical things
become categories and properties rather than moral principles.
The original objective of isolating a body of moral law from the
tribal encyclopedia had been largely achieved. The philosophic
problem of settling the status of the material world remained.

But to return to *doxa* or opinion: it is this word that, precisely
because of its very ambiguities, was chosen not only by Plato but
by some of his predecessors to crystallise those properties of the
poetised experience from which the intellectuals were trying to
escape. Both the noun, and the verb *doko*, are truly baffling to
modern logic in their coverage of both the subjective and objective
relationship. The verb denotes both the 'seeming' that goes on in
myself, the 'subject', namely my 'personal impressions', and the
'seeming' that links me as an 'object' to other people looking at
me—the 'impression' I make on them. The noun correspondingly
is both the 'impression' that may be in my mind and the 'impression' held by others of me. It would appear therefore to be the
ideal term to describe that fusion or confusion of the subject with

the object that occurred in the poetised performance and in the state of mind created by this performance. It is the 'seeming show of things', whether this panorama is thought of as within me or outside of me.

Doxa is therefore well chosen as a label not only of the poet's image of reality but of that general image of reality which constituted the content of the Greek mind before Plato. Its general significance prevailed in the end over its poetic one. If it originally united the two, this is precisely because in the long centuries of oral culture and oral communication it was the poet and his narrative that bore the responsibility for creating the general vision and preserving it and fastening it upon the minds of succeeding generations of the Hellenes.[45]

NOTES

[1] I have for convenience used one conventional translation of δόξα, though there is much to support the contention that it signifies 'thought' in general (cf. Rosenmeyer 'Judgment and Thought', etc.), a symbol of an unqualified 'state of mind' which precisely because it is unqualified Plato would demote to a status below that of the exact science which knows the Forms, their relations to each other, and to phenomena.

[2] Plato probably had precedent for this; below, n. 40; cap. 15, n. 5.

[3] 392d2 πάντα ὅσα ὑπὸ μυθολόγων ἢ ποιητῶν λέγεται διήγησις οὖσα τυγχάνει ἢ γεγονότων ἢ ὄντων ἢ μελλόντων, perhaps a reminiscence of *Iliad* 1.70 and *Theog.* 32 (above, cap. 6, notes 20, 21).

[4] 522a4-b1.

[5] 603c4-7.

[6] 595b5-6: cf. Book 6, 511d8.

[7] Cf. Paton, and also Notopoulos 'Parataxis', p. 14: 'This preoccupation with the particular is the natural state of mind of oral literature. . . Absorption in the particular unconcern with the logical relation of the parts to the whole is the unphilosophic condition of εἰκασία which Plato pictures for us in his account of the Cave.' With 596d8-e4 compare Book 6 509e1-510a3, where the objects include ἐν τοῖς ὕδασι φαντάσματα (also below, n. 12); at 598b3 a painting is called φαντάσματος μίμησις; Hamlyn would equate *eikasia* with sophistic.

[8] 598b1 ff.

[9] 598d4-5 διὰ τὸ αὐτὸς μὴ οἷος τ᾽εἶναι ἐπιστήμην καὶ ἀνεπιστημοσύνην καὶ μίμησιν ἐξετάσαι.

[10] 600e5; 601a4-5, b1-2.

[11] Omitting the excursus on the distinction between user and manufacturer 601c-602b.

[12] 602c10-12 καὶ ταῦτα καμπύλα τε καὶ εὐθέα ἐν ὕδατί τε θεωμένοις καὶ ἔξω, καὶ κοῖλα τε δὴ καὶ ἐξέχοντα διὰ τὴν περὶ τὰ χρώματα αὖ πλάνην τῆς ὄψεως.

[13] 602d6-e10.

[14] 603a11-b1 ὅλως ἡ μιμητικὴ . . . πόρρω . . . φρονήσεως ὄντι τῷ ἐν ἡμῖν προσομιλεῖ τε καὶ ἑταίρα καὶ φίλη ἐστίν. . . . On phronesis cf. above, cap. 11, n. 17.

[15] 604a10 ff.

[16] 605c1-3 οὔτε τὰ μείζω οὔτε τὰ ἐλάττω διαγιγνώσκοντι, ἀλλὰ τὰ αὐτὰ τοτὲ μὲν μεγάλα ἡγουμένῳ, τοτὲ δὲ σμικρά. . . .

[17] 475d1-e1 φιλοθεάμονες φιλήκοοι.

[18] 476b4 τάς τε καλὰς φωνὰς ἀσπάζονται κτλ. c2 ὁ οὖν καλὰ μὲν πράγματα νομίζων, αὐτὸ δὲ κάλλος μήτε νομίζων κτλ.

[19] 477a1-478d12.

[20] 479a5-b10.

[21] 479d3 τὰ τῶν πολλῶν πολλὰ νόμιμα.

[22] 480a6-13.

[23] 602e8-603a2 ἔφαμεν τῷ αὐτῷ ἅμα περὶ ταῦτα ἐναντία δοξάζειν ἀδύνατον εἶναι . . . τὸ παρὰ τὰ μέτρα ἄρα δοξάζον τῆς ψυχῆς . . . cf. 479e4 and 8 δοξάζειν.

[24] 480a1-7.

[25] 475d5-8.

[26] 475d3 and 476b4-5; cf. Laws 7.810e: the many poets, epic, iambic and the rest, serious and comic, are recommended as correct education for our young men who are thus rendered πολυηκόους as they learn whole poets by heart.

[27] 480a1 ff.

[28] Even the phrase at 476b6 πάντα τὰ ἐκ τῶν τοιούτων δημιουργούμενα is ambiguously relevant both to artifacts and to poems which describe them; cf. 10.596c5, d3, where χειροτέχνης and δημιουργός are applied to the case of painter and poet.

[29] 476c2, 479d3.

[30] 476a10 φιλοθεάμονάς τε καὶ φιλοτέχνους καὶ πρακτικούς.

[31] Apol. 22a8, c9 (but the order is varied).

[32] Above, n. 4.

[33] 10.603c10 ff.

[34] 478d1 ff.

[35] 479d7 ff.

[36] 523a10-b1 τὰ μὲν ἐν ταῖς αἰσθήσεσιν οὐ παρακαλοῦντα τὴν νόησιν εἰς ἐπίσκεψιν cf. 507c3 καὶ ἀκοῇ τὰ ἀκούομενα καὶ ταῖς ἄλλαις αἰσθήσεσι πάντα τὰ αἰσθητά.

[37] 523c4 ff.

[38] 524b4 πειρᾶται λογισμόν τε καὶ νόησιν ψυχὴ παρακαλοῦσα ἐπισκοπεῖν εἴτε ἓν εἴτε δύο ἐστὶν ἕκαστα τῶν εἰσαγγελομένων . . . εἰ ἄρα ἓν ἑκάτερον,

ἀμφότερα δὲ δύο, τά γε δύο κεχωρισμένα νοήσει . . . διὰ τὴν τούτου σαφήνειαν μέγα αὖ καὶ σμικρὸν ἡ νόησις ἠναγκάσθη ἰδεῖν . . . ἐντεῦθέν ποθεν πρῶτον ἐπέρχεται ἐρέσθαι ἡμῖν τί οὖν ποτ᾽ ἐστὶ τὸ μέγα αὖ καὶ τὸ σμικρόν.

39 525b5 διὰ τὸ τῆς οὐσίας ἁπτέον εἶναι γενέσεως ἐξαναδύντι.

40 In a subsequent volume: usage in Heraclitus and Parmenides is particularly pertinent.

41 Above, n. 36. von Fritz (1946, p. 24) points out that *aisthesis* is not pre-Socratic, but nevertheless (p. 31) characterises the antithesis *nous-aisthesis* as late pre-Socratic. Should it not be identified as Platonic, even though, as von F. demonstrates, Protagoras Democritus and Gorgias forced the issues which precipitated it?

42 476c2 νομίζων 479a3 νομίζει 476b5 ἀσπάζονται 480a3 φιλεῖν τε καὶ θεᾶσθαι.

43 602c7-8, 10.

44 Notopoulos 'Mnemosyne', pp. 482 ff., noting Plato's preference for the oral word, in the *Phaedrus*, interprets this not in connection with the dialectical process, but as a reassertion of the claims and powers of oral memory, now put to philosophic use. This compels him (p. 484) to interpret *Theaet.* 191d as though it referred to 'memory in philosophy' when it in fact refers to the wax tablet conception of the mind which Platonic epistemology finds impossible.

45 The account I have given of *doxa* in the *Republic* precludes the conclusion commonly held that in this dialogue the distinction between the respective objects of *doxa* and *episteme* is metaphysical, identifying two different 'worlds', in one of which the philosopher enjoys the 'vision of the Forms', but from which he is 'plunged in the swirling twilight world of compulsion', a world in which 'Plato has already resigned his hopes'—so Gould, p. 163. The difference is determined by considerations which are syntactical, not religious. It is to be noted that once the term 'world' is subtracted from statements like the above, they become meaningless (cf. also 'order' of being). There is no corresponding term in Plato's account.

CHAPTER FOURTEEN

The Origin of the Theory of Forms

WHEN Plato insists that his contemporaries must turn away from the panorama of sensual experience, and focus instead upon the abstracted object *per se* which is the only possible object of thought, he sometimes identifies this object as a Form and also speaks of the Forms (in the plural) as furnishing a methodology or intellectual discipline which is familiar to his readers. Obviously it was not familiar to the average Greek whose state of mind was still that of opinion. But Plato's language presumes a circle of some sort which was accustomed to use the term Form to identify this kind of object.[1] Since this *methodos* of the Forms seems to be presumed in dialogues earlier than the *Republic*, and since the critical dialogues following the *Republic* often examine the possible meanings of the term *Form* and the way it should or might be used, it has become usual among scholars to speak of Plato's Theory of Forms.

The phrase suggests a doctrinal position in which Plato wished to vest his philosophical prestige. But the actual tone of his writings does not support this; it is too non-professional. When in the *Republic* he first introduces the objects which 'are', he calls them Forms,[2] yet in the *Republic* itself he can more often than not employ the conception of the object *per se* without calling it a Form; and even in contexts where as often he reaffirms the absolute character of Platonic knowledge, he does not necessarily feel compelled to use the word.[3]

It is even more important to notice that he can use the term 'form' over and over again without benefit of capital letter, so to speak, to mean type or kind or class or category, in contexts where the possibility that this may also signify an object *per se* is not even in question.[4] In short he uses the word professionally and he also uses it casually and non-professionally. If one assumes that Plato's doctrine was systematic in the modern sense of that term, and also systematically expressed, one distinguishes sharply between the casual use of the word 'form' and its professional application as 'Form' and one ascribes the fact that the same term does double duty simply to an inadequacy of the Greek vocabulary. The assumption however may itself be at fault, and if so, the distinction between the two usages ceases to be sharp. If this is true, then the non-professional usage may shed light on the professional; nay, the professional may itself be only an attempt, not consistently pursued, to formalise the implications of the non-professional usage. It is to this conception of the problem that we address ourselves here.

Up to this point, in our pursuit of the meaning of Platonic doctrine, we have ourselves avoided the word Form, and this despite the fact that our area of investigation has focused on the *Republic* where the 'method'[5] of the Forms is explicitly avowed and used. Nor as we now take up this usage and the reason for it shall we attempt to find clues in those later dialogues where the problem of the Form and its relation to particulars is critically explored. By this time, Platonism had solved or felt it had solved the main issue which had given it birth, namely the urgent compulsion to break with the poetised tradition and with the poetised state of mind. Once a discourse of formal abstraction had become accepted as the proper instrument of science, whether moral or physical, the originally simpler if revolutionary motivation for the theory of Forms could be superseded; and the complexities of a new epistemology and a new logic of description with all its problems of predication and the like could properly come into the foreground. Our business here is with that simpler stage of development which produced the Form as an object of discourse in the first place. Clues to this stage in Plato's thinking are likely to be lost if they are sought in that refinement of language and analysis which came later and which was framed to cope with sophisticated dilemmas.

Why have we preferred to avoid mentioning the term Form until this point? Our search has been for those historical and linguistic necessities which prompted Plato to change the idiom of the Greek tongue. The direct evidence of these necessities is furnished not in the Forms but in his reiterated use of the 'itself *per se*', which is 'one', and which 'is', and which 'unseen'. This is Plato's fundamental language,[6] for by its own syntax it also betrays the syntax of that which he is breaking away from, that from which he is emancipating himself and from which he has to emancipate us. As has been explained, the converse of these attributes of the 'itself *per se*' is a pluralised series of events and acts which happen rather than are, and which are imagistically and therefore vividly portrayed, instead of being thought. In this series the integrity of the 'itself *per se*', conceived as category or as principle or as property or the like, gets broken up and scattered and dispersed through the pluralised instances, where we can say it may be present as a principle 'by implication', but where in fact it was not present in the Homeric discourse because that discourse lacked the linguistic facilities to name it.

This new Platonic language, then, discloses as no other language does the character of the revolution in Greek culture which it was the business of Platonism to announce. To understand the revolution we begin with this language and not with the Forms. As Plato himself puts it: 'For the majority of men it is impossible to entertain beauty itself instead of the many beautifuls, or any specific "itself" instead of the many specifics . . . so the majority can never be intellectuals.'[7]

The phrasing of the 'itself *per se*', stressing as it does the simple purity of the 'object', gathered together so to speak in isolation from any contamination with anything else, indicates a mental act which quite literally corresponds to the Latin term 'abstraction'; that is, this 'object' which the newly self-conscious 'subject' has to think about has been literally 'torn out' of the epic context and created by an act of intellectual isolation and integration. For example, the many (concealed) instances of proper conduct are gathered up into 'propriety *per se*, quite by itself'. This notion of propriety has had to be separated and abstracted from the image flow of events and situations where actors or agents happen to do proper or improper things.

It is fair then to speak of Platonism as posing an insistent demand that we think of isolated mental entities or abstractions and that we use abstract language in describing or explaining experience. What kind of abstractions did Plato, at the point where he wrote the *Republic*, have in mind? He nowhere gives a systematic list, but his answer to this question can be compiled as it were from a progressive series of contexts in each of which he is addressing himself to some aspect of this mental process.

When the "itself by itself" is first introduced in Book Five as a description of what the philosopher, and the philosopher alone, thinks about, the examples cited are beautiful, just, good, and their antitheses ugly, unjust, evil.[8] Indeed the fundamental character of the antithesis is itself used to argue for the existence of all these as abstract objects. This would mean that not only the positive moral principles or values but their negatives should be isolated and used in Platonic discourse. A little later as he presses the proof that only these objects are self-consistent, whereas the many exhibit only contradictory predicates, he reiterates the moral terms and adds double, half, great, small, light, heavy to the list.[9]

The next such list occurs in the parable of the Divided Line as he tries to describe the 'objects' which in section three of that Line are represented in the form of geometric figures. The examples given are odd, even, shape, three types of angle,[10] and 'the square itself' and 'the diameter itself'.[11] As to the fourth or uppermost section of the Line, he seems to imply that this represents that area of intellection where these and other abstractions are inter-related in a discourse which would be completely analytic, but he gives no examples.

Then in Book Seven, in the three-fingers passage, as he comes to examine the key issue of that contradiction contributed by the 'sensibilities', to which intellect must supply the answer by separating out and counting the 'objects' that have become confused with the fingers, he lists, as examples of these objects, size, smallness, hard, soft, heavy, light.[12]

Finally in Book Ten, repeating in effect the doctrine of the fingers passage in another form, and calling attention once more to contradiction in the sensibilities, he asserts that the calculative faculty has to come to the rescue and measure great, less, and equal; the error of 'mimetic' is that it fails to distinguish great and small.[13]

These lists when cross-compared reveal considerable community. The first and second, from Book Five, disclose, what we know well from elsewhere in Plato, that 'goodness' and 'rightness' (or the 'principle' of good and the 'principle' of right), which to us are moral categories or imperatives describing and also informing human behaviour, are for Plato on a par with shape and dimension (size and smallness) and proportion (double and half) and the like; that is, on a par with those simple basic mathematical categories which we use in discussing the physical world. They are on a par because they all alike represent the same kind of psychic effort which breaks away from the many and unifies experience into ones. The simple mathematical categories are then joined by arithmetical ones (odd and even) and by geometric postulates (square and diagonal). Then they are also joined by some of the basic 'properties' as we might call them of physical objects, for example penetrability (hard and soft) and weight (heavy and light).

With these clues to guide us, it is pertinent to hark back to that curriculum of the sciences which is offered in Book Seven as the essential prelude to dialectic. These sciences as Plato repeatedly stresses are not to be studied as closed subjects supplying blocks of information or bodies of rules for mental absorption. Their entire purpose is to accelerate the intellectual awakening which 'converts' the *psyche* from the many to the one, and from 'becoming-

ness' to 'beingness'; this, if our thesis is correct, is equivalent to
a conversion from the image-world of the epic to the abstract
world of scientific description, and from the vocabulary and
syntax of narrativised events in time towards the syntax and
vocabulary of equations and laws and formulas and topics which
are outside time.

Now, in this connection it is pertinent to notice in Book Seven
that the sciences offered, from arithmetic to harmonics, are
arranged in ascending series according to the abstract definition
of their fields of operation. They are each a thought-world, so to
speak, disposed within a set of co-ordinates; these co-ordinates
form an ascending series which increases in complication. Within
geometry we grasp the field of the plane 'in two dimensions'.
Then follows the 'three-dimensional' which 'partakes in volume'
and this must be grasped 'itself *per se*'. Then comes the 'three
dimensional in motion' or 'motion applied to volume', and its
field of mental vision is occupied by 'the speed that is' and 'the
slowness that is' or 'the truth of equal or double or any other
proportion'. Finally comes 'motion in sound'; for 'motion has
several forms'.[14]

It should be pointed out that these phrases are used in Plato's
text to define areas of the known, or objects of knowledge.[15] He
speaks as though the detailed disciplines of the sciences are really
useful only to open up the mental vision of systems of co-
ordinates which govern them. Is it to be concluded that in this
whole passage of the *Republic* Plato is appealing to the Greek mind
to think about body and space, motion and velocity and the like,
as such? or, we might say, to think about physical experience in
these terms and using this kind of vocabulary? This is surely the
clue to that passage, so startling to empirical scientists, where he
damns and dismisses the study of the 'visible heaven'.[16] What he
is appealing for is to get away from that kind of story of the
heavens of which Hesiod's calendar is the epic prototype and from
those ingenious orreries and constructs which confined themselves
to trying to model and reproduce the visible appearances and the

motions of the heavenly bodies. A star-map is an example of
what he rejects. He is demanding instead a discourse which shall
rearrange these phenomena under general headings or categories
of the physical so that they then can be expressed in the language
of natural law. The visible heavens are to function only as a paradigm from which to elucidate the universal behaviour of bodies,
expressed in equations which 'are' and do not 'become' or change.
In the absence of a laboratory technique, he has to use the visible
heaven as his controlled experiment in mechanics.[17] His appeal
to the pupil is double-barrelled, and has to be, in the existing state
of the Greek vocabulary. First, he says, start thinking not about
how fast this particular object you see is moving or how big it is;
think about speed and size as general co-ordinates; second, don't
tell me 'look, A is rising faster than B'; try instead to say: the
speed temporarily embodied in A is twice that of the speed
temporarily embodied in B; and then say: the velocities of these
two bodies are in given ratio to a theoretical common velocity;
and this will bring you to consider what are the laws or formulas
according to which apparent speeds vary. Thus invisible astronomy becomes a device for thinking in terms of what (a) is purely
abstract and (b) can be stated in a timeless syntax as that which
always 'is' and never 'is not'.[18]

Here is a new frame of discourse and a new kind of vocabulary
offered to the European mind. We take it for granted today as the
discourse of educated men. It does not occur to us that once upon
a time it was necessary for it to have been discovered and defined
and insisted on, so that we could easily and complacently inherit
it. This discovery is essentially Plato's, even though he is building
on a great pioneering effort in this same direction which had
preceded him. The fact that Greek words which we are here
able to translate as 'motion' or 'body' had already existed is not
the point. It is their syntactical relationship that has changed, and
as it has changed, the word is shorn of particularity and becomes
stretched to the dimensions of a concept. In pre-Platonic usage
(if we here except certain of the pre-Socratics) the words had

never been used as subjects of the timeless is. They had symbolised the flight of an arrow or the corpse of a particular man as they had fitfully presented themselves in the narrative series, and now they are going to mean just 'any and every motion' and 'any and every corpse in the cosmos' without qualification. They have been abstracted and integrated out of all the pictures of runnings or flights of arrows or men and of bodies of fighters and corpses of the dead. They have been made into 'invisibles'.[19]

Goodness and rightness (with evil and unrighteousness), proportion and size, dimension and weight and shape, odd and even, the square and the diagonal, solidity, motion, velocity, and volume—what does this kind of terminology represent to us? As terms of a sophisticated vocabulary, these are many different things: they are moral values; they are also axioms; they are physical properties; and also relations. In combination with each other they furnish the terms in which we state both moral principles and physical formulas, both equations and laws. They bespeak the language of categories, and also of universals. The only modern term that would apply to all alike would be the word 'concept'. For these share the common characteristic that as categories, classes, relationships or principles or axioms, they have been coined by the mind to explain and to classify its sensual experience or have been extracted from that experience and have been inferred from it. As Plato says, the one thing you can say about them all is that you cannot see or taste or hear them. Some other faculty of man's brain is responsible for this kind of language. If we call them 'concepts' it is to oppose them to the 'image'. If we call them 'abstract' it is to oppose them to the concrete visualised event or the concrete visualised things that behave in an event. And it is fair to say that Platonism at bottom is an appeal to substitute a conceptual discourse for an imagistic one. As it becomes conceptual, the syntax changes, to connect abstractions in timeless relationships instead of counting up events in a time series; such discourse yields the abstracted objects of 'intellection'.

Plato can never separate any discussion of these objects from the

PREFACE TO PLATO

activity of 'thinking' that apprehends them. They are *noeta* or they are nothing. And they are so often put before us less for their own sake than to illustrate and underline the difference between knowledge on the one hand and opinion on the other, or between an act of the intellect and an act of the sensory mechanism. It is more important to learn to think about this new kind of object than to decide on the precise names and numbers of the objects that there may be. This is the reiterated impression one receives from Plato's own account of the matter.[20]

Why then did he refuse to label them as concepts? He could have devised Greek for this purpose. Some of his predecessors, themselves aware of what was going on in the Greek mind, had for example spoken of 'thoughts' or 'notions' (*phrontides, noemata*)[21] as though they represented a new phenomenon in the Greek experience. Yet to describe these various phenomena, of language and of mental effort, which we have characterised as abstracted objects, Plato used a Greek term (in two variants) which avoids any suggestion of mental construction and is translatable only visually as 'shape' or as 'form'.

The Homeric meaning of this word refers to the 'look'[22] of a person, but it had already been specialised to some extent before Plato's day, at least by intellectuals, who if they were mathematicians used it to describe a geometric figure or construct,[23] and if they were cosmologists or medical men might use the word to describe a 'common look' shared by a group of phenomena;[24] it was thus a 'general shape' or, in the Latin equivalent, the *species*. It was probably these two[25] previous usages which encouraged Plato to exploit the word professionally and apply it, as apparently he intended at the time when he wrote the *Republic*, to almost any concept which was useful as a method of classifying phenomena or of determining principles of action or of generalising the properties of things or of determining their relationships.

Why did he prefer this sort of word to describe the results of conceptual activity, if it was for this kind of activity on the part of the Greek mind that he was appealing? It is better first to ask:

Why did he have to shun any term which would approximate to our 'concept'? The answer is probably very simple. A concept, at least at this stage of Greek speculative development, would mean any and every thought devised and put into words by the *psyche* of the aroused intelligence. The possibilities of abstraction are limitless, and of meaningful abstraction hardly less so. But in the sphere of morals, which is always for Plato the primary illustration of the need for conceptual thinking, he was completely devoted to the thesis that the principles of morality are fixed and finite and do not form an endless series and are not framed in terms of empirical adjustment to temporal circumstances. Here his fervent opposition to relativism surely warned him that to propose justice and goodness as abstract *conceptions* which we have to refine upon by our own intelligence would open the way to the endless invention of new formulas and new conceptions of what morality might be. Against this relativist acceptance of a morality which might have been developed historically by man for man's needs he had a revulsion which went beyond argument and reached into the depths of his consciousness. Probably it should be admitted that social background and class prejudice committed him very early in life to the proposition that social relations between men should be not only stable but also authoritarian.[26] And if so, the principles of justice which describe these relations must themselves be independent of human invention or improvement.

At any rate, the need to symbolise moral abstractions as final was the primary motive, we suggest, for calling them Forms. For the Forms, in order to be such, have to enjoy a kind of independent existence; they are permanent shapes imposed upon the flux of action, and shapes which, while they can be viewed and understood by my *psyche*, cannot be invented by it. So the Forms are not the creation of the intellect and this means that the 'objects' represented by such linguistic devices as 'the itself *per se*' are not the creations of the intellect either.

He had a second motive, perhaps equally strong. A great

multiplicity of these objects was used to describe not the sphere of moral action but the behaviour of the physical environment. Plato inherited from his predecessors an underlying conviction that as we experience physical phenomena we are somehow in contact with a world, an order, a system which exists outside ourselves and independently of our knowledge of it. As we have said in an earlier chapter, it was fundamental to the Greek genius, and we can see this in Greek art, that the external world should not be taken lightly or dismissed as non-existent. What was required was that its structure and logic be appreciated. This structure for Plato as for most Greek thinkers was itself abstract. It was also coherent and finite, a closed system, an object of intelligence, not of intuition. The senses in their report of it yielded only dilemmas and contradictions.

If so, then the mental categories we use in order to describe and to understand it, such as its figures and proportions, its spatial relations, its volumes and densities, its weights and its velocities cannot be merely arbitrary conveniences of the human intellect. They must somehow represent the cosmic structure itself. We do not invent them though we have to learn with great effort to think about them. So they too are Forms, the real existence of which is guaranteed independently of our cognition even though our cognition is geared exclusively to apprehend them.

So the abstractions demanded of the Greek mind become Forms, and not concepts. We may cavil with this outcome, but in the historical context it makes sense. If we view them in relation to the epic narrative from which, as a matter of historical fact, they all emerged they can all be regarded as in one way or another classifications of an experience which was previously 'felt' in an unclassified medley. This was as true of justice as of motion, of goodness as of body or space, of beauty as of weight or dimension. These categories turn into linguistic counters, and become used as a matter of course to relate one phenomenon to another in a non-epic, non-poetic, non-concrete idiom. Simply put, a narrativised experience says: 'The storm-god launched the river against the wall and swept it away.'[27]   An abstract version rearranges this to say 'The river had a force of such and such (which would mean a proportion of some universal or ideal unit of force which always 'is') and the wall had a weight (or mass or inertia) of such and such; the weight and the force when calculated and compared yield the result that the wall has to give way before the stress imposed on it'.   But this particular result now depends on concepts of force and weight which just 'are' and which become the terms of equations which 'are'.   These in Platonism would become the 'Forms' of force and weight, and their participation in each other becomes a law governing the relation of pressure to inertia.   Then the application of this law to the given instance shows the 'Forms' participating in the particular situation of the wall plus the river.

Or again, Agamemnon challenged by Calchas to give up the priest's daughter is very angry; yet he adds: 'For all that I will give her back if that is better.   Rather would I see my people whole than perishing.   Only make you ready a prize of honour forthwith lest I alone of all the Argives be disprized, which thing is not proper.   For you all behold how my prize is departing from me.'[28] This series of acts and events sharply but separately imagised—'I will give her back—the people must not perish—but get me a substitute—I am king—I am the only one to lose my prize'— these can be rearranged as the expression or illustration of moral principle or social law: 'The good of the army is paramount and this forces me to return the girl.   Nevertheless my status is also paramount; justice therefore requires that I receive a substitute.' Here the 'good' of the army, the 'status' of Agamemnon, and the 'justice' of his demand are cast in a language which presumes some general standard of good and of propriety and of justice, by which the particular good and the particular propriety of the present situation can be estimated.   The standards have to be expressed in ideal laws which just 'are'.   They can participate in a given situation which 'is and is not', but only by providing the norms which persist through the situation and are obeyed in the course of the actions and events which constitute it. These too, then, would be Platonic Forms.

For Plato, we repeat, these terms and the formulas made out of them were not just linguistic devices, nor inventions of the intellect, but entities of some sort existing outside of the mind. Yet the effort it takes to discover and to name them and to learn to use them provides the central preoccupation of Book Seven of his *Republic*, the book devoted *par excellence* to the curriculum of the Academy. The 'method' of the Forms is in a practical sense prior to the Forms themselves, if we realise that the abstract 'objects' do not come gliding into our consciousness suspended on clouds of illumination. Rather, we have to grapple with the many and seek their conversion into ones, an operation which first discloses these 'objects' as possible in language and in thought.

To call them Forms threw the main emphasis not on how we actually find and apply them but on their 'objectivity' *vis-à-vis* the 'subject' who has to think about them. Plato as he prepares to use and exploit the Form is becoming convinced of the ultimate separation of objective knowledge from the knowing subject, and convinced that it is this facet of the truth which above all he must dramatise. We may complain that he thus underplays the historical relationship of the new formal and abstract language to the old epic language. The one, we say, emerged from the other, just as the intellect emerged out of the Homeric consciousness. But if we remember the centuries of old habit, which had fused subject with object in sympathetic self-identification as a condition of keeping the oral tradition alive, we can realise how this inherited state of mind was for Plato *the* enemy, and how he would wish to frame his own doctrine in language which met it head on, and confronted it, and destroyed it. The net effect then of the theory of Forms is to dramatise the split between the image-thinking of poetry and the abstract thinking of philosophy. In the history of the Greek mind, it puts the stress on discontinuity rather than on continuity. This is ever the way with makers of revolutions. In their own day and to themselves and their own audiences they are prophets of the new, not developers of the old. Socrates to be sure conceived of himself as a midwife of the soul, a metaphor which presupposes perhaps some continuity between the Socratic dialectic and previous experience. Plato's language, as it elevates the philosopher above the common run of men and the Forms above the common idiom and thought, is more stringent. A term less challenging than Form would not perhaps have accomplished his purpose.

Was this new idiom not in fact ushering in a completely new stage in the development not only of the Greek but of the European mind? It was; yet Plato was aware also and rightly so that only his genius had been able fully to realise that this was a revolution, and that it had to be pushed with urgency. Others before him had been moving in this direction, had been experimenting tentatively with the new syntax and had been aware that the poetic tradition was an obstacle. But only Plato saw the issue steadily and as a whole. If he therefore sought to populate the universe and the mind of man with a whole family of Forms which had emerged from God knows where, this was in a sense a necessity for him. For he was seeing into the heart of a profound change in the cultural experience of man. They were not his personal whim; they were not even his personal doctrine. They announced the arrival of a completely new level of discourse which as it became perfected was to create in turn a new kind of experience of the world—the reflective, the scientific, the technological, the theological, the analytic. We can give it a dozen names. The new mental era required its own banners to march under and found it in the Platonic Forms.

Viewed from this perspective, the Theory of Forms was a historical necessity. But before we leave it in the enjoyment of this status, it is proper to ask whether the choice of the term did not also carry with it certain grave disadvantages. What we are now going to say will strike many readers as controversial, especially those who feel the spell of Plato's mysticism. Our contention will be that a thinker whose historical task was to destroy

the effect of one spell should not have re-introduced another, and
as it were by the back door. The trouble with the word Form is
precisely that as it seeks to objectify and separate knowledge from
opinion it also tends to make knowledge visual again. For as
'form' or 'shape' or 'look' it is something after all which you tend
to see and watch and visually contemplate. Plato is so convinced
of the reality of goodness and of odd and of even that he tries to
make us see them.[29] But should he have tried?

No doubt the previous use of the word for a geometric figure
played its role in his own imagination.[30] He is careful in the
parable of the Line to point out that geometric figures incorporate
Forms but are not themselves wholly abstract; they still are
visibles, or use visibles.[31] But it may be doubted whether he
always succeeded in shielding himself rigorously against this
visual contamination. The proof of the matter lies in the idiom
and syntax he would himself sometimes employ to describe our
relationship to the Forms. We ourselves he can say may 'imitate'
them. After he wrote the *Republic*, he probably came to reject
this way of expressing the relationship.[32] It is symptomatic
however of its danger that it remains to this day the most facile
method of explaining to students the operation of the Forms. Are
they not patterns to which we liken our actions and ourselves?
This gives rise to the doctrine that the philosopher 'imitates the
objects that are' and 'likens himself to them' and finally likens
himself to God. 'For one imitates that with which one enthusiastically consorts.'[33] The last phrase sounds like an echo of Plato's
analysis of the relationship between auditor and poem in Book
Three. But now the context is not pejorative. Yet can Plato have
it both ways? Is it not true that this kind of statement is simply
rhetorical and obscures rather than reveals the essence of Platonism? For the objects being discussed are really graspable only after
a tough dialectical effort which breaks up the dream and removes
our habit of identification, substituting for it a separate and isolated objectivity. It would seem that in such metaphors, used not
infrequently, Plato allows himself to fall back into the idiom of

precisely that psychic condition which he is setting out to destroy.[24]

Our relationship to these objects is not one of 'imitation', and never should be. Rather it is one of an anxious, puzzled, and often frustrated inquiry until we have grasped and named them, and an equally arduous effort of syntax and of composition as we apply them in meaningful statement. The notion of 'imitation' replaces all the Socratic sense of urgent effort by a new type of receptive passivity.

That this over-facile conception, this shortcut to the significance of the use of the Forms, was assisted by the choice of the word Form itself can be illustrated from a passage in the *Republic* which we have deliberately reserved for this place. No passage is more familiar to modern students of the theory precisely because no passage is so easy of comprehension. You have the unique and eternal Form of 'bed' corresponding to the common name 'bed'. Then you have a copying of the Form by the craftsman, who makes this bed or that, and incorporates the pattern therein. Finally you have the artist, whether the painter or poet, who 'imitates' the craftsman's copy, as he just paints the bed or sings about it.[35]

The reason why the Theory of Forms here uses this particular illustration is clear. The artist and the poet in common Greek idiom were both craftsmen.[36] Plato wants a trilogy which will put another craftsman on top of them in a superior status, and the philosopher in turn above him. This will dramatically, but we suggest only rhetorically, degrade the artist to third place and not just second and so clinch the Platonic dismissal of him. To get this hierarchy, a Form has to be chosen from which an artifact can be derived. Presumably a shoe or a saucepan, a clothes bag or a safety-pin, would have done as well, nay any artifact whatever which a given civilisation happens to have turned out. This raises the question whether in a culture that did not happen to use beds or nails (and such is conceivable) the corresponding Forms any longer exist.[37] But aside from the metaphysics of the problem, the real limitation of this example of a Form is that it remains so patently an ideal 'shape' which you can indeed imitate by copying it as a sort of outline and which can easily be imagined existing as such even in the mind of God who, Plato incautiously suggests, may be responsible for its origin.[38] The visual content of the Form predominates over its dialectical use.

Hence also it is made here to correspond to a common name, that is, to a noun that denotes a concrete physical object. So used, the Form amounts only to the demand that we recognise all common nouns as indeed 'common'; they can be regarded as symbolising classes. The effort of abstraction which this requires of us is minimal and it does not yield the terms of an abstract discourse, for the term bed will still go on being used as bed. What the theory of Forms was properly designed to affirm was the existence of abstract properties and relations of physical objects and so forth. This is amply demonstrated by Plato's lists of examples in the *Republic* itself. No artificer tries to make 'dimension' or 'justice' or 'velocity' or 'equality'. And these abstractions considered as linguistic devices are all of adjectival origin. One could indeed ask whether a Greek noun denominating in the first instance a specific thing should ever be associated with a Form.[39]

But the Form of bed undeniably suggests visual relationships— an ideal geometry of a bed—even at the highest level, and so on down the scale of intellection to the poet's imperfect visualisation. This type of example is not exploited again[40] in this way by Plato. But one can say that repeatedly, in striving for a language which shall describe that new level of mental activity which we style abstract, he tends to relapse into metaphors of vision, when it would have been less misleading to rely always on idioms which stress the critical effort of analysis and synthesis. The crucial example is his use of the Greek word for 'view' or 'contemplation' (*theoria*), which to be sure has properly and happily transmuted itself into our word 'theory', signifying a wholly abstract level of discourse, but which in Plato continually suggests the 'contemplation' of realities which once achieved are there to be seen.[41] The mental condition is one of passivity, of a new sort perhaps. The poetic type of receptivity gained through imitation was an excited condition emotionally active. The new contemplation is to be serene, calm, and detached. It is to be like the 'inspection' of a religious rite as opposed to participation in a human drama. Plato has changed the character of the performance and has reduced us to silent spectators. But we remain sightseers. Are we not simply being invited to avoid hard thinking and relapse into a new form of dream which shall be religious rather than poetic?

This would conduct us along the path which leads to mystic contemplation of truth, beauty, and goodness. It is not to be denied that Plato sometimes invites us to travel it. Yet we contend that it would not have been so easy to travel, if he had not tried to symbolise his newly-discovered abstractions in visual terms. The Forms thus made concrete, again acceptable to our senses and our affections, could proceed to populate a physical cosmos which had been prepared for their occupancy and their habitation. The *Timaeus* is Plato's final tribute to this kind of speculative vision. But it is a vision, not an argument. Dare we suggest that in the *Timaeus*, for this very reason, he also accomplished the final betrayal[42] of the dialectic, the betrayal of that Socratic *methodos* which had sought for formulae in order to replace the visual story by the purely abstract equation? There is to be sure a kind of algebra in the *Timaeus*. But it is well overlaid with the dream-clothes of mythology, and precisely for that reason the dialogue became the favourite reading of an age which clung to faith rather than science as its guide. Yet the day would come when the original drive of the Platonic method would revive, and the phenomenal flux would once more be examined and penetrated and subordinated to categories of explanation which possess a wholly abstract integrity. And when this day came, science would awaken again.

NOTES

[1] 475e6 ff.; 504e7-8; 505a2-3; 507a8; 596a5-7.

[2] 476a5; strictly speaking, the language which affirms the existence and importance of the 'object' is first used at the beginning of Book 2, but its elucidation is postponed to this place (above, cap. 12, notes 6, 20).

[3] In the exposition (476a-485a) which follows upon the introduction of the Forms, and which depends on them, the term is used only twice, at 476a5 and 479a1. In the account of the university curriculum (including dialectic) which fills so much of Book 7, it is used only at 530c8, 532e1, 534c1, and of these instances the first two are 'non-professional' (vid. next note). In the Phaedo the term is not introduced until 103e (below, n. 6). In the Theaetetus, it does not appear at all.

[4] Some exx. are Book 2. 357c, 358a, 363e; Book 3. 396b, 397b; Book 4. 395b, etc., 432b, 435b-e, 443c.

[5] Above, n. 1.

[6] Thus, aside from the Republic, where we have sufficiently illustrated, in cap. 12, the way in which Platonic epistemology is dominated by the auto to (Book 2 init., Book 5 476a-Book 6 485a, and the whole of Book 7), we find that the same is true of the Phaedo (e.g. 65b ff., 78d ff., 100b ff., in fact up to the point where the Forms are first used, vid. above, n. 3) and of the Theaetetus.

[7] 493e2-494a2 αὐτὸ τὸ καλὸν ἀλλὰ μὴ τὰ πολλὰ καλά, ἢ αὐτό τι ἕκαστον καὶ μὴ τὰ πολλὰ ἕκαστα, ἔσθ᾽ ὅπως πλῆθος ἀνέξεται ἢ ἡγήσεται εἶναι; . . . φιλόσοφον μὲν ἄρα . . . πλῆθος ἀδύνατον εἶναι cf. 490b1-4; 500c2-3.

[8] 475e9-476a4, repeated at 507b2-8, but without 'the just'.

[9] 479a1-b8.

[10] 510c4-5.

[11] 510d7-8.

[12] 523e3-524a10.

[13] 602d6-e6; 605c1-4. These last examples do not objectify the great, small, etc., as auta ta, but the mental processes which distort the metra and those which correct them are described in terms reminiscent of the contrast between doxa and episteme and their respective objects, and reminiscent also of that process by which reason corrects sensation as described in Book 7 (above, cap. 13, pp. 240 ff.).

[14] 528a9-b3 μετὰ ἐπίπεδον . . . ἐν περιφορᾷ ὂν ἤδη στερεὸν λαβόντες, πρὶν αὐτὸ καθ᾽ αὐτὸ λαβεῖν· ὀρθῶς δὲ ἔχει ἑξῆς μετὰ δευτέραν αὔξην τρίτην λαμβάνειν· ἔστι δέ που τοῦτο περὶ τὴν τῶν κύβων αὔξην καὶ τὸ βάθους μετέχον 528e1 ἀστρονομίαν . . . φορὰν οὖσαν βάθους 529d2-4 ἃς τὸ ὂν τάχος καὶ ἡ οὖσα βραδυτὴς ἐν τῷ ἀληθινῷ ἀριθμῷ καὶ πᾶσι τοῖς ἀληθέσι σχήμασι φορᾶς τε πρὸς ἄλληλα φέρεται καὶ τὰ ἐνόντα φέρει 529e5 τὴν ἀλήθειαν . . . ἴσων ἢ διπλασίων ἢ ἄλλης τινὸς συμμετρίας 530c8 πλείω . . . εἴδη παρέχεται ἡ φορά 530d7 ἐναρμόνιον φοράν.

[15] 529b5 μάθημα . . . ἐκεῖνο δ᾽ ἂν περὶ τὸ ὄν τε ᾖ καὶ τὸ ἀόρατον 529d4-5 ἃ δὴ λόγῳ μὲν καὶ διανοίᾳ ληπτά, ὄψει δ᾽οὔ 529d8 τῆς πρὸς ἐκεῖνα μαθήσεως

ἕνεκα 530b8 χρήσιμον τὸ φύσει φρόνιμον ἐν τῇ ψυχῇ ἐξ ἀχρήστου ποιήσειν c6 τῶν προσηκόντων μαθημάτων.
16 529c7 ff. and especially 530b7 τὰ δ'ἐν τῷ οὐρανῷ ἐάσομεν.
17 529d7 παραδείγμασι χρηστέον c2 διαφερόντως γεγραμμένοις καὶ ἐκπεπονημένοις διαγράμμασιν 530b6 προβλήμασιν . . . χρώμενοι.
18 Cherniss, pp. 67-70, argues that the organised or 'official' curriculum of the Academy restricted itself to geometry, and cogently cites the evidence of a basic text of the subject, perhaps arranged by an Academic, which was quickly followed by an improved edition of the same, certainly by an Academic. The 'improved arrangement and greater generalisation of many theorems' in the latter he ascribed to 'pedagogical considerations in accord with Plato's conception of mathematical studies' (p. 68). However, to restrict the propaedeutic curriculum to 'plane and solid geometry and number theory' (p. 67), on the ground that Plato's sciences of ideal astronomy and ideal harmonics did not yet exist, seems to me too narrow a conclusion. If they did not exist, the Platonic purpose, plainly stated, was to create them in the course of instruction, or at least to introduce the pupil, before the 'dialectical age' of thirty, to problems or propositions concerning moving bodies and musical harmonies out of which he would be constrained, for example, to grasp motion as a purely abstract conception, expressing a genus which exists in two different species, and to contemplate the necessity of composing analytic formulae or 'definitions' which translate particular motions in terms of general laws. Hence the story that he 'set it as a problem for astronomers to determine what are the uniform and ordered motions, the assumption of which will account for the apparent movement of the planets' (Cherniss, p. 64) should be taken to reflect that kind of mental training which Plato calls for in the astronomical section of his propaedeutic curriculum. Its object in fact was not to produce a definitive solution to a particular problem, but to train pupils to grasp the notion of 'ideal motion in depth' and to reveal to them that any solution can be expressed only in statements which relate a given apparent motion to ideal motion, that is, to 'the speed which is and the slowness which is, in true (final) number and final figures' (n. 14) which is not a bad description of what Plato demanded in setting this particular problem. The fact that Eudoxus and Heraclides came up with quite different solutions would be a matter of comparative indifference to Plato. They were responding to what Cherniss calls 'the same stimulus' (p. 64) and it is to be guessed that the average academic pupil experimented tentatively and imperfectly with different solutions, by way of training in the abstract (hence as Cherniss says 'he never became a mathematical specialist'), before passing on to a dialectical examination of the basic norms which control (or should control) human action and cosmic phenomena.
19 The pre-Platonic history of phora, kinesis, soma and kindred physical terms, as they were converted from an epic context in the event-series, and transmuted into abstractions by the pre-Socratics, will be explored in a later volume.
20 507b9 is typical: τὰ μὲν δὴ ὁρᾶσθαί φαμεν, νοεῖσθαι δ'οὔ, τὰς δ'αὖ ἰδέας νοεῖσθαι μέν, ὁρᾶσθαι δ'οὔ. The fact that Speusippus, while presumably remaining under Plato's influence, was able to reject the Forms altogether, while Xeno-

crates provided a substitute by converting them into mathematical (not ideal) numbers (Cherniss, pp. 33-47), may indicate how that Academic training and discussion in which all shared was focused simply on the sheer process of isolation and abstraction, as the primary task of philosophy. The theory of Forms, i.e. the conversion of the *auto to* into *eidos* and *idea*, remained Plato's own. 'The Academy was not a school in which an orthodox metaphysical doctrine was taught, or an association, the members of which were expected to subscribe to the theory of ideas' (Cherniss, p. 81).

[21] Support for this statement is furnished not by the remains of the pre-Socratics (*vid.* Diels-Kranz, index, *s. vv.*) but mainly by the indirect testimony of the *Clouds*, where *phrontis* is used not only (like *phronesis*) in the generic sense of thinking as a mental activity (lines 229, 233, 236, 740, 762) but specifically of a single mental act, or (isolated) thought (137, and, in the plural, 952; add *phrontisma* at 154). Correspondingly, in the same play, the 'think' verbs can be used with the cognate internal accusative to express 'thinking a thought' (695, 697, 724, 735) as well as with direct object (225, repeated 1503, and 741). *Noema* is used generically at 229 (in conjunction with *phrontis*, above), but specifically at 705 ἀλλὸ νοήμα φρενός and 743 τι τῶν νοημάτων. The use of *merimna* in the plural (952, 1404) may also symbolise specific 'thoughts' (cf. *Emped.* B. 2.2, repeated 110.7; and also 11.1; and cf. cap. 15, n. 3). *gnome* in sing. and plur. occurs commonly (169, 321, 730, 744, 747, 761, 896, 923, 948, 1037, 1314, 1404, 1439), in the senses of 'mind', 'sentiment' or 'opinion', 'expression', and (perhaps) as 'a thought'. The enlargement of 'domain' assigned to *nous, phren, merimna* in the last half of fifth century has been determined by von Fritz (1946, esp. p. 31), but not the possible significance of the plural usage *noemata, phrontides, merimnae.*

[22] Cf. Grube, pp. 9-10 (citing von Fritz, Natorp and Wilamowitz i. 346).

[23] Taylor, *Varia Socratica*, pp. 246-67; cf. ὁρωμένοις εἴδεσιν at *Rep.* 510d.5.

[24] Emped. B 98.5. The same philosopher frequently uses εἴδη in the sense of 'typical shapes', intermediate between the 'look' of a particular and the 'look' of a class or kind to which the particular belongs: B 22.7; 23.5; 71.3; 73.2; 115.7; 125.1.

[25] The influence of the atomist εἴδη and ἰδέαι on Plato remains problematic, and the equivalency between εἶδος and φύσις (Taylor, p. 228) still more so.

[26] Cf. Havelock, *Liberal Temper*, introd.

[27] Cf. *Iliad* 12.17 ff.

[28] *Iliad* 1.116 ff.

[29] Cf. *Euthyphro* 6e εἰς ἐκείνην (sc. τὴν ἰδέαν) ἀποβλέπων and *Cratylus* 389a ποῖ βλέπων ὁ τέκτων τὴν κερκίδα ποιεῖ; b βλέπων ... πρὸς ἐκεῖνο τὸ εἶδος ... and the many metaphorical uses of sight in the *Republic* (below, n. 41).

[30] R. G. Steven notes (p. 154) Plato's visual preference for line over colour, which was aesthetically conservative. *Eidos* might therefore evoke that 'outline' which is closer to the formalism of archaic art, and the suggestion of which is retained in the translation 'Form' but obliterated if we substitute 'Idea'. Henry Jackson carried things too far when he inferred that the Ideas were very thin

matter of some sort, but there was nothing wrong with his judgment on Plato's Greek.

31 510d5 ff.

32 The *Parmenides* (132d ff.) examines and rejects this metaphor.

33 500c2–7.

34 It is this usage, as repeated for example in the *Phaedrus* and *Timaeus*, which has encouraged the construction of a Platonic theory of aesthetic, according to which artistic *mimesis* can be carried out at the metaphysical level; cf. above, cap. 2, n. 37. For A. Diès, p. 594, imitation is 'at the centre of his philosophy'.

35 596a10 ff.

36 Above, cap. 13, n. 28.

37 The problem posed by the Forms of artifacts is raised in the *Parmenides* 130c; cf. *Cratylus* 387a ff. It is possible that Plato never finally made up his mind on this point (Grube, p. 36).

38 Above, cap. 2, n. 28.

39 Cherniss, p. 5, treats *Republic* 596a as supplying 'one of the cardinal propositions of this doctrine of ideas'; cf. p. 34, where he argues the proposition is a necessary foundation for the doctrine, expounded in the *Phaedo*, that there is a separate idea for each number. But 'twoness' and 'bedness' surely enjoy different epistemological status: the former in fact is one of those abstractions which have adjectival origin. Grube loc. cit. notes the doubts raised in the *Parmenides* about the existence of ideas of artifacts.

40 Assuming that the *Cratylus* is earlier (above, n. 37).

41 E.g. 475e4, 500c3, 532c6, and the entire parable of the sun (507c6–509b10), which relies on an analogy between two types of vision. It is notable that the actual description of dialectic (532d8–535a2) avoids the metaphor, stressing instead the search, the question-answer, the *elenchus*, and the effort of ratiocination.

42 How seductive this defection may be can be seen from Cornford's translation, p. 251, where he borrows from *Tim.* 46c to infer that in *Rep.* 7 'astronomy and harmonics . . . lead the mind to contemplate the beautiful and harmonious order manifested in the visible heavens and in the harmonies of sound . . .' This corresponds to *Timaeus* doctrine, but it contradicts what has just been said in the *Republic* about the visible heavens and audible sounds. Knowledge as presented in the *Rep.* is conceptual and dialectical, and in this sense also 'Socratic'; in the *Timaeus*, it is concrete, poetic and mythical.

CHAPTER FIFTEEN

'The Supreme Music is Philosophy'

A HISTORY of the Greek mind furnishes a stage on which the players in the great comedy of ideas conduct their business with each other. These are not men and women but rather words and thoughts which cluster in competing formations and manoeuvre to challenge us and win our attention while they seek to elbow each other off the boards. Two protagonists have confronted us, in the shapes of two different types of mentality: there is the player we have labelled the Homeric, largely because that is the label Plato himself prefers for him;[1] but he is really the pan-Hellenic performer of yesterday, the revered archetype of a long line of poets who is still good for one more turn. And there is his Platonic antagonist, young, sophisticated, discontented, who aggressively challenges his rival's prestige.

The third person in this comedy stands between them and can be identified in Greek terms as the goddess 'Music', or as 'Paideia'. She cannot grow old or die. She is the teacher of Greece and also the tradition of Greece. She is a way of thinking and feeling and also of living. But what are the lines we should give her in this play? What is her mode of address to be? Does she have a mind of her own? For a long time now, she has been the mistress of the Homeric player, that image-thinker, and he has told her what to say and how to say it. Now young Plato demands her affections and offers her his own. But if she is to listen to him she must put off the archaic mannerisms which have made her so agreeable to Homer and learn instead a new diction to please Plato; she must not only speak a new idiom but think new thoughts. For if she is going to live with Plato in his Academy, that new house that he

is building for her, she has got to learn new habits of household management.

To Plato, this competition for her hand is a contemporary issue;
it is still being decided at the opening of the fourth century before
Christ and he appeals passionately to her, and through her to the
Hellenes to whom he addresses his *Republic*, that they and she will
sympathise with and understand the new language he uses, and so
favour his suit.

Yet had not Homer lived not less than three and a half centuries
before him? That is a long time. During this time, had his
prestige remained entirely undimmed, and his authority unques-
tioned? In this comedy of the mind, had there not been some sort
of prologue to warn of the future plot, a curtain-raiser of some
sort? The plot has now quickened to a crisis. But was young
Plato really the first to raise his voice against the old master? Is it
indeed credible, since his is a voice of revolution, that the forces
of that revolution had not already begun to gain some momentum
before he came on stage and spoke his piece?

They had indeed; and as a kind of epilogue to our description
now completed of Plato's own position, it is just and appropriate
before we close the record to look back in time however briefly
to the prologue. It is an act of justice to Plato himself, for he is not
that kind of thinker who is just ingenious, not an eccentric in the
stream of history who produces to be sure a formidable body of
doctrine but a doctrine of his own making. Rather he is one of
those thinkers in whom the seminal forces of a whole epoch
spring to life. He thinks the unconscious thoughts of his contemporaries. He can predict the thoughts which they will wish to
think but which they do not yet know that they wish. We might
say that he gives to the intellectual currents of his age their
direction and drive. It would be better to say of his peculiar and
pioneering task that it sought to create the current of intellectualism
itself, by charting and digging the channel along which similar
efforts previously dispersed might now flow in full tide.

Does he himself not bear witness that there had indeed been

efforts in the same direction before his day, and that since these
had provoked from poetry an angry reply they must, like his own,
have been directed against her and perhaps have challenged her
monopoly over education? His words on this historical background to his own position are given as he concludes his own
frontal assault in the tenth book:

> Let us warn poetry before she condemns us for being inflexible and un-
> civilised towards her to remember that there has been a quarrel between
> philosophy and poetry which goes back a long way. Think of that 'snarling
> bitch that bays at her master', that 'hero of the talking-shop of fools', that
> 'rabble of the super-intelligent', those 'hair-splitting concentrators who
> cannot earn a living'. Yes, those and a thousand other testimonies to the fact
> that these two have been confronting each other for a long time now.[2]

It may be significant of these quotations from unnamed sources
that their common target appears to be the idiom and vocabulary
of their opponents and the intellectualism implicit therein. They
attack the way one talks, not the substance of any doctrines that
may be expounded.[3] Is this a hint that the main sin of philosophy
in the eye of tradition had been simply that it had proposed to
invent the language of the abstract, and to substitute the concept
in place of the image? This conclusion is premature at this point.
But it is pertinent to ask at once, since poetry's opponent is
named by Plato as 'philosophy', who does he mean by this
character, whom he here so to speak substitutes for himself on the
stage of intellectual history?

The text books of the history of philosophy seem to supply the
obvious answer: Plato's reference must be to the pre-Socratics,
identified since Aristotle as a group of physical thinkers ranging
from Thales to Democritus. He need not be speaking of all of
them: Xenophanes and Heraclitus are the most probable candi-
dates since they refer to Homer and Hesiod by name and with
irreverence. So the commentators usually nominate these two
thinkers for the role of representing 'philosophy' in this ancient
quarrel.[4] Nor, from the side of philosophy, is much made of
their attacks on poetry. These have been dismissed on the whole

as having little intrinsic connection with the ideological positions taken up by the pre-Socratics.

Somehow, all this seems a little inadequate to explain the rather fundamental feeling which is detectable in Plato's description of the quarrel. The trouble with this way of identifying what he calls 'philosophy' is not that in itself it is wrong, but that it is too narrowly based. It leaves out too many names, and it presents a false portrait of the kind of thing that 'philosophy' might mean, when applied by Plato to the period before Plato, and the kind of men that had practised this 'philosophy'. The basic assumption always made is that the pre-Socratics were professional thinkers equipped with a vocabulary and a set of concepts adequate to construct systematic doctrine. This doctrine, being abstract and metaphysical, is then capable of being classified as materialist or idealist or monist or pluralist and the like as though these terms revealed the basic intentions of the thinkers in question.

But if our previous thesis is correct, or is even near the mark, if the Homeric mind and idiom was the controlling mind and idiom of the Hellenes until Platonism substituted a thoroughly conceptual idiom; if indeed the Hellenes had first to learn to think in a professional sense: how could it be that pre-Platonic thinkers were already equipped with the conceptual apparatus and language, and were consequently already thinkers, before the problems and methods of thinking had been fully explored, before the thinking subject had been identified and separated from the known object, before the character of conceptual relationships as timeless and as invisible and as integrations of previous experience had been fully established? We would be prepared surely to entertain the notion that the pre-Socratics found themselves involved in a struggle similar to Plato's, that their activity anticipated however dimly his own conviction that the poetised idiom must be abrogated, that the problem was for them as for him one of new vocabulary and syntax, and even that with this there went a dawning recognition of the need to identify the autonomous personality and the powers of the thinker. If they were indeed pioneers in these endeavours, then the long quarrel cannot have been confined to Xenophanes and Heraclitus. Perhaps we have been looking at the target too narrowly.

In Plato the poetic mind has been identified with 'opinion', the state of mind of the many. With this clue in our hands is it not possible to reread, certainly Parmenides and Empedocles, and even with some probability an Anaxagoras and a Democritus, to discover that they too are continually attacking the same target, either the poets or men in the mass, and like Plato are identifying the mass mind as a state of mind hostile to thinking, and perhaps to be labelled 'opinion'? Are they not equally committed to the assertion that a different state of mind must be created in Greece, one which they seek to link with knowledge or science, and that the problem of energising this mind is one of energising a new language?

Finally, are these preoccupations wholly confined to the pre-Socratic cosmologists? Is it not likely that that character called 'philosophy' who had been provoking this quarrel with poetry must symbolise an entire movement, a current of effort which involved all who had need of a conceptual language in which to describe phenomena whether human or natural? Could this include geographers and historians? Could it involve the early medical writers? Would it not certainly embrace those leaders of the Athenian enlightenment whom we have been taught to style 'sophists'?[5]

These are suggestions, offered here only to provoke some fresh investigation of pre-Platonic speculation, undertaken from this standpoint. The real barrier to such an effort exists in the form of a modern presumption, in which we all share, as to what the word 'philosopher' signifies. In the first place it would appear that this noun did not become a label of the pre-Socratics until early in the fourth century. It scarcely occurs in any document written before the last quarter of the fifth century. Heraclitus may have used it, not necessarily of himself.[6] Herodotus uses the verb 'philosophise' in connection with Solon's travels and his desire to see the

THE SUPREME MUSIC IS PHILOSOPHY

world, and the same verb occurs in a famous context in Pericles' funeral speech 'we philosophise without effeminacy and we *philokalise* (we embrace the noble) with economy'.[7] The words read like an aphorism; they certainly do not make philosophy sound very professional, and indeed 'philosophy' as a feminine noun, the name of a character so to speak on the stage of Greek intellectual history, seems to have made her entrance only about the time Plato wrote his *Republic*, or a little earlier.[8]

Any assiduous search for usage in the fifth century is in danger of missing the main point, which is that the clues to the history of the word 'philosopher', and therefore to a history of the idea of philosophy, are first fully supplied in the *Republic* itself, where the type of person symbolised by this word is identified simply as the man who is prepared to challenge the hold of the concrete over our consciousness, and to substitute the abstract. It is treated as a word which needs definition. It is not one already in professional use, on which Plato was trying to place a new and fanciful interpretation. The latter is the assumption that translators usually adopt when they confront the passage in the *Republic* where the philosopher is at last brought on stage, so that his presence in the state is made the central issue of the dialogue. There is no basis for this assumption, no contemporary evidence that the 'philosopher' identified the kind of person we mean by that term, that is, that he represented a member of a 'school of thought' among other schools equipped with doctrines expressed in formulas which were appropriately systematic.

It is in the fifth book[9] that Plato literally thrusts the *philosophos* at us as the sole claimant for chief political authority in the state. The proposal is meant to arrest and shock, and it does. Such a novelty forces us to examine what we mean by a 'philosoph'. The answer begins by concentrating on the implication of the first syllable in the word. Phil- is the label of a psychic urge, a drive, a thirst,[10] an all-consuming desire. The 'philosoph' then is a man of special instincts and energies. We then ask: Towards what are these directed? and reply: The object is *sophia*,[11] equiva-

lent to the remaining syllable of the word. (The current translation of this as 'wisdom' carries as many unfortunate and misleading connotations as does the word 'philosopher' itself.)[12]
What then is this *sophia*? Is it that experience sought through the
poetic performance? No, it is a cognition of those identities
which 'are', and 'are forever', and are 'imperceptible'; these are
the Forms.[13]

We have seen in an earlier chapter precisely what these represent,
and the context which they occupy in the unfolding history of the
Greek consciousness. A 'philosoph' therefore in Plato's terms is at
bottom a man with the capacity for the abstract, and in the
present circumstances of Greek education this type was bound to
be rare. He was one therefore who had by conscious and we
might say eccentric effort defied the ethos of his own culture.
Plato drives home the point:

> They who embrace each itself *per se* as that which is are to be identified
> as devotees of *sophia* instead of devotees of opinion. The latter embrace the
> specific sounds and colours they see . . . etc.

and again

> We can agree on this conclusion about the native characters that are
> 'philosophic': in any mental discipline they are drawn passionately toward any
> aspect of it which is demonstrated as pertaining to that isness which always is
> and which does not vacillate under the influence of becoming and perishing.

and again

> The mass of men cannot accept the idea that there is a beauty itself rather
> than many beautiful things, nor that there are the several itselves *per se* instead
> of the many specific things. Thus the mass of men cannot be philosophic.[14]

According to these and other affirmations, the Greek term
philosophia would identify something in the human scene at once
much simpler than the modern 'philosophy', and also in a historical sense much more profound. It is that capacity which turns
a man into a student by defying the pressure of his environment.
But this pressure is also sharply defined in contemporary Greek
terms as that of the poetised tradition with its habit of passionate

emotional identification with persons and stories of heroes, and with the play of action and episode. Instead, the 'philosoph' is one who wants to learn how to restate these in a different language of isolated abstractions, conceptual and formal; a language which insists on emptying events and actions of their immediacy, in order to break them up and rearrange them in categories, thus imposing the rule of principle in place of happy intuition, and in general arresting the quick play of instinctive reaction, and substituting reasoned analysis in its place as the basic mode of living.

Plato is describing what he regards as a natural élite, distinguished from their fellows by a proclivity for reducing every situation to abstract terms. If in our language we were asked to describe who these people are, by any one word which like the Greek *philosophos* presumes a type and not an accident, we might call them the 'intellectuals'. The word has that same colour of doubtful fame, it conveys the same ambiguity of social evaluation, which Plato describes as characteristic of the new *philosophos* in his society. We have grown used to the intellectuals now, because the habit of rearranging experience out of the obvious into the theoretic has been accepted into our western culture and made part of it. It was not always so. Therefore Plato does not in these pages select a previously familiar profession, that of the philosopher, and urge that it be equipped with qualities of a more general character. On the contrary, he is trying for the first time in history to identify this group of general mental qualities, and seeking for a term which will label them satisfactorily under a single type. We might almost say he is inventing the idea of the intellectual in society, were it not for the fact that like all such inventions in the realm of semantics the conception and the word had begun to emerge over the horizon in the generation previous to his own.[15] He it was who hailed the portent and correctly identified it. In so doing, he so to speak confirmed and clinched the guesses of a previous generation which had been feeling its way towards the *idea* that you could 'think', and that thinking was a very special kind of psychic activity, very uncomfortable,

but also very exciting, and one which required a very novel use
of Greek.

Both the new vocabulary and the personal commitment that
went with it, as they disrupted the poetised experience, were also
rightly felt to be a grave affront to tradition. As they were a
seduction to some, they were suspect to many more. This is the
kind of context in which the life and the dialectic of Socrates
makes historical sense. But since our purpose here is not with the
Socratic problem narrowly considered, but rather with an over-
all revolution in Greek culture which was to make Platonism
inevitable, we can keep our gaze fixed on the 'philosophers', and
on 'philosophy' as the banner of the revolution, provided we
translate the word into 'intellectualism'. It was the signal of a
warfare which was waged not in lecture rooms between competing ideas, but in the heart and the hearth of the city state itself.
It invaded the apparatus, whatever that may have been, of the
educational system, as Plato correctly discerned.

The whole issue, as it became a social-political issue, far trans-
cending the narrow preoccupations of specialists, is compressed
into the words which form the title of this chapter: 'the supreme
music is philosophy'. Few phrases, because of the semantic changes
that have overcome the words used, are more capable of total
misunderstanding. The words do not mean that the message of
professional philosophy is one grand sweet song. They are pronounced by Socrates as Plato represents him in prison on the last
day of his life. He had often heard a voice in a dream exhorting
him 'to make music and work hard at it'. That is, in traditional
terms, he had felt himself to be in the great educational tradition
which had been, in the largest sense, Homeric. Yet he had to put
his own interpretation on what education meant, and he had
formed a very untraditional conception of what this might be.
'Intellectualism' might be 'the supreme form of education', trans-
cending and cancelling the previous poetic method. However,
he adds ironically, in these last days with nothing more left to do
he has in solitude been turning back to poetry.[16]

At his trial, according to Plato's representation, he had identified his mission as simply that of 'intellectualising', one that was recognised and rejected bitterly by the community. Would he accept a release from the charges against him on condition that he stop this procedure?:

As long as I breathe and have my faculties, never, never will I stop philosophising. . . .

And what is it that he does when he does this? What is 'philosophising'? Plato allows him to answer our question in the formula with which, so he says, he constantly approaches and confronts his fellow citizens:

Why do you not concentrate on thinking and give thought to it and to the truth and to your *psyche* to make it as excellent as possible?[17]

These words reduce to its simplest and most essential terms that *methodos*, or discipline of the abstract, to which Plato devotes the central doctrines of his *Republic*.

Was it a *methodos* which public opinion would identify solely with Socrates? We might think so at first from the missionary character with which in Plato's *Apology* it is invested. But the philological evidence for what it is worth points to a larger group than the Socratics as pioneer 'intellectuals'. A little earlier in the same speech, Socrates describes the general prejudice against him, which crystallises in the charge that he 'demoralises the younger generation'. How do people substantiate such a charge? he asks. They cannot really do so, but they try by producing the stock arguments 'against all the philosophisers', whose field of interest he says covers cosmology and irreligion and reversal of values ('making the worse argument appear the better').[18] Both pre-Socratics and Sophists then, by the close of the fifth century before Christ, if the *Apology* does indeed reproduce the idiom of that period, were accepted by public opinion as representative of the intellectualist movement. If they were called 'philosophisers', it was not for their doctrines as such, but for the kind of vocabulary

and syntax which they used and the unfamiliar psychic energies
that they represented. Sophists, pre-Socratics, and Socrates had
one fatal characteristic in common; they were trying to discover
and to practise abstract thinking. The Socratic dialectic pursued
this goal with more energy, and perhaps insisted more ruthlessly
that it was along this path and this alone that the new educational
programme must be conducted. That was why the lightning of
public opprobrium struck Socrates down.

The idiom of Pericles' Funeral Speech reproduces an earlier and
more relaxed attitude towards the intellectuals, before the educational crisis had become sharpened, before the split between the
older and younger generation had become an angry social issue,[19]
before the stresses and strains of war had bred suspicion and fear
of the future and prompted a reaction toward the past. Yet even
in this speech, there is a note of apology: 'We Athenians can
intellectualise without sacrifice of manliness.'[20] Probably the
words would not have occurred in such a context a decade earlier.
Is it in fact credible that Pericles the practical statesman ever used
them? Yes, barely so, if we choose to regard the phrase as a
reflection of the sophistic influence which had surrounded his
policies. But it may mirror the historian's present conception, as
he looks back from the close of the century to its Periclean golden
age. Would a contemporary idiom have used this particular
word?

At any rate, the phrasing expresses by implication the threat
that the new offered to the old. If poetry was to cease to be the
vehicle of education, what became of the heroic and aristocratic
tradition and its values, expressible as they were solely in poetry?
A course in mathematics and dialectic might produce analysts and
planners and critics, and society might one day embrace them.
But would it any longer produce heroes 'without softness'?

In the *philo-sophos*, meaning a man who is instinctively drawn
to intellectualism and had an aptitude for it, Plato thought he saw
a fresh human type emerging from the society he knew. As a
type, it was symbolised effectively in the conjunction of the verb

'to like' or 'love'[21] with the adjective *sophos* which more than any other had stamped a man as 'intelligent'. *Sophos* and its noun *sophia*, the 'intelligent' person and his 'intelligence', had been traditional terms, and as such we would not have expected them to denote the new 'intellectualist' form of intelligence. Yet it was indeed precisely for this meaning that they became adapted. This was to be their destiny. Their earlier usage had in fact contained the essential seed-germ of their future history. For in Homer as in later authors they had meant not 'wisdom' or 'experience' or 'sagacity' in a general sense, but the 'skill' or 'know-how' in a very specific sense of the craftsman.[22] From this, their development in usage indicates a progress which reflects the changing cultural situation. By the late sixth century, at least, they had been appropriated for that skill *par excellence* to which the Greeks gave prestige, namely the skill of the bard. His was pre-eminently a skill in the command of effective communication, both of word and of content.[23] *Sophia* therefore might denote his power as a musician or versifier, but equally his authority as a teacher, the voice of the traditional experience which lay behind his verse. With the slow transition from verse to prose and from concrete towards abstract the man of intelligence came to represent the master of a new form of communication equally consecrated to educational purposes, but now anti-poetic. In short, *sophia* always remained 'skill of speech' and 'skill of mind', but the kind of speech and the kind of mind changed. The Seven Sages were so identified, presumably by the end of the fifth century, as reputed masters of the idiom of the aphorisms attached to their names.[24] The skill thus represented was still oral. Socrates on the other hand is styled 'an intelligent man' in the hostile sense of being 'too intelligent'[25] because he uses a new and sophisticated idiom in which to express experience. It is therefore as fatal to translate *sophia* as wisdom as it is to translate *mousike* as music. For wisdom, of which all approve whatever the intellectual climate, is a word which so far from revealing the connotations of the Greek word *sophia* actually conceals them. No one is brought into court for being a 'wise man'. But a man might get into trouble for being 'too skilful'.

The semantic histories of *sophos* and *sophia* and their compounds (which we have touched on without exhausting them)[26] is relevant to the understanding of the situation of those before Plato who may have been pioneers in developing the skill of the abstract. For one thing, if such words could be used at the end of the fifth century in connection with a few men who had lived earlier,[27] this does indicate that certain pioneers in the abstract were thought to have existed. But for another, this also indicates how essentially ambiguous was the situation of these would-be prophets of a new order of language. They claimed a superior skill in intelligence for themselves. Yet what could this seem to be, except a variant of the poetic intelligence in which they had been initially trained, and the prestige of which they felt they shared? And for this too the traditional label had been *sophia*.[28] The pre-Socratics, to take their case first, began as men who on the one hand composed as poets, or like Heraclitus as poetic epigrammatists, responding to the conditions of an oral situation. They therefore felt themselves to be in the great oral tradition. Yet obviously they felt repugnance to it and fought it, identifying it in the person of 'the many' and also in the persons of Homer and Hesiod whom they sometimes name as opponents. They therefore lay claim to the superior 'intelligence' of the minstrel as the teacher of Greece, yet seek to adapt this conception to a new order of intellectualism, which is destined to supplant the poetic intelligence. They are in a cleft stick, and we can watch the words *sophos* and *sophia*, as well as others like them, changing very slowly from poetic ability towards abstract ability during the sixth and fifth centuries.[29]

We must therefore prepare ourselves for the hypothesis that early Greek philosophy represents an enterprise which faced the same problems of abstraction that Plato solved, and that in part it anticipated his solution. We must open our minds to the possibility that what the pre-Socratics said was less important than

how they tried to say it.[30] If we observe in them a constant preoccupation with language, and a continual complaint against its
limitations, and a constant appeal for new efforts of cognition, we
should be prepared, instead of passing over these admonitions and
complaints as though they were a routine exercise,[31] to ask: How
large do these preoccupations bulk in their surviving fragments?
Proportionately, how much attention do the pre-Socratics seem
to give to these matters as compared with what might be called
systematic doctrine? If the proportion seems to favour the
former, we should adjust our perspective accordingly; that is, we
must be prepared at least to find that their besetting preoccupation
was with what Plato would call *methodos* rather than with the
taking up of fixed philosophical positions or the making of doctrinal affirmations. If we detect in some of them an undercurrent
of hostility towards the poets, and on the other hand a continual
denunciation of popular idiom and thought, we should be prepared to connect these two targets, as they are connected in
Plato, who identifies poetry with opinion.

Yet equally, remembering that these men were pre-Platonic
and so much closer in time and circumstances to the heroic and
archaic culture of Greece, we must be prepared to find that their
own idiom is not as advanced as that of Plato's, that they in fact
start as poets—how else indeed could the announcement of an
important piece of preserved communication be published, except
as it was framed both concretely and visually? Yet their enterprise was undertaken in order to destroy concretion and visibility.
How were they to do it? How desperate and paradoxical their
situation! Where were they to get a philosophical vocabulary,
except as they wrung it out of the previous idiom of the oral
culture and submitted the vocabulary and syntax of Homer and
Hesiod to queer twists and unbearable strains? If then it turns out
that the earlier pre-Socratics composed either in verse or in poetic
aphorism; and that even the later ones could manage a prose of
ideas only as they strung together lapidary sentences into paragraphs of meaning, we should not suppose, as is too commonly

supposed, that they were philosophers by intent and poets by accident. On the contrary, the only possible early conception of themselves would be that they were a school of minstrelsy, offering to be sure a brand of poetic education such as Greece had never heard before.[32]

To such an approach to early philosophy the received tradition both ancient and modern offers a formidable obstacle. Aristotle may take the credit for inventing the idea of the history of philosophy in a professional sense.[33] Important as the invention was, it could be carried out only at the price of reducing pre-Socratic thought to sets of first principles, to party platforms as it were, to sets of doctrinal positions which could be expounded in logical-historical order. This method of writing the history of the Greek mind was then codified by Theophrastus in a text book, which remained thereafter the magisterial source for any authoritative account, both in antiquity and to this day.[34] Therefore a plea that we cease to insist of the pre-Socratics and the Sophists that they were materialist or monist or pluralist or idealist or relativist—to suggest instead that what they all had in common was of greater importance than what separated them—this may indeed seem an unpalatable approach to the period. Yet it may be that the documentation, now available, of the actual words and syntax that they used, if rigorously evaluated in terms of the language of their own centuries, the sixth and fifth before Christ, and not in terms of our own, would force us to precisely this conclusion.

The pre-Socratics, however, and the Sophists, were not the whole story. There may have been other composers of the Greek word, poetic or prosaic, who also became involved in or played some role in this history. We are dealing, be it remembered, with a crisis in the character of preserved communication. Under what precise conditions did its character change? If there was some sort of revolution, what was its general shape? Let us go back to our earlier chapters and recall the essential Homeric situation, meaning by that the cultural situation in Homeric and near-Homeric times.

We began with the hypothesis that any linguistic-ethnic group conforms to common patterns of custom and uses certain common types of technology. It also shares in some sort of common world-view, embracing an account of the history both of the human group and of the environment in which it lives. These items add up to a system, in the very loosest sense, of public and private law, forming a corpus of hoarded experience. Historians have been prone to assume that this corpus, or 'the tradition', as we might call it, transmits itself from generation to generation without benefit of organised effort. We have argued on the contrary that any body of knowledge accumulated through experience can be lost again, unless it is incorporated in some kind of educational discipline, and that all societies *qua* societies have to have this discipline, the content of which is partly the imitation of behaviour but very largely the imitation of words.

To become available for transmission through the educational apparatus, the tradition has therefore to be verbally preserved in something like permanent and unaltered form, and the next question is how? In the Homeric or pre-Homeric period, say between twelve hundred and seven hundred, any written version was impossible, and indeed we have argued that even in the earlier epoch of syllabic writing systems, no complete written version of the tradition was possible either. Preservation of such a corpus had to rely on the living memories of human beings, and if these were to be effective in maintaining the tradition in a stable form, the human beings must be assisted in their memorisation of the living word by every possible mnemonic device which could print this word indelibly upon the consciousness. The devices that we explored were first the employment of standard rhythms engaging all possible bodily reflexes, and second the reduction of all experience to a great story or a connected series of such stories. These narratives enabled useful experience to be remembered in the form of vivid events arranged in paratactic sequence, while the compendious plot served as an over-all reference frame. The narrative is from this point of view to be regarded not as an end in itself but as a vehicle for transmitting the material of the tribal encyclopedia, which is presented not as such, but as dispersed into a thousand narrative contexts. Here then in the compendious epic of Homer is contained all philosophy and all history and all science. The epic is primarily a didactic device, and it therefore does not make very much sense to classify a poet like Hesiod as the 'first' didactic poet. In what special sense he was didactic will however be explored in a moment.

In the eighth century we see a new technology of communication become available which provided a second and quite different method of preserving the tradition. It requires historical imagination at first to see how drastic the revolution was, and to understand how it was destined in the end to penetrate and alter every cultural condition and social relationship in Europe. This however still lay in the future. The new method, employing alphabetic signs which were capable of fluent transcription and unambiguous recognition, committed the tradition to a material which could then be left lying around available for consultation at will. This passive preservation is accomplished without the aid of the living memory, which can afford to forget. For the tradition is now safe and can enjoy a separate life of its own in what we call 'Greek literature'.

However this at first makes little practical difference. The old and the new, the oral and the written techniques of preservation, go on side by side. Poetry can be written down, but it remains poetry. The first new phenomenon caused by the invention of the alphabet was the preservation of non-didactic poetry composed for private occasions or on themes disconnected from the educational apparatus. These songs, always plentiful we must assume, would in the normal course of things be forgotten and their place taken by others, in turn to enjoy only an ephemeral life. But once put on to parchment or papyrus in written signs they become capable of recollection and re-use.[35] Hence the phenomenon in Greece of the so-called 'lyric poets' who are simply the first of their company to have enjoyed the possibility of preservation. It is worth noting in passing that this evolution of literary events, with Archilochus the first surviving lyrist, provides patent proof that those who on epigraphical evidence have argued for a late date for the invention of the Greek alphabet are undoubtedly right.[36]

As a method of preservation, the acoustic technology of epic had been rendered obsolete by the technology of the written word. But in the slow march of history it takes time for obsolescence to be recognised, and there were rather special reasons why in this case time had to be taken. The way was now open for the composition of the encyclopedia without benefit of rhythm and without the setting of narrative. This would also, one would think, enable the encyclopedia to be amplified and extended in a thousand ways, once freed from the constrictions which the economy of mnemonic necessity had imposed. But in fact no such liberating revolution immediately occurred. The psychic habits of centuries could not be broken quickly, especially when— and this is very important—they had exploited all the resources of the sensory pleasures.

Besides, the full use of the written word required a condition which immensely complicated its progress. Writing is not a technique like swimming which can be indulged with complete satisfaction by the isolated individual in a pond of his own choosing. To be sure a writer can write for his own convenience in order to re-read and reorganise what he has written, and we may be sure that the first Greek writers did just that. They found that oral compositions were recallable more easily, and that their organisation and complication could therefore be increased. But writers in order to fulfil the full potentiality of their writing require readers, just as minstrels require an audience. And these became available in quantity only as the social apparatus was organised behind the effort to create them. In short the 'literacy' which a writer can exploit depends on whether the educational system creates readers for him, and the degree to which he feels able to exploit it will depend upon the degree of 'readership' in his linguistic group.

The progress towards full literacy in fact took over three hundred years, if we are right in dating its arrival in Athens not long before the conclusion of the Peloponnesian War.[37] In between Homer and Plato there intervened various stages of craft and of semi-literacy. The precise degrees and shadings from one into the other will probably never be reducible to exact history. The net result was that long after Homer had been alphabetised, the main stream of the Athenian tradition continued to rely first on repeating Homer, second on the composition of supplements to Homer, in the form of hymn, ode and chorale and, at Athens, the drama. These works were composed by writers, who however composed under audience control, so that they had to conform to the idiom and the genius of preserved oral communication. That is, in addition to retaining the devices of rhythm, they adhered also to the language of image and of event and of situation in which the thing-happening predominates over the idea, and the concrete symbol over the abstract concept.

But the alphabetic technology had in theory made it possible for preserved knowledge to discard both the rhythm on the one hand and the syntax of the image-series on the other. These had been companion but separate devices for framing words in memorisable form. How interesting therefore it becomes to notice that to carry out this double task at a single blow seems to have been too much for the energy even of the Greek mind. Of these two verbal modes, each at first might be discarded, separately from the other, but not the two together. Thus when the more obvious choice was made, and meter was dropped, the result was not a prose of ideas (whether or not we would style this as 'philosophic') but a prose of narrative, which retained the paratactic genius of epic, reporting experience still in the guise of events happening and of actions performed. Thus 'history' is born on the coasts of Ionia, and also a descriptive geography presented as history.

On the other hand the much more difficult enterprise of making some break with the spell of narrative and trying to rearrange

experience in categories rather than events was first attempted and
for long continued within the confines of rhythm. The first
'proto-thinkers' of Greece, if we may so style them, were still
poets.[38] They had to do their thinking out loud so that their compositions could still be recited and memorised. Yet while the
formulas employed were oral, the essential genius of these compositions was not. They exhibit a paradoxical character, on the
one hand formidably didactic, obviously conceived as a programme of instruction rather than of pleasure, yet on the other
hand clinging to the epic formulas, the imagery, the visual
quality of their verbal inheritance with an almost desperate zeal,
as though the effort to think had to be compensated for by
leaning as much as they dared upon the familiar age-old idiom.
Thus the idiom had the effect of continually compromising and
blunting their conceptual intention. The *archegos*[39] as Aristotle
might call him, the dominant figure who set in motion these
forces, which as they gathered momentum were finally to disrupt
the Homeric mind and break the spell of the concrete, and substitute the discipline of the abstract, was Hesiod. His successors[40]
in the same enterprise were the early pre-Socratics.

Hesiod is easiest to estimate in the first instance as a cataloguer.
This is not in itself the key to a deep understanding of him but it
can serve to illuminate the character of the revolution in the
technology of preserved speech which he initiated. The *Theogony*
is superficially a catalogue of the names of gods and their functions
arranged in families. The *Works and Days* is a catalogue of
exhortations, parables, proverbs, aphorisms, sayings, wise saws
and instances, interlarded with stories. We agreed in an earlier
chapter[41] that the catalogue in its pure or isolated form was not
likely to survive in a wholly oral medium. To find its place in
the living memory, it required attachment to a narrative context,
and itself needed to be phrased with a maximum of active verbs
and adjectives in order to dress up the information as action. The
Greek Catalogue of Ships in the second book of the *Iliad* illustrated
both these points in the oral tradition.

In Hesiod the catalogue has parted company with the narrative. It has been isolated or abstracted, we suggest, out of a thousand contexts in the rich reservoir of oral tradition and in particular out of the two poems we identify as Homeric. Not all of the material in Hesiod is Homeric,[42] but a good deal of it is, and the Homeric core in the two poems may have served as a nucleus round which to gather congruent material from other oral epics now lost but known to Hesiod. In short, the material of the tribal encyclopedia previously suspended and carried along in the river of narrative is now being recognised as such in embryo form and is being sieved out of the stream. A general world view is emerging in isolated or 'abstracted' form. Since this effort of isolation violates the canons of easy oral memorisation, it presumes that Hesiod is operating with the help of the written word.[43] The act of organisation which carries beyond the plot of a story in order to impose a rough logic of topics is an act performed by the eye not by the ear. It reveals the architectural capacity made available by a rearrangement of written signs, as opposed to the acoustic patterns of echo and response characteristic of a purely oral poem.

In their larger perspective, then, these two poems are not simply catalogues; rather they represent twin efforts of massive mental integration which has got as far as recognising two main areas of human experience: the physical environment (in the *Theogony*) and the moral environment (in the *Works and Days*). The *Theogony* under the guise of its hundreds of divine names and its plentiful stories about them does in the main attempt to vision forth the visual cosmos, its skies, seas, earth, rivers, mountains, its atmosphere, weather, storms, stars, sunshine, its fires, floods, and earthquakes. It is a document which opens up the prospect of thinking in terms which are spatial.

This would be an abstract achievement, and is obviously beyond the actual achievement of Hesiod. The instinct to narrativise experience as a series of doings is still too strong, and the world emerges in the form of a story about the actions of gods. But semantically, one vital step is taken which points forward to the future substitution of a vocabulary of the abstract. The device exploited by the poet for organising his panorama of living forces is the family—the *genos*, or *genee*. This concrete device is used to arrange a hundred phenomena in congruent groups. A step has been taken towards classification[44] and even towards establishing a chain of cause and effect. The *genos* is on the way to becoming the 'genus' or class.

The *Theogony* does not merely attempt an integration of spatial experience. It combines this with an attempt to integrate the role of the public law in the human community. This is symbolised in the person of Zeus and his progeny, and in the attributes of civilisation which are represented as supervening upon the arrangement and control of physical forces. After the wind and the storm comes the reign of law and peace.[45] Thus the organisation achieved by the poet is not yet tightly logical. Distinct areas of future knowledge are not yet distributed neatly and abstractly into physics versus politics and ethics. He is preparing the way for these tighter integrations, but that is all.[46]

The *Works and Days*, however, devotes itself almost wholly to the organisation of public and private law.[47] This was a much more difficult task, because the material to be rearranged in this new form was not primarily visual at all. The environment could be organised in a pattern of apparent visibles, even if this was to be a preparation for invisibles. But the human comedy, the body of custom, habit, usage, and precept, was just words and acts. We can only wonder at that effort of genius which succeeded in welding together with some degree of coherence a picture of Greek moral directives and approved habits, as we have it in the *Works and Days*. This 'proto-morality', as we shall call it, is a semi-abstract system which, as any reader will recognise, continually breaks down into the concrete. Rule and precept are interrupted by anecdote and story; the composer seems to lose control over his themes only to regain it again. Equally, a struggle has begun to use Homeric language in generalised contexts, that is, to change the syntax. Words for instance which had meant simply

'men' come to be used in a context which suggests an overriding notion of a 'general mankind'.[48] Words which had
symbolised the 'ranging' and the 'going to and fro' of men and of
animals can be set in contexts to suggest the 'general range' or
'law'[49] and the over-all habit pattern under which men live. The
composer of the *Theogony*, seeking to rearrange and regroup
narrative situations, had found great linguistic assistance for his
task in the words for 'family'. Used with facile frequency in his
composition, these then reappear in the *Works and Days*, to furnish
the conception of a 'type', at what would appear to be an increasing level of sophistication. Thus the author composes what
he calls a *logos* of the five 'families' of mankind,[50] which as they
succeed each other begin to demonstrate typologies of moral
conduct, and the abstract possibilities of the same word are carried
even further when, as he launches his poetised discourse, he draws
a distinction between two 'families' of strife, one beneficial and
one destructive.[51] These indeed are truly formal categories which
in the terminology of a later logic would be distinguished as two
species within the same genus. These examples are to lead in the
long run to the Platonic assertion that such typologies are the
'themselves *per se*', the 'objects' of intellection. They have been
cited here however to show how a vocabulary of the semi-
abstract grows out of epic concreteness, not by substituting new
words for old, but by altering the syntax in which the old words
are found. It is the conjunction of the word 'family' with the
word for 'strife' that first prompts the suggestion that a family is
now being used in a rather special metaphorical sense. In this
way all abstractions advanced by exploiting the resources of
metaphor.

We are here only raising the curtain upon the pre-Platonic
struggle to achieve conceptual thought, a struggle which prepared the way for Platonism but used linguistic weapons more
primitive than Plato's. We have suggested for Hesiod an outline
sketch, but no more than that, of the direction in which his two
compositions are moving. Let us now leave him unexplored and

undocumented in detail in order to watch the next step taken by the Greek mind towards the goal of conceptualisation.

The step is taken mainly though not exclusively within the area of the physical experience as opposed to the moral. It is the possibility opened up in the *Theogony* of a conceptual synthesis and analysis of the environment which is first pursued to its conclusion, before the mind of Greece returns, in the period of the Sophists, to the task of further organising the area of moral discourse represented in the *Works and Days*. As we have suggested, there was a sound psychological reason for this priority. A story which accounted for the appearances in the visible heavens by narrating their births and their wars and the like, in fact a 'cosmogony', could lead more easily towards an effort of mental integration, and so to a 'cosmology' of permanent relations, because the visible apparatus of the cosmos was itself already, *qua* visible, also a kind of 'whole', a roughly symmetrical and therefore single phenomenon which could lead to the notion of a 'one'. The mind could be drawn to entertain the idea of an abstract pattern governing the disposition of the heavens and earth more easily than it could entertain the notion of a pattern informing the manners and mores of society, simply because a visual prototype of the first was already available in the apparently closed and semi-circular area contained between firmament and earth. So *cosmos*[52] had priority over *dikaiosune*—physical over moral theory.

The *Theogony*, describing the despatch of the Titans to Tartarus, had appended to this episode a kind of vision[53] of the over-all cosmic arrangement, with earth suspended symmetrically between Heaven and Hades in a kind of space where dwelt Night and Day who alternately emerged to occupy the atmosphere. This poetised account, in the main a sequence of images, in part a construct, broods as it were over the efforts of the early cosmologists to construct a more satisfying account of the world's history and its present disposition. Their cosmologies begin with Hesiod, yet continually try to get away from him. They imitate him even as they continually correct him. Their own accounts, considered as attempts to connect up the heavenly bodies and the atmosphere and the earth and the waters and the underworld in plausible schematisms, would remain antiquarian curiosities, nor would their authors have held pride of place in the history of the European mind, if they had been content with cosmology.

What however they also do is to seize upon the fact, already implicit in Hesiod, that, even in the attempt to cosmologise, something is happening to their use of the Greek language and something is happening also to their minds. They become aware that as they construct a picture of a cosmos they are offering in effect something new, namely an idea of order conceived as an overriding premise of description, or as a method of organisation. The epic account had broken up the phenomena into running stories and kept them dispersed in concrete contexts. The pre-Socratics become aware they are integrating these phenomena out of stories into patterns, and as they become aware, they attempt the vital step of expressing the idea of integration itself, as a governing principle of their method. This was an abstraction, not an event, and it could not be expressed in the vocabulary of the syntax of events. So they simply take the Greek word for 'one thing' and attach it either to God, or to nothing, leaving it suspended in the neuter singular. The idea of 'unification', of 'schematisation', of 'system', has been born, and born as an idea. They realise almost as quickly that this sort of word and the concept it represents cannot be put into a story; it requires the kind of statements which are framed in timeless syntax. The 'one' just 'is'. And so the 'is' comes to occupy pride of place alongside the 'one'.[54]

Thus they are in the position of trying to describe the ground rules of what they were doing. Their centre of attention is no longer on the cosmic picture as such, but rather upon the method which made any new arrangement of experience possible. Since this involved mental operations and linguistic devices of a novel order they also become preoccupied with the urgent need to develop a new level of consciousness and a new language, and correspondingly they find themselves automatically involved in a warfare against the old consciousness and the old language. They cannot attempt to define the former without contrasting it with the latter. That is, the only way in which they can define it is by negatively describing what they must escape from, namely 'being born' and 'happening' and 'ceasing to be' and 'the shift of shape and colour'[55] and the endless pluralisation of the episode, the endless variety of situation in the epic series.

This conflict of theirs with an idiom which at the same time they had often to use themselves, for want of a better, conditions them in their time and place, and stamps them as contenders in an arena which no longer exists today in the shape in which they found it. But their conflict produced essential and permanent contributions to the vocabulary of all abstract thought: body and space, matter and motion, permanence and change, quality and quantity, combination and separation, are among the counters of common currency now available because the pre-Socratics first brought them near the level of consciousness. They did this by altering the syntactical context of the words, and sometimes by new coinages in the impersonal singular. No longer, as we have said, was it a matter of 'this corpse on the battle field' but of 'body' anywhere and everywhere.[56] No longer was it 'this basket which happens to be empty and will be full in a moment': it is the cosmos which is empty or has emptiness always and everywhere.[57]

To the stock of physical concepts like these they also added a minimal vocabulary of mental process.[58] Such dichotomies as reason versus emotion, or intellect versus the senses, are so familiar to us that it takes time to notice how the pre-Socratics had to feel their way towards such conceptions, as they sought to disentangle and distinguish the different levels of psychic effort and activity which their new language and their new method of inquiry were revealing in themselves. Essentially this kind of terminology was promoted by an introspective regard of their own effort to integrate and to abstract, and by a primary awareness of how different was the previous Homeric experience in which this had never been attempted. For each of these types of experience they sought the appropriate name, and also names for the entire core of personal consciousness within which these changes were taking place.

The thinkers whose activities we have been outlining here were proto-thinkers, in the sense that they had to discover conceptual thinking itself as idea and as method before the products of thought, that is systems, could emerge fluently. Their names range from Xenophanes to Democritus. The so-called Milesian School cannot unfortunately be included for the fundamental reason that within the context of the growth of the Greek mind towards abstraction any contribution they may have made has been lost. Their *ipsissima verba* have all perished, and with them is lost any index to their conceptual gropings.⁵⁹

When in the age of Democritus or a little earlier we turn to gaze on Athens, the first thinker of Athens turns out to be a man who devotes his entire energy to defining more precisely the character of this Greek drive towards abstraction. The notion that the teaching of Socrates represents some reversal of previous trend is untenable, even though it may seem to receive some encouragement from Plato's *Apology*.⁶⁰ If the pre-Socratics had sought the necessary vocabulary and syntax, and had given voice to an awareness of the mental powers that were required for this purpose, they may be said to have done so without always knowing what they were doing. It was the genius of Socrates which detected what was going on and defined the psychological and linguistic consequences. The method of abstraction is by him put forward as a method; the problem is specifically recognised as linguistic (*logos*) and also as psychological. The character of the abstraction is correctly formulated as an act of isolation, separating the 'itself in itself' from the narrative context, which only tells us *about* this 'itself' or illustrates it or embodies it. A great deal of Socratic energy probably went into defining the thinking subject (*psyche*) who now was separating himself critically from the poetic matrix where all experience had been represented in image-sequence. And as he separates, he thinks 'thoughts' or abstractions which form the new content of his experience. There is no contemporary evidence that for Socrates these concepts became Forms; it is safer to regard this as a Platonic addition.[61]

Socrates himself in the unfolding history of Greek culture presents a figure of paradox as contradictory as any of his predecessors. Just as Parmenides for example remained a minstrel attached to the oral tradition, yet defiantly struggling to achieve a set of non-poetic syntactical relations and an unpoetised vocabulary, so Socrates remains firmly embedded in oral methodology, never writing a word so far as we know, and exploiting the give and take of the market place, yet committing himself to a technique which, even if he did not know it, could only achieve itself completely in the written word and had indeed been brought to the edge of possibility by the existence of the written word.

The Socratic enterprise undertaken by a native Athenian in the heart of his own community attached itself intimately to the educational problem of the city-state. The efforts of the cosmologists, so far as they avoided the problem of conceptualising human behaviour and ethical imperatives, also avoided direct entanglement in the educational controversy. But with Socrates we enter that period sometimes known as the Greek Enlightenment in which the conceptual drive is diverted away from the environment and towards man's own habit patterns, and so to the politics and ethics of the city-state. Not that 'politics' and 'ethics' yet existed as recognised areas of discourse and knowledge. It was precisely the task of Socrates and of the Sophists to integrate these as areas and to recognise them as topics, in order to prepare the way for them to become disciplines. In so doing, they also began to deploy within these areas the abstract counters required for the currency of moral discussion. So the Right and the Good, the Useful, the Pleasurable, and the Expedient, the Natural and the Conventional, all arise out of the Greek consciousness and find their appropriate names, usually in the neuter singular.[62] As they arise, they join the company of body and space and motion and matter to provide that basic fund of common conceptions which make sophisticated discourse possible. Under the aegis of the Sophists and of the Greek Enlightenment, then, we are returned to Hesiod, but this time to the *Works and Days*. The more difficult task of integrating the human panorama, and conceptualising it and analysing it, as opposed to the cosmic panorama, is at last taken up.

It is in the same period that the entire drive towards the abstract begins to be recognised as such. The Athenians become historically self-conscious; they recognise something new has intruded into their language and into their experience, and they begin to call it 'philosophy'. Even the meagre remains that survive of Sophistic writings reveal at once the measure of their effort to achieve a new level of discourse (*logos*) and a virtuosity òf conceptual vocabulary, which seek to classify both the psychic processes (for example emotion, reason, opinion, and the like) and also human motivation (as for example, hope, fear) and also moral principle (as for example utility or justice).

If these were pursued by Socrates in disconnection from any discourse about the physical,[63] this was not true of his contemporaries. The focus of intensity was on human behaviour but the conceptual and linguistic problems still involved the cosmic behaviour also. That is why all alike involved in this enterprise are defined in Plato's *Apology* as 'philosophisers'.[64] Greece was now committed to a dangerous and fascinating game, in which the combats of Homeric heroes found themselves being translated into battles between concepts, categories, and principles.

With the vocabulary of ideas, there was also born a prose of ideas, which finds its most effective and vivid expression in the speeches of Thucydides.[65] Had we more of the Sophistic writings, the historian might not get such exclusive credit. It is plain on the surface how deeply he is in their debt. The very few Hippocratic writings of this period demonstrate the same influence. They are essentially essays in the arrangement and the behaviour of the human body, and its environment, under categories. They are in this sense all of them Sophistic tracts, part of the common enterprise which had begun so long before in Hesiod and was soon to gather final momentum in order to burst into the pages of Plato.

For the stage was now set for a genius, could he be found, who as a writer but not as a poet would organise once and for all a prose of ideas; who would expound once and for all in writing what the syntax of this prose must be, and who would explore the rules of logic which should govern it. This genius was found, and he in turn found another genius for his disciple, who could correct and systematise the logic of his master's discoveries. Their joint efforts created 'knowledge' as an object and as the proper content of an educational system; divided into the areas of ethics, politics, psychology, physics, and metaphysics. Man's experience of his society, of himself and of his environment was now given separate organised existence in the abstract word.

Europe still lives in their shadow, using their language, accepting their dichotomies, and submitting to their discipline of the abstract as the chief vehicle of higher education, even to this day. The 'supreme music' had indeed become 'philosophy' and the Homeric *paideia* would now slip insensibly into the past and become a memory, and as it did, the peculiar genius of Greece, as it had exhibited itself in the archaic and high classical periods, would become a memory also.

We have been raising a curtain on Plato's predecessors only to let it drop again. They have been revealed briefly, speaking the prologue to Platonism. But that prologue itself calls for expansion, till it takes on the proportions of a new play. The great Greek comedy of ideas had begun three hundred years before Plato and Aristotle wrote. A Preface to Plato is no sooner completed than it demands a Preface to the pre-Socratics and to their archetype Hesiod.

NOTES

[1] *Rep.* 595b10–c2, 598d7–8, 600e4–5, 605c10–11, 607a2–3.

[2] 607b3 ff., reading (with Adam) at 607c1 κράτων.

[3] Denniston (*vid.* also above, cap. 3, n. 14), noting presence in Aristophanes, particularly in *Clouds* and *Frogs*, of one group of terms 'which I will describe as intellectualist', cites λεπτός (and derivatives) and μέριμνα (plus its verbs and compounds) as occurring also here in Plato. He also infers from comedy that γλῶττα was 'a popular sobriquet for an intellectual of any kind' and he might for good measure in the same context have included ἀδολέσχης and its derivatives. Just as these words place stress on the unpleasing vocabulary of intellectualism as its chief hallmark, so also do λακέρυζα and κενεαγορίαισιν in the present passage. This point is missed by Atkins (p. 14) who would explain the quarrel as provoked through the doubts cast by philosophers 'upon the Olympian mythology'.

[4] Ferguson note ad loc. adds Pythagoras and Empedocles.

[5] The preoccupations of pre-Platonic thinkers with problems of language and of cognition, and their hostility to the poets and to *doxa*, will be explored in a later volume.

[6] φιλόσοφος Heracl. B 40 (authenticity suspected by Wilamowitz, defended by Diels, ad loc.; cf. also Nestle, pp. 16, 249, n. 3) and Gorgias *Helen* 1.3.

[7] φιλοσοφεῖν Herod. 1.30; Thuc. 2.40.1; Plato *Apol.* 23d (of cosmologists), 29c, etc. (of Socratic dialectic).

[8] φιλοσοφίη Hippoc., *Anc. Med.* 20; in Plato, perhaps first at *Charmides* 153d3 ἐγὼ αὐτοὺς ἀνηρώτων τὰ τῇδε, περὶ φιλοσοφίας ὅπως ἔχοι τὰ νῦν, περί τε τῶν νέων, εἴ τινες ἐν αὐτοῖς διαφέροντες ἢ σοφίᾳ ἢ κάλλει ἢ ἀμφοτέροις ἐγγεγονότες εἶεν where context identifies term with the ethos of Socratic circle, but not yet with a disciplined body of knowledge; then *passim* in *Gorg.*, *Phaedo*, *Rep.*, etc. Ueberweg-Praechter's *Grundriss*, paragraph 1, usefully reviews 'Der Begriff der Philosophie', but obscures the historical sequence of usage. What survives of Old Comedy, while it lavishes satire and pun upon *sophistes* and its many derivatives, never mentions the three phil-words, which points to the absence of any professional usage before the Socratics, and implies that even they did not take up the word till the later years of Socrates' life. *Sophistes* had long been the standard term for an 'intellectual', but it had included poets (above, cap. 9, n. 27). The phil-words mark the final break with the previous 'poetised' intelligence; cf. also above, cap. 9, n. 28. The origins, in Heraclides Ponticus, of the fable that 'philosophy' was the name first given to a way of life by Pythagoras, are exposed by Jaeger, pp. 97–8. Morrison has lately sought to revive its credibility, but at the price of submitting the philological evidence to a species of third degree. He is forced to admit that *philosophia* in *Anc. Med.* and *philosophein* in Thuc. 'cannot be Pythagorean by any stretch', and also that *philosophein* as used by Socrates in the *Apology* is not Pythagorean either. But he wishes to see the hypothetical Pythagorean sense revived in *Gorgias* and later dialogues. This gives, in chronological order, (a) an original Pythagorean brand of 'philosophy', and then (b)

a later fifth-century brand, and then (c) a Socratic brand for which Plato feels temporary addiction, and then (d) a return by Plato to the Pythagorean vintage, as he emerged from the Socratic influence. Stages (b) and (c) are explained in the ff. sentence: 'If, as seems unlikely, any Pythagorean colour still attached to the word *philosophia* and its cognates by the last quarter of the fifth century, it is clear that for Plato it would have been obliterated by the vivid personal experience he had from Socrates, whom he makes declare in the *Apology* that god had enjoined him to live a life of philosophy.' A semantic career, so tortuous and improbable as this, reveals to what lengths one may be forced to go to protect that privileged position in the history of early Greek thought which Pythagoreanism, in defiance of all the evidence (or rather lack of evidence), has come to enjoy.

⁹ The *philosophos* is first introduced at 375e10 and equated with the *philomathes* (376c2) on the grounds that the *pathos philosophon* (376b1) is that which can distinguish between the known and unknown (376b4).

¹⁰ 474c8-475b10: even the *philoinos*, the 'addict', is considered to furnish an appropriate analogy for this thirst (475a5).

¹¹ 475b8.

¹² Below, n. 22.

¹³ At 475e4 the true philosophers are τοὺς τῆς ἀληθείας φιλοθεάμονες; at 480a11 they have become τοὺς αὐτὸ . . . ἕκαστον τὸ ὂν ἀσπαζομένους.

¹⁴ 480a11-12; 485a10-b3; 493e2-494a2.

¹⁵ Above, cap. 9, n. 28.

¹⁶ *Phaedo* 60d8-61b7.

¹⁷ *Apol.* 29d4-5, e1-3; cf. above, cap. 11, n. 17.

¹⁸ 23d4-7.

¹⁹ The testimonies of Old Comedy on this point will be examined in a later volume. The proportion of titles, plots and themes in which the educational controversy is exploited in one way or another is quite extraordinary.

²⁰ Above, n. 7.

²¹ The significance of this prefix, on which Plato lays such stress (above, n. 10), can perhaps be interpreted in the light of what Collingwood (p. 266) calls 'the emotional charge' upon the activity of intellect (cf. also p. 297: 'Poetry then, in so far as it is the poetry of a thinking man and addressed to a thinking audience, may be described as expressing the intellectual emotion attendant upon thinking in a certain way; philosophy, the intellectual emotion attendant upon trying to think better.') We would have to add that for Plato only the latter is as a rule viewed as valuable.

²² Snell (above, cap. 9, n. 27) placed all historians of Greek philosophy in his debt when he examined the usage of *soph-* (pp. 1-19) and its correlate *episteme* (pp. 81-96). Cf. also Nestle, pp. 14-16, who attempts a somewhat arbitrary typology of *sophos* under six heads.

²³ Snell, op. cit. p. 8, with the citations from Athenaeus and Cicero.

²⁴ Above, cap. 9, n. 27.

²⁵ *Apol.* 18b7, 23a3.

308   PREFACE TO PLATO

²⁶ Cf. also cap. 9, notes 27 and 28.

²⁷ Above, n. 18.

²⁸ Above, notes 23 and 26.

²⁹ On the historical behaviour of prestige words, *vid.* above, cap. 9, n. 28.

³⁰ We might say in Hume's language that they were preparing the method by which impressions are converted into ideas, but only if Hume's 'impressions' are interpreted broadly and his 'ideas' narrowly, the former describing both 'something given by sensation' and 'something perpetuated by consciousness or imagination', whereas the latter would refer to 'something constructed inferentially by the work of the intellect' (Collingwood, p. 214, cf. p. 233, n. 1; but contrast p. 171, where Hume's 'ideas' are interpreted as solely the work of the imagination).

³¹ As Kirk-Raven appears to have done, in the cases of Heraclitus and Empedocles.

³² The postulate of the early priority of a prose of ideas in Greek literature dies hard; cf. even Snell, p. 8: Xenophanes, Parm., and Emped. employed verse 'obwohl die Zeit schon vergangen war, in der allein in metrischen Gewand einem Gedanken literarisch-praegnante Form gegeben werden konnte'. This presumption is kin to that belief which would place the introduction of the alphabet as early as possible (above, cap. 3, n. 4).

³³ Specifically in *Met.* A 3-10, aside from shorter notices of 'opinions' scattered through his works.

³⁴ Aristotle's methods of rewriting the opinions of his predecessors are exhaustively analysed by Cherniss, *Aristotle's Criticism.* The account by Theophrastus (Diels, *Dox. Gr.*, pp. 475-95) of their various *archae* or first principles, that is, of the traditional pre-Socratic metaphysics, when examined by McDiarmid, turns out to be based very directly upon excerpts from Aristotle's notices rather than on whatever originals may have been available to him. Upon this account in turn the various epitomes and handbooks of the history of Greek philosophy in use in Hellenistic and Roman times depended. The problem of the collision between the language of this 'doxographic' tradition and that of the original remains of the pre-Socratics is central to the history of the early Greek mind, and must be examined in a later volume.

³⁵ Xenophanes, B 1, itself an elegiac poem, proposes that symposiac poetry should take on didactic responsibilities (lines 13-16, 19-24), a reflection, we suggest, of its new status as preserved (written) communication.

³⁶ This point has already been argued above, cap. 3, n. 4.

³⁷ Above, cap. 3, n. 6.

³⁸ This statement, controversial in the eyes of all who have been conditioned to accept the Milesians as writers of philosophical prose, will be defended in detail in a later volume (cf. also Nilsson Κατάπλοι). The credulity of Kranz has sought to enlarge the stock of Anaximander's *ipsissima verba* (contrast FVS 4th edition, where Diels still omitted any B section, with fifth and subsequent editions; Kirk-Raven and Kahn defend a surviving clause as authentic; the language attri-

buted to Anaximenes is rightly suspect). Xenoph., Parm. and Emped. are incontrovertibly poets, and as for the sayings of Heraclitus, their title to be considered as oral communication, designed to be heard and memorised but not read, rests in the first instance on the fact that each statement is self-contained, a fact which inhibited Diels from organising them in any systematic order. The paraphrases of later antiquity have in some instances modified the terseness, rhythm, and parallelism of the originals. On the 'style' of Anaxagoras and Diogenes vid. above, cap. 3, n. 16.

[39] Plato, Rep. 10 595c1-2 τῶν καλῶν ἁπάντων τούτων τῶν τραγικῶν πρῶτος διδάσκαλός τε καὶ ἡγεμών; 598d8 τὸν ἡγεμόνα αὐτῆς (sc. τραγῳδίας) ὅμηρον; Aristotle Met. Α. 3.983b20 Θαλῆς . . . ὁ τῆς τοιαύτης ἀρχηγὸς φιλοσοφίας.

[40] As has recently been increasingly recognised; cf. Kirk-Raven, pp. 24-32, nos. 24-8, on 'Hesiodic Cosmogony', and Gigon, Ursprung.

[41] Above, cap. 5; vid. also 7, n. 19.

[42] Notopoulos, 'Homer, Hesiod, etc.', produces arguments for the persistence in Hesiod of 'vestiges' derived from Achaean epic, as it survived orally on the mainland in independence of our present Homeric text.

[43] Webster, pp. 273-5, argues the case for a separation between Iliad and Odyssey on the one hand (with which he groups the Delian Hymn) and Hesiod (with whom he groups the cyclic epic) on the other: 'Up to the Odyssey the poets were still composing in the old (oral) measure . . . Hesiod is already beginning to break away from the old technique.' Notopoulos (previous note) argues strenuously that Hesiod is still 'oral poetry'. These two opinions are not irreconcilable. Solmsen, p. 10, n. 28 (above, cap. 6, n. 23), cites the 'majority' of recent German authorities who would date Hesiod before the Odyssey, but himself inclines to disagree.

[44] Cf. Nestle, p. 45: 'doch waehlte auch er fur seinem Zweck ein menschliche Vorbild, naemlich das des Stammbaums.' This was an act of 'integration', which in very rudimentary (and non-abstract) form may be discerned in Homer's habit, when giving lists (noted by Richardson, p. 51), of first naming a collective and then itemising the members of the list. This applies not only to the arming scenes in the Iliad (above, cap. 4, n. 39) but to simpler examples like Odyssey 9.218 ff.: 'we entered the cave and looked at all the several things in it. The baskets were heavy with cheeses, and packed were the pens with sheep . . . and swimming with whey were all the vessels, (even) the scoops and bowls, wrought vessels into which he milked . . .'; or Iliad 2.261 ff.: '. . . if I do not take you and strip your own garments off you, (even) mantle and tunic, (even) they that cover your genitals, and as for you yourself, pack you off weeping to the ships . . .' These examples are instructive because their syntax (if we are careful to include the whole context and do not artificially isolate a fragment of the situation) belongs not to a true effort of abstraction, but rather to the mental act of 'concrete vision' which first grasps the whole event or action (above, cap. 10) and then at leisure repeats itself by going over the items that make up the vision. Odysseus and his men confront the experience of a spectacle consisting of several groups

of objects. These are not presented as objects in a still-life catalogue, but as successive situations; hence the pens are packed, the baskets heavy, the whey brimming; consequently, the verb twice takes precedence over the noun. Then the mind, by an act of 'collecting itself' or 'recollection', goes over the items that produce this total vision. Similarly, the essential threat of Odysseus comes first, to take a man and then strip him: the total drastic act is first expressed, and then explicated. In both these instances, after the itemisation, the syntax returns to the original single vision; the 'wrought vessels', 'the man himself'. The difference between this process and true categorisation of species under a genus could be expressed by saying that (a) the genus is here experienced visually and dynamically as an act or situation, (b) the items that follow are in a kind of apposition with the situation (hence the felt need to include some word like 'even' in the translation) while in true categorisation they are subordinate.

⁴⁵ *Theog.* 881 ff.

⁴⁶ Nestle goes too far when he says of Hesiod 'So siegt die Reflexion ueber die Kunst, der Verstand ueber die Phantasie . . . etc.' (p. 52).

⁴⁷ Above, cap. 4, pp. 62 ff.

⁴⁸ e.g. *WD* 279.

⁴⁹ Above, cap. 4, n. 5.

⁵⁰ *WD* lines 106 ff.

⁵¹ *WD* line 11, a correction (as Wilamowitz noted, *Erga*, ad loc., cf. also Nestle, p. 46) of *Theog.* 225 ff., which in turn rationalises *Iliad* 18.107-10. The Homeric statement, poetised, specific and concrete, becomes the 'topic' of the Hesiodic correction, as also of the Heraclitean (Her. B.80, cf. A 22).

⁵² First in the 'metaphysical' sense at Heracl. B.30 (Anaximenes B 2 being suspect).

⁵³ In three variant versions, *Theog.* 719 ff., 736 ff., 807 ff.

⁵⁴ Xenoph. B 23, 24, 26; Heracl. B 10, 30, 32, 41, 50, 57, 89; Parm. B 2, 4, 8 *passim*, and similarly in their successors.

⁵⁵ Though this phraseology is taken from Parmenides, the language used by his colleagues is equally committed to an assertion of identity, continuity and unity.

⁵⁶ Melissus B 9, Diogenes B 7, Democ. B 141; cf. above, cap. 14, n. 19.

⁵⁷ Melissus B 7, Emped. B 13; cf. also Diller for usage of *cosmos*.

⁵⁸ The work of Snell and von Fritz in this field (*vid.* bibliog.) is fundamental: 'This difficulty (sc. separation of original terminology and concepts from those of the tradition) can be overcome only by a careful analysis of the history of the terminology'—von Fritz (1946, p. 32).

⁵⁹ Kirk-Raven attempt a reconstruction, but Kirk has already well said, p. 7: 'It is legitimate to feel complete confidence in our understanding of a Presocratic thinker only when the Aristotelian or Theophrastean interpretation, even if it can be accurately reconstructed, is confirmed by relevant and well-authenticated extracts from the philosopher himself.'

⁶⁰ 19c8 ff.

⁶¹ Above, cap. 14, n. 20.

[62] Cf. the Greek ethical terms cited in the course of Nestle's chapter on 'Protagoras', pp. 264-301.

[63] Above, n. 60; a vexed question, much disputed by participants in the 'Socratic problem'; cf. Havelock, 'Evidence'.

[64] Above, n. 18.

[65] Above, cap. 3, n. 16.

BIBLIOGRAPHY

OF AUTHORS AND WORKS CITED OR DISCUSSED IN THE FOOTNOTES

JAMES ADAM: *The Republic of Plato* (ed. and comm.), Cambridge 1920.
W. F. ALBRIGHT: *The Archaeology of Palestine*, Penguin Books 1949.
'Some Oriental Glosses on the Homeric Problem', *AJA* 54 (1950) 162-76.
'Northeast-Mediterranean Dark Ages' in *The Aegean and the Near East*, ed. S. S. Weinberg, N.Y. 1956, pp. 144-64.
J. I. ARMSTRONG: 'The Arming Motif in the Iliad', *AJP* 79 (1958), pp. 337-54.
J. W. H. ATKINS: *Literary Criticism in Antiquity*, Cambridge 1934.
JOHN BURNET: *Early Greek Philosophy*, 4th edn., London 1958.
The Socratic Doctrine of the Soul (Proc. Brit. Acad., vol. 7), Oxford 1916.
The Ethics of Aristotle (ed. and comm.), London 1900.
C. M. BOWRA: *Problems in Greek Poetry*, Oxford 1953.
Tradition and Design in the Iliad, Oxford 1930.
Heroic Poetry, London 1952.
RHYS CARPENTER: 'The Antiquity of the Greek Alphabet', *AJA* 37 (1933), pp. 8-29.
'The Greek Alphabet Again', *AJA* 42 (1938), pp. 58-69.
H. M. and N. K. CHADWICK: *The Growth of Literature*, Cambridge 1932-40.
H. F. CHERNISS: *The Riddle of the Early Academy*, Berkeley 1945.
Aristotle's Criticism of Presocratic Philosophy, Baltimore 1935.
R. G. COLLINGWOOD: *The Principles of Art*, Oxford 1938.
R. M. COOK and A. G. WOODHEAD: 'The Diffusion of the Greek Alphabet', *AJA* 63 (1959) 175 ff.
F. M. CORNFORD: *The Republic of Plato* (tr. and notes), New York 1945.
Before and After Socrates, Cambridge 1932.
PHILLIP DELACY: 'Stoic Views of Poetry', *AJP* 69 (1948) 241-71.
A. DELATTE: *Les Conceptions de l'enthousiasme chez les philosophes presocratiques*, Paris 1934.
J. D. DENNISTON: 'Technical Terms in Aristophanes', *CQ* 21 (1927) 113-21.
H. DIELS: *Doxographi Graeci*, Berlin 1879 (3rd edn., 1958).
Fragmente der Vorsokratiker, Berlin 1922, 4th edn.
H. DIELS and W. KRANZ: *Fragmente der Vorsokratiker*, Berlin 1934-8, 5th edn.
A. DIÈS: *Autour de Platon*, Paris 1927.
E. R. DODDS: *The Greeks and the Irrational*, Berkeley 1956.
STERLING DOW: 'Minoan Writing', *AJA* 58 (1954) 77-129.
'The Greeks in the Bronze Age', XIe Congrès International des Sciences, Stockholm 1960.
T. J. DUNBABIN: *The Greeks and their Near Eastern Neighbors*, London 1957.
G. F. ELSE: ' "Imitation" in the Fifth Century', *CP* 53 (1958) 73-90 and 'addendum' 245.
H. C. EVELYN-WHITE: *Hesiod Homeric Hymns* etc. (Loeb), London 1950.

JOHN FERGUSON: *Republic* Book Ten (text and comm.), London 1957.

M. I. FINLEY: *The World of Odysseus*, N.Y. 1954.

H. FRAENKEL: *Wege und Formen fruehgriechischen Denkens*, Munich, 2nd edn. 1960.

P. FRIEDLAENDER: *Plato* (tr. Meyerhoff), Vol. I, N.Y. 1958.

K. von FRITZ: '*NOOΣ* and *NOEIN* in the Homeric Poems', *CP* 38 (1943) 79-93.
'*NOOΣ NOEIN* and their derivatives in Pre-Socratic Philosophy', Part I, *CP* 40 (1945) 223-42; Part 2, *CP* 41 (1946) 12-34.

O. A. GIGON: *Der Ursprung der griechischen Philosophie*, Von Hesiod bis Parmenides, Basel 1945.

JOHN GOULD: *Development of Plato's Ethics*, Cambridge 1935.

W. C. GREENE: 'Plato's View of Poetry', *HSCP* 29 (1918), pp. 1-75.

B. A. VAN GRONINGEN: *In the Grip of the Past*, Leiden 1953.

G. M. A. GRUBE: *Plato's Thought*, London 1935.
'Plato's Theory of Beauty', *Monist* 1927.

W. K. C. GUTHRIE: *The Greeks and their Gods*, London 1950.

R. HACKFORTH: 'The Modification of Plan in Plato's Republic', *CQ* 7 (1913) 265-72.

G. M. A. HANFMANN: 'Ionia, Leader or Follower', *HSCP* 61 (1953) 1-37.

E. A. HAVELOCK: 'Why Was Socrates Tried?': Studies in Honour of Gilbert Norwood, Toronto 1952, pp. 95-109.
'The Evidence for the Teaching of Socrates', *TAPA* 65 (1934) 282-95.
The Liberal Temper in Greek Politics, London and New Haven 1957.

JENS HOLT: *Les Noms d'action en -σις (-τις)*, Aarhus 1940.

F. HOUSEHOLDER: Book Review of Emmett Bennett and Others, *CJ* 54 (1959) 379-83.

F. JACOBY: *Hesiodi Carmina Pars I: Theogonia*, Berlin 1930.

W. JAEGER: *Aristotle* (Eng. trans), 2nd edn., Oxford 1948.
Paideia, Vol. I (Eng. trans.), Oxford 1939.

L. H. JEFFERY: *The Local Scripts of Archaic Greece*, Oxford 1961.

MARCEL JOUSSE: *Le Style Oral rhythmique et mnémotechnique chez les Verbomoteurs*, Paris 1925.

G. S. KIRK: *Heraclitus: The Cosmic Fragments*, Cambridge 1954.

G. S. KIRK and J. E. RAVEN: *The Presocratic Philosophers*, Cambridge 1957.

W. KRANZ: See under Diels.

A. LESKY: *Geschichte der griechischen Literatur*, Bern 1957-8.

R. O. LODGE: *Plato's Theory of Art*, London 1953.

ALBERT LORD: *A Singer of Tales*, Cambridge (Mass.) 1960.
'Homer Parry and Huso', *AJA* 53 (1948) 34-44.

H. L. LORIMER: *Homer and the Monuments*, London 1950.
'Homer and the Art of Writing', *AJA* 52 (1948) 11-73.

J. B. McDIARMID: 'Theophrastus on the Presocratic Causes', *HSCP* 61 (1953) 85-156.

A. MEILLET: *Les Origines Indo-européennes des metres grecs*, Paris 1923.

GORDON M. MESSING: 'Structuralism and Literary Tradition', *Language* 27.1 (1951).

J. S. Morrison: 'The Origins of Plato's Philosopher-Statesman', CQ N.S. 8 (1958) 198-218.

W. Mure: A Critical History of the Language and Literature of Ancient Greece, London 1850.

J. L. Myres: 'Folk Memory' (Presidential Address), Folklore 37 (1926) 13-24.

K. O. Mueller: A History of the Literature of Ancient Greece, 1841 (in German), 1858 (Eng.).

W. Nestlé: Vom Mythos zum Logos, Stuttgart (2nd edn.) 1942.

R. L. Nettleship: Lectures on the Republic of Plato, ed. Charnwood, London 1925.

M. P. Nilsson: Homer and Mycenae, London 1933.
ΚΑΤΑΠΛΟΙ, Rh. Mus. 60 (1905) 161-89.
'Die Uebernahme und Entwicklung des Alphabets durch die Griechen' (1918), reprinted op. sel., vol. 2, Lund 1952.

J. A. Notopoulos: 'Mnemosyne in Oral Literature', TAPA 69 (1938) 465 ff.
'Parataxis in Homer', TAPA 80 (1949) 1-23.
'Homer, Hesiod and the Achaean Heritage of Oral Poetry', Hesperia 29 (1960).

Denys Page: History and the Homeric Iliad, Berkeley 1959.

F. A. Paley: The Epics of Hesiod, London 1861.

Adam Parry: 'The Language of Achilles', TAPA 87 (1956) 1-7.

Milman Parry: l'Epithète Traditionelle dans Homère, Paris 1928.

H. J. Paton: 'Plato's Theory of εἰκασία', Proc. Arist. Soc. 22 (1922) 69-104.

H. N. Porter: 'The Early Greek Hexameter', YCS 12 (1951) 3-63.

L. J. D. Richardson: 'Further Observations on Homer and the Mycenaean Tablets', Hermathena 86 (1955) 50-65.

Richard Robinson: Plato's Earlier Dialectic, Ithaca, N.Y. 1941.

S. H. Rosen: 'Collingwood and Greek Aesthetic', Phronesis 4 (1959) 135 ff.

T. Rosenmeyer: 'Gorgias, Aeschylus and Apate', AJP 76 (1955) 225-60.
'Judgment and Thought in Plato's Theaetetus' (mimeograph.), presented at Soc. Anc. Greek Phil., New York, December 1959.

Jacques Schwartz: Pseudo-Hesiodea, Leiden 1960.

Paul Shorey: The Unity of Plato's Thought, Chicago 1903.
Plato's Republic (Loeb), London 1935.

E. E. Sikes: The Greek View of Poetry, London 1931.

H. W. Smyth: Greek Melic Poets, London 1900.

Bruno Snell: Die Ausdruecke fuer den Begriff des Wissens in der vor-Platonischen Philosophie, Philol. Untersuch., 29 Berlin 1924.
The Discovery of Mind (tr. Rosenmeyer), Oxford 1953.

Friedrich Solmsen: 'Gift of Speech in Homer and Hesiod', TAPA 85 (1954) 1-15.

Alice Sperduti: 'The Divine Nature of Poetry in Antiquity', TAPA 81 (1950) 209-40.

R. G. Steven: 'Plato and the Art of his Time', CQ 27 (1933) 149-55.

J. Tate: ' "Imitation" in Plato's Republic', CQ 22 (1928) 16-23.
'Plato and Imitation', CQ 26 (1932) 161-9.

A. E. TAYLOR: *Varia Socratica*, Oxford (Parker) 1911.
   Socrates, Edinburgh 1932.
E. G. TURNER: 'Athenian Books in the Fifth and Fourth Centuries B.C.', Inaug.
   Lect. Univ. Coll., London (H. K. Lewis), 1952.
Ueberweg-Praechter: Grundriss der Geschichte der Philosophie, Vol. I, 13th
   edn., Basel 1951.
B. L. ULLMAN: 'How Old is the Greek Alphabet?', *AJA* 38 (1934) 359-81.
M. VENTRIS and J. CHADWICK: *Documents in Mycenaean Greek*, Cambridge 1956.
W. J. VERDENIUS: *Mimesis*, Leiden 1949.
H. T. WADE-GERY: *The Poet of the Iliad*, Cambridge 1952.
CALVERT WATKINS: 'Indo-European Origins of a Celtic Metre', Proc. Int. Conf.
   on Poetics, Warsaw, August 1960 (Inst. Lit. Stud. Polish Acad. Sc.).
T. B. L. WEBSTER: *From Mycenae to Homer*, London 1960.
   'Greek Theories of Art and Literature down to 400 B.C.', *CQ* 33 (1939)
   166-79.
   'Homer and the Mycenaean Tablets', *Antiquity* 113 (1955) 14 ff.
C. H. WHITMAN: *Homer and the Heroic Tradition*, Cambridge (Mass.) 1958.
U. VON WILAMOWITZ-MOELLENDORF: *Platon*, Vol. I, 3rd edn., Berlin 1948.
   Hesiodos Erga, Berlin 1928.
RODNEY S. YOUNG: 'Late Geometric Graves and a Seventh-Century Well in the
   Agora' *Hesperia*, Supp. 2 (1939).
   'Review of Dunbabin', *AJA* 64 (1960) 385-7.
ZELLER-NESTLE: *Die Philosophie der Griechen*, 13th edn., Leipzig 1928.
T. ZIELINSKI: 'Die Behandlung gleichzeitiger Ereignisse im antiken Epos',
   Philologus Supplementband 8 (1901).

ADDENDA

H. H. BERGER: *Ousia in de dialogen van Plato*, Leiden 1961.
HANS DILLER: 'Der vorplatonische Gebrauch von $KO\Sigma MO\Sigma$ und $KO\Sigma MEIN$' in
   Festschrift Bruno Snell zum 60. Geburtstag etc., Muenchen 1956, 47-60.
K. VON FRITZ: 'Das Prooemium der Hesiodischen Theogonie' in *Festschrift
   B. Snell* 29-45.
D. W. HAMLYN: 'Eikasia in Plato's Republic', *Phil. Quart.* '8 (1958) 14-23.
C. R. KAHN: *Anaximander and the Origins of Greek Cosmology*, New York 1960.
G. S. KIRK: 'Dark Age and Oral Poet', in *Proceedings Camb. Philol. Soc.* 1961 34-48.
KAROLY MAROT: *Die Anfaenge der griechischen Literatur*, Hungary Acad. Sci. 1960.
H. I. MARROU: *Histoire de l'éducation dans l'antiquité*, 4th edn., Paris 1958.
E. D. PHILLIPS: 'A Suggestion about Palamedes', *AJP* 78 (1957) 267-278.

General Index

Abou Simbel, 54[10]
abstraction, not Homeric, 188, 189; in *Iliad* versus *Odyssey*, 191[9]; mathematical, 230; of subject from object, 233[48]; as act of isolation, 256, 257; responsible for sciences, 259; equivalent to integration, 261; creates concepts, 261–3; applied to Homeric narrative, 265; responsible for Forms, 266; pursued in early Academy, 274[20]; function of philosophy, 282, 283; Presocratic and Sophistic, 285, 286, 288; semi-abstraction in Hesiod, 297, 298; Socratic, 302–4
Academy, 14, 15, 19[44], 19[45], 31, 210, 266, 273[18], 274[20]
action and agent, essential to memorised record, 167–9, 237, 239
Adeimantus, 12, 21, 24, 223
Adeimantus and Glaucon, 17[31], 220–2, 231[13]
'advisedly', see 'fitting'
Aegean, 123, 161[3], 176
Aegisthus, 181
Aeschines, 56[18]
Aeschylus, 58[22], 59[22]; *Supp.*, 53[7], 55[15]; *P.V.*, 53[7], 86[40]
Aetius, 162[28]
Agatharchus, 55[16]
Agathon, 54[10]
agent, see action
Aglaia, see Graces
agora, 107, 108
aisthesis, 253[41]; see sensation
aitia, in Herodotus, 54[8]
Ajax, 186
akoe, 53[8]
Alcman, 96[9]

Alexandria, 201
'all', Platonic, 228; see integration
alphabet, 39 ff., 45, 49[4], 55[12], 115, 117, 129[6], 129[7], 137, 189, 208, 292–4, 308[32]
amanuensis, 137
amathes, 54[12]
Ameipsias (*Connos*), 212[17]
analytic, see syntax
Anatolia, 73, 118
Anaxagoras, 55[16], 56[16], 280, 309[38]
Anaximander, 308[38]
Anaximenes, 309[38]
anthologies, 55[16], 56[16]
Antiphon, 56[16]
Antisthenes, 16[15]
aorata, 219; see also invisibles
aorist, see gnomic
apate, 58[22], 113[19]
aphorism, Presocratic, 289
Aphrodite, 98
apodexis, 53[8]
Apollo, 64–6, 71, 72, 74, 76, 77, 79, 80, 83, 98, 101, 110, 112[4], 124, 154, 163[29], 169, 170, 184, 185, 187
Apology of Plato, 49[2], 55[16], 162[28], 191[12], 209, 211[2], 213[17], 230[3], 245, 252[31], 285, 302, 304, 306[7], 307[8], 307[17], 307[25]
aporetic, 18[37]
aporia, 210, 230[1]; cf. dilemma
Arabia, 139
arbitrators, 67, 108, 121
archae, 308[34]
Archilochus, 52[4], 293
Ares, 101, 178
arete, 108, 193[31], 213[17]
Argos, 77
Aristides, 54[10]

317

Index of Modern Authorities